THE CREDO OF CHRISTENDOM

and other
Addresses and Essays on
Esoteric Christianity
(1916)

> Contents: Biographical Preface; The Credo of Christendom; The Hermetic Fragment Kore Kosmou, the Virgin of the World; The Method of the Mystics; Karma; Bible Hermeneutics; Violationism or Sorcery in Science; The Systematisation and Application of Psychic Truth; The Constitution of Man; Concerning Reincarnation; The Doctrine of Shells; Extraneous Spirits and Obsession; The Historic "Jesus"; Fate, Heredity, and Reincarnation; The Mystic Kings of the East; Christian Mysticism; Animals and their Souls; The Trinity; Index.

Anna Bonus Kingsford
and
Edward Maitland

ISBN 1-56459-446-7

**Kessinger Publishing's Rare Reprints
Thousands of Scarce and Hard-to-Find Books!**

We kindly invite you to view our extensive catalog list at:
http://www.kessinger.net

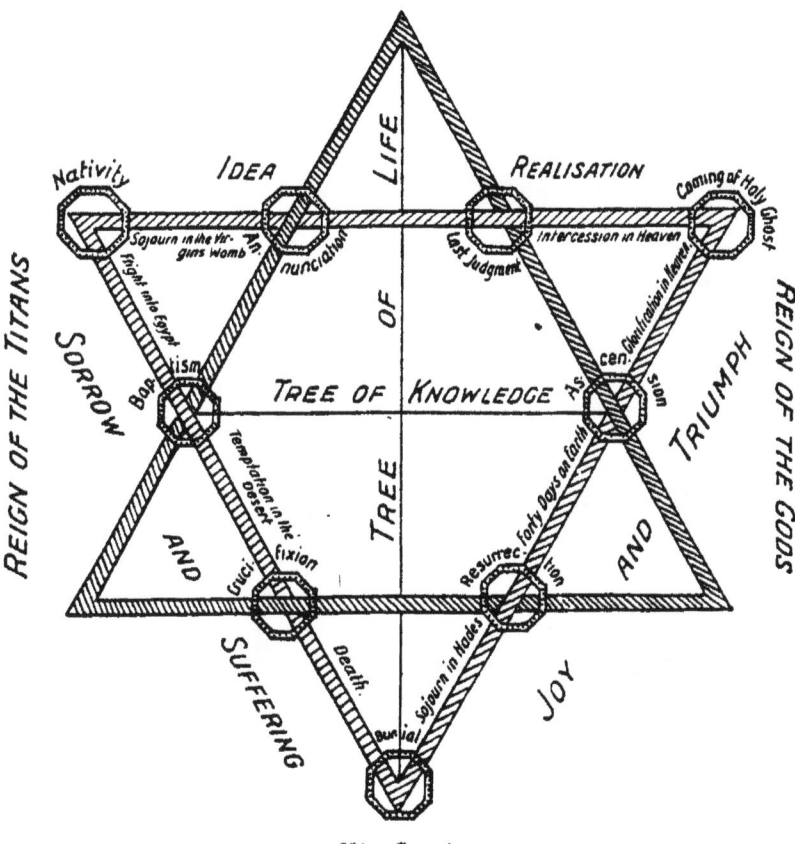

Via Crucis

Reproduction from a rough drawing by Anna Kingsford shewing the seven Stations, States, or Acts of the Human Soul comprising the Lower Triangle of the Sacred Hexagram or "Seal of Solomon," and representing the interior evolution of such Soul.—S. H. H.

CONTENTS

	PAGE
BIOGRAPHICAL PREFACE	1

LECTURES

THE CREDO OF CHRISTENDOM	94
THE HERMETIC FRAGMENT KORÉ KOSMOU, THE VIRGIN OF THE WORLD	127
THE METHOD OF THE MYSTICS	140
KARMA	143
BIBLE HERMENEUTICS	146
"VIOLATIONISM," OR SORCERY IN SCIENCE	157
THE SYSTEMATISATION AND APPLICATION OF PSYCHIC TRUTH	170

ESSAYS AND LETTERS

THE CONSTITUTION OF MAN	184
CONCERNING RE-INCARNATION	191
THE DOCTRINE OF "SHELLS"	197
EXTRANEOUS SPIRITS AND OBSESSION	203
THE HISTORIC "JESUS"	205
FATE, HEREDITY, AND RE-INCARNATION	220
THE MYSTIC KINGS OF THE EAST	225

	PAGE
CHRISTIAN MYSTICISM	230
ANIMALS AND THEIR SOULS	236
THE TRINITY	243
INDEX	245

ILLUSTRATIONS

"VIA CRUCIS"	*Frontispiece*

	PAGE
THE LOWER TRIANGLE	104
THE UPPER TRIANGLE	105

" O hear ye this, all ye people: ponder it with your ears, all ye that dwell in the world; high and low, rich and poor, one with another:—My mouth shall speak of Wisdom: and my heart shall muse of Understanding. I will incline mine ear to the parable: and shew my dark speech upon the harp."—Ps. xlix. 1–4.

" Hear my law, O my people: incline your ears unto the words of my mouth. I will open my mouth in a parable: I will declare hard sentences of old, which ye have heard and known, and such as our fathers have told us: that we should not hide them from the children of the generations to come."—Ps. lxxviii. 1–4.

" Blessed are they that hear the word of God, and keep it."—Luke xi. 28.

THE CREDO OF CHRISTENDOM

AND OTHER

ADDRESSES AND ESSAYS ON ESOTERIC CHRISTIANITY

BIOGRAPHICAL PREFACE

" I found him whom my soul loveth, I held him, and would not let him go, until I had brought him into my Mother's house, and into the chamber of her that bore me."—Cant. iii. 4.

" Some put their trust in chariots, and some in horses, but we will remember the name of the Lord our God. They are brought down, and fallen: but we are risen, and stand upright."—Ps. xx. 7, 8.

" Thou shalt break the ships of the sea through the east wind."—Ps. xlviii. 7.

" INTERIOR knowledge, earnest aspiration, and purity of thought and life, are the keys by which alone can be opened the gates of the inmost and highest sphere."[1] The Bible tells us that " the words of the Lord are pure words—even as the silver, which from the earth is tried, and purified seven times in the fire;"[2] from which we are intended to understand that *God's truth is spiritual*, and that all divine revelations are to be understood, not in a literal but in a spiritual sense. The Kingdom of God is not of this world. He who would know the truth must seek it above and within, where alone it is to be found. The heart must be lifted up, and the door of the outer senses must be shut. When Samuel heard the voice of the Lord, we are told, he was " laid down in the temple of the Lord, where the ark of God was";[3] and so must it be with us, if we would hear that voice. " Truth itself is unutterable, save by God to God."[4] " When man," says Anna Kingsford, " has wearied himself to despair in futile endeavours to seize and fix truth on the plane of sense

---

[1] *C. W. S.*, pt. i. No. xxxix.
[2] Ps. xii. 6. [3] 1 Sam. iii. 3. [4] *C. W. S.*, pt. i. No. iv.

and fact, if he be worthy and faithful God reveals to him the higher plane of the Noumenal and Divine, where alone truth eternally abides." In these pregnant words is to be found the keynote of the present volume of Lectures, Essays and Letters given and written by the late Anna Kingsford,[1] to which have been added some letters written by her friend and collaborator, the late Edward Maitland.

Most of the Lectures in this volume were given by Anna Kingsford to the Hermetic Society, which she founded, and of which she was the President, but which, owing to her early death, came to an untimely end. As, however, the value of Anna Kingsford's life is to be measured not by the number of years she lived—she was but in her forty-second year when she died—but by its quality and great achievement, so the importance of the Hermetic Society, which had a life of but little over two years, must be measured not so much by the short period of its existence as by the value of the work accomplished by means of or through its agency—for, as will be seen, it was for the purpose of creating a then much-needed platform for the dissemination of teaching, such as is represented by these Lectures, that the Hermetic Society was founded. And it served its purpose, for had it not been for such Society, these Lectures would not have been given—lectures which were intended to "raise the level of the national religious ideal; and, by withdrawing it from the external and natural to the interior and spiritual plane, to defeat the designs of materialism upon the stronghold of the moral life."

The circumstances which led to the formation of the Hermetic Society are fully set forth in that priceless record, *The Life of Anna Kingsford*,[2] and it is chiefly therefrom that the following particulars have been obtained.

In the months of May, June, and July, 1881, Anna Kingsford and Edward Maitland gave to a private audience in London

---

[1] In the case of her Lectures on the Creed, I have been able to give only *abstracts* of such Lectures, the original MSS. (if any) thereof having been lost or destroyed. The Articles and Letters which are given in this volume have been to a great extent taken from *Light*. Anna Kingsford and Edward Maitland are said to have been "the ablest contributors that *Light* ever had" (Mad. de Steiger in a letter to *Light*, 1886, p. 71).—S. H. H.

[2] *The Life of Anna Kingsford*, by Edward Maitland, in two large volumes: first edition, 1896; third edition, complete with additions, 1913. All references in this book to *The Life of Anna Kingsford* are to the third edition.—S. H. H.

some wonderful lectures on Esoteric Christianity, which, in the following year, were published anonymously under the title of *The Perfect Way, or the Finding of Christ*.[1] Giving these Lectures brought them across some members of the then recently formed Theosophical Society,[2] and, as will be seen, it was owing to the hostile attitude taken up by certain prominent members of that Society towards Esoteric Christianity that it became necessary later on to found the Hermetic Society. Speaking of the audience of the " Perfect Way " Lectures, Edward Maitland says : " Among these were sundry members of a body with which we now first formed acquaintance, bearing the name of the British Theosophical Society. These were a group of students of the occult science and mystical philosophy of the East, who formed a branch of a parent Society founded originally in New York by a Russian lady, Madame H. P. Blavatsky, and an American, Colonel H. S. Olcott, but whose headquarters were then in India."[3]

Anna Kingsford's and Edward Maitland's purpose was " the restoration of the true, esoteric, and spiritual Christianity,"[4] and they regarded it as a very remarkable coincidence that while the object of their collaboration had been, and was, " the restoration of the esoteric philosophy or Theosophy of the West, and the interpretation thereby of the Christian and kindred religions," the collaboration between Madame Blavatsky and Colonel Olcott had a similar object in regard to the esoteric philosophy or Theosophy of the East ; and " both parties had until then been working on lines thus parallel in complete ignorance of each other's existence." But, Edward Maitland says, " while our knowledges were derived directly from celestial sources, the hierarchy of the Church invisible in the holy heavens,[5] theirs claimed as their source certain ancient Lodges of Adepts said to inhabit the inaccessible heights of the Thibetan Himalayas, an order of men credited with the possession of knowledges and powers which constituted them beings apart and worthy of divine honours."[6]

[1] A fourth edition of this book was published in 1909.—S. H. H.
[2] The Theosophical Society was founded in America in 1875. In the following year a branch was formed in London.—S. H. H.
[3] *Life of A. K.*, vol. ii. p. 15. [4] *Ibid.*, p. 277.
[5] Edward Maitland says : " The revelation made to us was identical in source, method, and kind with that which had been delivered to the inspired of old, and of which the Bible is the chief surviving depository, being described by the Rabbins of the Kabala as given by God to Adam in Paradise, and to Moses on Sinai, expressions which denoted the state of illumination."—*Life of A. K.*, vol. ii. p. 31.
[6] *Life of A. K.*, vol. ii. p. 16.

While the Theosophical Society was new, Theosophy was ancient. As Edward Maitland has pointed out: "It was known very long before eight centuries ago. For it was no new thing in the days of St Paul, who says (1 Cor. ii. 7), 'We speak Theosophy (Θεου σοφια) in a mystery,' and Moses is declared (Heb. xi. 26) to have esteemed it 'greater riches than the treasures of Egypt.' For, in its true sense, it has ever meant the science of the perfectionment of the human ego—theologically called 'regeneration'—whereby man demonstrates the potential divinity of humanity, by realising it in his own person. In other words, Theosophy, in its supreme aspect, is that 'Mystery of Godliness,' the process whereby God is manifest in the flesh (1 Tim. iii. 16)."[1] To the reviewer of one of her books who had fallen into the error of regarding Theosophy as "a thing of recent invention, or, at least, importation," Anna Kingsford replied: "Theosophy—both the term itself and the system properly so called—has subsisted in the Church from the beginning; and what I have done is to restore and develop it—not as lately 'come over to Europe,' but as held by St Paul, by St Dionysius 'the Areopagite,' by the scholastics, and by the host of Christian mystical philosophers, to whom alone it is due that Christianity is now in any degree a spiritual religion, instead of having degenerated into a mere fetish-worship. I propound no 'Modern Theosophy' which is not also 'Olden Mysticism.'"[2]

Among the members of the British Theosophical Society who attended the above-mentioned Lectures were Charles Carlton Massey, Dr George Wyld, the Hon. Roden Noel, and Isabel de Steiger.

During the year, 1881, A. P. Sinnett came over from India "for the purpose of publishing a book which was to introduce the alleged thaumaturgists of the East, whom the Theosophical Society claimed as its 'Masters,' to the notice of the Western world." Edward Maitland says: "We were naturally curious to know what he had to say, and he, on his part, was curious to make the acquaintance of those who—if all were true which he had heard about us—were in certain respects setting themselves up as rivals of his own venerated chiefs. It was arranged, therefore, that he should pass an evening with us. There were several points on which we desired information, especially the existence and powers of the alleged 'Mahatmas,' and the system of thought which

---

[1] E. M.'s letter, dated 22nd October 1891, to the *Echo*.
[2] *Life of A. K.*, vol. ii. p. 257.

constituted their 'esoteric doctrine.' That there should be persons such as the Mahatmas were stated to be was not impossible for us, it followed from the teaching we had already received, and which was contained in our eighth Lecture,[1] though we had never before heard it said that such persons actually existed in the world now. We knew, too, that Reincarnation, under the name of Transmigration, was an Eastern tenet, and, consequently, the doctrine of Karma, which we had received in such plenitude of detail without ever having heard of that term for it. We were, therefore, greatly surprised to learn from Mr Sinnett that these tenets formed no part of the doctrine of the Theosophical Society, being neither contained in their chief text-book, the *Isis Unveiled* of its founders, nor communicated to it by its Masters, and on these grounds Mr Sinnett rejected them, sitting up with us until long after midnight arguing against them, and saying, among other things, of the doctrine of Reincarnation, that even of the Spiritualists only a few who followed Allan Kardec accepted it. Whereupon we stated our conviction that it would yet be given to his Society by its Eastern teachers, and that, as for Allan Kardec's writings, we knew of them enough to know that they were far from trustworthy, and his presentation of that doctrine especially was unscientific and erroneous. For the sole source of his information was ordinary mediumship, as exercised by some sensitives who could see only in the astral, and represented, therefore, no true spiritual vision, but only the ideas of living persons, whom they reflected. And when his own book, *The Occult World*, made its appearance, as it did in the course of that same year, we were able to infer from it that, if there really was a true system of esoteric philosophy in the East, it had not yet been imparted to the Theosophical Society, if only for the reason that the doctrine of that book was sheer materialism, and had no room for the *Theos*, who forms so essential an element in that which is denoted by the term 'Theosophy.'

"Thus far our experience of that body was a disappointing one, or at least would have been so had we yet anticipated much of it. Recognising, as we did, the time as having come for the unsealing of the world's Bibles, and our own appointed mission as that of unsealing the Bibles of the West, we should have welcomed eagerly a corresponding movement having for its purpose the unsealing of the Bibles of the East. The Theosophical

[1] See *The Perfect Way*, Lect. viii.

Society was, however, still in its infancy, and we resolved to wait patiently and hopefully for its further unfoldment."[1]

Referring to this time, Edward Maitland says: "Meanwhile, another notable sign of the times occurred to mark the year 1881. This was the publication of the Revised Version of the English Bible. The fact of a new translation was welcomed by us, if only as constituting a blow to the idolatrous veneration in which the letter of the old translation was held, a striking example of which we recognised in the ground of the opposition to the proposed revision raised by the excellent Lord Shaftesbury—that it would deprive many pious persons of some of their favourite texts; by which it would appear that men's blunders were more worthy of conservation than the inspirations of the Holy Ghost, to which he implicitly ascribed the Bible. The manner in which the work was accomplished would have been in the highest degree disappointing to us had we anticipated any other result than was actually attained. For we knew as did no others that the time was the winter solstice of the human soul, and spiritual perception was at its lowest ebb, so that, be the learning expended on it what it might, there would be no insight to guide it. The very first verse of Genesis more than confirmed our gloomiest anticipations. In the Authorised Version, the Hebrew word wrongly rendered 'heaven' in the first chapter was rightly rendered 'heavens' in the second chapter. In the Revised Version, both were wrongly rendered 'heaven.' This error in Hebrew as well as in doctrine was for us, with chapters vii.-x. of the Greater Mysteries[2] in our hands, proof positive the translators had not begun to understand the system of thought which underlies the Bible, and of which the Christ is the personal demonstration. And it was not without a sense of elation that we reflected that the real and vital translation of the Bible, its translation from the Letter to the Spirit, had been withheld from the magnates of the dominant orthodoxy, backed by the national purse, to be committed to such inconspicuous and poverty-stricken instruments as ourselves. There was an irony

---

[1] *Life of A. K.*, vol. ii. pp. 19, 20. See also letter, dated 3rd July 1882, from A. K. to Lady Caithness, giving an account of this interview with Mr Sinnett (*ibid.*, p. 74).

[2] The reference is to certain divine Illuminations which had been received by Anna Kingsford, and which—with other of her Illuminations —were subsequently published in *Clothed With the Sun*. The Illuminations referred to appear as chapters vii.-x. of part ii. of that book.—S. H. H.

BIOGRAPHICAL PREFACE

about it which argued a keen sense of humour in the divine disposers of events."[1]

The year 1881 also saw the founding in London of the Spiritualist paper *Light*.[2]

On the publication, in the following year, of *The Perfect Way*—which, it will be remembered, was published anonymously—a copy of the book was sent to the editors of the *Theosophist*[3] for review. At the same time, Anna Kingsford, without disclosing her name,[4] wrote to Madame Blavatsky a letter, in which—referring to *The Perfect Way*—she said: "It would not have been in my mind to write thus to you, but that I find in the *Theosophist* for February (on p. 114) certain words concerning 'Initiates' which cause me to desire you should know something of the genesis of the book of which I have spoken. I have said that all that book contains came forth from my heart and lips. Yet I know nothing of your literature—and between you and me there is, nevertheless, perfect agreement and accord. Steadily, and not once nor twice, have I refused invitations to join the Theosophical Society in London, lest, perchance, it should be said that I had learnt somewhat from its members. See then, that it is possible to be initiated of one's own interior Spirit, through whom the voice of the Gods speaks to man, if but his life be pure and free from lust. You, who are initiated, will know whether I have the truth. There is more—far more—that *I am straitly forbidden to publish*. If, in what is written, there be any error, that is the fault of the writer or of the seer, but not of that which was seen.

"Madam: I pray you to ask your Brothers whether I have the truth. Tell them, if they need to be told, how it came to me, and whence I obtained it, and on what conditions.

"You are doing a splendid work in India. I, too, hate the tenets of modern Christianity, and labour continually to destroy its idols. I, too, am a follower of holy Buddha, and not the less of the ideal Christ.

"The first knowledge I had of you was from the author of the *Occult World*, who came to see me in London last summer. To

---

[1] *Life of A. K.*, vol. ii. pp. 22–23.
[2] This paper, Edward Maitland says, "proved a channel for the enunciation of our knowledges when the general Press was entirely closed against us, and therein a stimulus to ourselves to write what otherwise would have remained unsaid" (*Life of A. K.*, vol. ii. p. 49).—S. H. H.
[3] The *Theosophist* was founded in India in October 1879.
[4] The letter is signed "One of the Writers of *The Perfect Way*."—S. H. H.

him I told something of the method of my own initiation, and he was astonished. If you ask him about me, and learn from him—or from any other person—my name, pray consider it secret."

In the same year, 1882, she and Edward Maitland resumed their meetings which, in the previous year, had proved such a success.[1]

Two remarkable Lectures which were given by her at this time are reprinted in the present volume. I refer to the Lectures entitled "'Violationism,' or Sorcery in Science" and "The Systematisation and Application of Psychic Truth" respectively. They were both given to the British National Association of Spiritualists. Edward Maitland says that the former was "especially designed to rouse the Spiritualists from their indifference on the subject of vivisection by shewing them that their very claim to positive knowledge of the soul's reality and persistence constituted an obligation on them to oppose a practice which is utterly at variance with all that the soul is and implies." But, he adds, "as the result proved, the Spiritualists were too exclusively absorbed in their phenomenal experiences to care for the higher issues of their belief; and between spiritualism and spirituality there was a gulf which had yet to be bridged, and so far as they were concerned the appeal fell on deaf ears."[2] The object of the latter Lecture was "to raise the spiritualistic movement from the level of mere phenomenalism,"[3] but, judging from some editorial comments thereon which appeared in the following number of *Light*,[4] it is clear that her message was unacceptable to the "Spiritualists" of her day. Her platform was too high for them.

Edward Maitland says: "The latter part of May brought us from India a copy of the *Theosophist* for that month, with the first portion of a review of *The Perfect Way*, written, we were given to understand, by our visitor of the preceding summer, the author of the *Occult World*, Mr A. P. Sinnett. Coming, as did this review, from the one quarter in the world—so far as we were then aware—which laid claim to special knowledge of the

---

[1] *Life of A. K.*, vol. ii. p. 50.
[2] *Ibid.*, p. 47. As regards Spiritualism, Edward Maitland says: "It is simply a practice consisting in holding or seeking intercourse with unembodied intelligences or forces; and nothing in the world can make it anything else" (*Light*, 1884, p. 519).—S. H. H.
[3] *Life of A. K.*, vol. ii. p. 60.
[4] *Light*, 1882, pp. 269-270.

subjects dealt with in our book, this review could not fail to have great interest for us; and it was, accordingly, with much satisfaction that we found it described at the outset as an 'upheaval of true spirituality; a grand book by noble-minded writers, and one that if every man in London above a certain level of culture should read attentively, a theological revolution would be accomplished.' . . . But though thus highly appreciative of the book from some aspects, the reviewer took violent exception to it from others, for he not only dissented from some of its teachings on occult matters, but objected to the symbolism in which, in order to interpret the Bible, we had followed the Bible —and notably the adoption of the term 'Woman' to denote the Soul and the Intuition; and he even ventured to assert positively that, instead of the Gospel narrative having been written expressly to illustrate a certain doctrine, as stated by us, the doctrine was but an ingenious application of the facts of the spiritual consciousness to a story which was altogether unintended to bear such relation; so that we were putting into the Gospels meanings of which their writers never dreamed, as if mystical theology had been of subsequent invention to the Christian era? instead of pervading—as we had shewn that it does pervade—the Bible from the beginning, and is declared in the Bible itself to do so; as, for instance, when St Paul declares of the books of Moses, 'which things are an allegory,' and Jesus finds the Christ-doctrine of which He was the personal illustration in the books of Moses. . . . Recalling his persistent denial of Reincarnation on his visit to us in the previous year, we were interested to find him now accepting the doctrine.[1] . . . Thus, while profoundly gratified by the review in some respects, we were almost as profoundly antagonised by it in others. And the result was a controversy in the pages of the *Theosophist* not altogether devoid of bitterness. . . . It was, however, finally and happily composed. Our reviewer concluded his part of the correspondence by describing us as 'having produced one of the most—perhaps the most—important and spirit-stirring of appeals to the higher instincts of mankind which modern European literature has yet evolved.'

---

[1] After seeing A. K. and E. M., in 1881, he had received instruction from his Guru about the subject, but his instruction appears to have been partial only, because in a letter, dated 3rd July 1882, to Lady Caithness, A. K. says: "he does not yet know all the truth concerning it, and so finds fault with our presentation of that side of it which, as yet, he has not been taught" (*Life of A. K.*, vol. ii. p. 74).—S. H. H.

To which we returned a conciliatory reply, pointing out at the same time certain respects in which he had mistaken us. And the controversy wound up with the following characteristic enunciation by the editor, Madame Blavatsky, in which, as will be seen, she entirely threw over Mr Sinnett in his repudiation of an intended mystical sense as underlying Christianity."[1] In the *Editor's Note* Madame Blavatsky said: "It is most agreeable to us to see our reviewer of *The Perfect Way* and the writers of that remarkable work thus clasping hands and waving palms of peace over each other's heads. The friendly discussion of the metaphysics of the book in question has elicited, as all such debates must, the fact that deep thinkers upon the nature of absolute truth scarcely differ, save as to externals. As was remarked in *Isis Unveiled*, the religions of men are but prismatic rays of the one only Truth. If our good friends, the *Perfect Way-farers*, would but read the second volume of our work, they would find that we have been all along precisely of their own opinion that there is a 'mystical truth and knowledge deeply underlying' Roman Catholicism, which is identical with Asiatic esotericism; and that its symbology marks the same ideas, often under duplicate figures. We even went so far as to illustrate with woodcuts the unmistakable derivation of the Hebrew Kabala from the Chaldæan—the archaic parent of all the later symbology—and the kabalistic nature of nearly all the dogmas of the Roman Catholic Church. It goes without saying that we, in common with all Asiatic Theosophists, cordially reciprocate the amiable feelings of the writers of *The Perfect Way* for the Theosophical Society. In this moment of supreme effort to refresh the moral nature and satisfy the spiritual yearnings of mankind, all workers, in whatever corner of the field, ought to be knit together in friendship and fraternity of feeling. It would be indeed strange if any misunderstanding could arise of so grave a nature as to alienate from us the sympathies of that highly advanced school of modern English thought of which our esteemed correspondents are such intellectual and fitting representatives."[2]

---

[1] *Life of A. K.*, vol. ii. pp. 64–67.

[2] *Life of A. K.*, vol. ii. pp. 67–68. The two parts of the review appeared in the *Theosophist* of May and June 1882, and the articles in discussion in September and October of the same year, and A. K.'s and E. M.'s final reply and the above editorial in January 1883. On 3rd July 1882, Anna Kingsford wrote to Lady Caithness, warning her not to be misled by the " misrepresentations " of *The Perfect Way* contained in the above-men-

BIOGRAPHICAL PREFACE

In the latter part of the year 1882, being then in Switzerland, where they were engaged in an anti-vivisection crusade, Edward Maitland received from England a letter, in which the writer—Mr G. B. Finch—informed him as follows:—

"The Theosophical Society in England has arrived at a crisis. Dr Wyld resigned the Presidency some time ago, and Mr C. C. Massey has been elected. On his election he wrote to Colonel Olcott, asking whether it was any good keeping up the Society, and entering into full particulars about the state of affairs here. I learned these things from Mr Massey, to whom I had gone to see whether something could not be done to keep what seemed to be a useful agency going. M. says that members are admitted too freely; that he had urgently proposed to put it on an ascetic basis, but that Madame Blavatsky had rejected this. She apparently wished the Society to be catholic. But it can be this and at the same time eclectic, for they have sections; and it would be in accordance with the practice of the Society elsewhere to have a section on the ascetic base, or any other base within the purview of the Society's aims. M. seemed to wish for some such section, and if Mrs Kingsford were in it, I think he would be greatly pleased. . . . I should like to be a member of some such section as I have described, if you and Mrs Kingsford were members."[1]

Edward Maitland says: "This was the first suggestion to us of a conjunction with the Theosophical Society, and the idea had not occurred to us before; nor, now that it was suggested, and this by those whom we held in high esteem, did we feel drawn to it. On the contrary, we already knew enough about the origin, motives, and methods of the Theosophical Society to distrust it. Its original prospectus committed the glaring inconsistency of declaring the absolute tolerance of the Society of all forms of religion, and then of stating that a main object was the destruction of Christianity. Its founders had committed it also to the rejection of the idea of a God, personal or impersonal, and this while calling it *Theo*-sophical. And it claimed for its doctrine a derivation from sources which, even if they had any existence—a matter on which we had no proof—were not to be compared with those from whom ours was derived,[2] while the doctrine

---

tioned review, and pointing out one of the "mistakes" therein contained which, she said, was "so gross and palpable," that she found it hard to believe it had been committed innocently (*Life of A. K.*, vol. ii. p. 73).—S. H. H.

[1] *Life of A. K.*, vol. ii. p. 79.   [2] See p. 3, *ante*.

itself was palpably inferior so far as yet disclosed, and this both in substance and form .... The matter went no further at this time; but we were struck by learning that Mary [1] had been recognised by the mysterious chiefs of the Theosophical Society as 'the greatest natural mystic of the present day, and countless ages in advance of the great majority of mankind.'" [2]

The receipt of the above-mentioned letter was followed by some correspondence with C. C. Massey, the result of which was that Anna Kingsford consented to her nomination as President of the British Theosophical Society, whereupon C. C. Massey notified the Society of his intention to nominate her as its President for the ensuing year. In the notice, issued to the members, C. C. Massey referred to "the well-known fact that Anna Kingsford was one of the literary authors of that remarkable work *The Perfect Way, or the Finding of Christ*," [3] and he added: "I may say that I have not decided on making this proposal without the most careful deliberation and consultation, and that I regard its adoption as of *vital importance*." [4]

Edward Maitland says: "When at length we gave consent, we did so on condition that we retain absolute freedom of opinion, speech, and action, acknowledging no superiors, nor any allegiance save to our own Illuminators, [5] and reserving the right to use as we might deem fit any knowledges we might acquire. For, having obtained what we had already received expressly for the world's benefit, we were resolved to remain unfettered in this respect. Our association was thus so ordered as to have for its purpose a simple exchange of knowledges. They should tell us what they knew, and we should tell them what we knew, both sides reserving the right of criticism, acceptance, and rejection, the Understanding alone, and in nowise Authority, being the criterion." [6]

The election of Anna Kingsford as President, and Edward Maitland as Vice-President, of the British Theosophical Society

---

[1] The initiation name given to Anna Kingsford by her Illuminators.—S. H. H.

[2] *Life of A. K.*, vol. ii. pp. 80–81.

[3] They were informed that the Chiefs of the Theosophical Society recognised in this book "knowledges of which the Eastern adepts had believed themselves to be the exclusive possessors, having been safeguarded by them from the remotest ages" (Article on "Mr Edward Maitland" in *Light*, 1893, p. 104).—S. H. H.

[4] *Life of A. K.*, vol. ii. pp. 103–105.

[5] Celestial personalities whom they knew as the Gods. (See *Life of A. K.*, vol. i. pp. 244, 257; and see p. 7, *ante*.)—S. H. H.

[6] *Life of A. K.*, vol. ii. p. 105.

for the ensuing year took place on Sunday the 7th January 1883, the day being that following the feast of the Epiphany. Dr G. Wyld, the late President, was also elected a co-Vice-President along with Edward Maitland.

The following letter written at this time by Anna Kingsford to Madame de Steiger is of interest : [1]—

"21 AVENUE CARNOT, PARIS,
"11th January 1883.

"DEAR MADAME DE STEIGER,—I salute you in my new character of President of the British Theosophical Society; and, though I shall not be able for some time to come to take my place among you in the body, yet I hope that my new dignity will serve as a fresh link in the tie of friendship already existing between us, and that you will from time to time send me some account of your proceedings in the Society, and of your own personal reflections on the teaching we are now promised from the East.

"I pointed out to Mr C. C. Massey in a recent letter the singular coincidence that it was on Epiphany Sunday, the festival of the Magi, that the T. S. elected as its President for the new year a *King's ford*; and I suggested that we might regard this fact as a happy augury for the prosperity of the Society in the immediate future; since now indeed the way seemed at last opened for the passage of the Kings of the East, and, as it is said in the Apocalypse, the River is dried up that the way of the Kings of the East may be prepared. . . . It gives me considerable surprise, and puzzles me not a little, to learn that Dr Wyld is still not only a member of the Theosophical Society, but is absolutely accepted as co-Vice-President with Mr Maitland ! I quite understood from Dr Wyld himself, and also from the circular issued by Mr Massey, that the aims and programme of the T. S. had become so distasteful to the Doctor that he had determined to resign his connection with it. Strange that he should withdraw deliberately from the *Presidency*, only to come forward as *Vice*-President so shortly after ! Can you explain this riddle ? I should be very glad to have it solved.

"I have requested Mr Massey to retain his place as my *locum tenens* until I return, and feel sure that, as he is so manifestly in harmony both with our Indian correspondents and with myself, you will be glad of this arrangement. . . .

"ANNA KINGSFORD."

---

[1] *Life of A. K.*, vol. ii. p. 106.

On the 20th May following they returned to England, when Anna Kingsford commenced her duties as President of the British Theosophical Society, which, on her suggestion, was afterwards designated the London Lodge of the Theosophical Society.[1]

Writing, at this time, to Lady Caithness, Anna Kingsford says: "I am going to do my utmost to make our London Lodge a really influential and scientific body. ... Besides, we do not want to pledge ourselves to Orientalism only, but to the study of all religions esoterically, and especially to that of our Western Catholic Church. Theosophy is equally applicable to such study; but Orientalism can relate only to Brahmanism and Buddhism."[2] And, in a further letter, she says: "I have a plan which I earnestly hope I shall somehow have the means of carrying into practice next spring. It is to give lectures in London at one of the Lodge halls on 'Esoteric Christianity.' I should explain the hidden and true significance of the Catholic doctrines,—as much, of course, as is possible,—and the interior meaning of all sacred myths. I have already sketched out a little scheme which, if only it can be realised, will, I feel certain, do more for our Theosophy than any number of printed books."[3]

Anna Kingsford made her first public appearance in her new rôle as President of the British Theosophical Society at the reception which, on the evening of the 17th July 1883, was given by the Society, at the Princes' Hall, Piccadilly, to Mr Sinnett, who had then recently returned from India to this country. An account of the reception, which appeared in *Light*,[4] says: "Some 270 guests assembled, and among them were many faces well known in Society, and not a few men of letters and science whose judgment and opinion the world is accustomed to treat with deference. The company would be described in the language of the ordinary reporter as at once fashionable and influential." The proceedings were opened by Anna Kingsford, when she gave an eloquent address on Theosophy and the aims and objects of the Theosophical Society.[5] One of Mr Sinnett's objects in returning to this country had been the publication of his book *Esoteric Buddhism*, which had then recently appeared, but which, at that

---

[1] *Life of A. K.*, vol. ii. p. 119.
[2] Letter dated 8th June 1883. *Life of A. K.*, vol. ii. p. 119.
[3] Letter dated 25th June 1883. *Life of A. K.*, vol. ii. p. 120.
[4] *Light*, 1883, p. 335.
[5] The Address was reported in *Light*, 1883, pp. 337-338; and in a Supplement to the *Theosophist*, October 1883; and it is reprinted in *The Life of A. K.*, vol. ii. pp. 123-126.

time, they had not had an opportunity of carefully and critically studying.[1] Speaking for herself as "a Catholic Christian," and referring to the fact that the guest of the evening was a Buddhist,[2] she laid particular stress upon the fact that all the great religions of the world were fundamentally one and the same, claiming that " once the veil of symbolism is lifted from the divine face of Truth all Churches are akin, and the basic doctrine of all is identical"; and, she said, " Some of us have dreamed that our English Branch of the Theosophical Society is destined to become the ford across the stream which so long has separated the East from the West, religion from science, heart from mind, and love from learning. We have dreamed that this little Lodge of the Mystics, set here in the core of matter-of-fact, agnostic London, may become an oasis in the wilderness for thirsty souls,—a ladder between earth and heaven, on which, as once long since in the earlier and purer days, the Gods may 'come and go 'twixt mortal men and high Olympus.'" Speaking of Mr Sinnett's address on this occasion, Edward Maitland says: " Admirable as it was for its purpose, it struck some notes which we recognised as scarcely harmonising with the conceptions formed by us, and which therefore might not impossibly develop into an irresolvable discord."[3]

The first duty which devolved upon Anna Kingsford and Edward Maitland as the chiefs of the London Lodge of the Theosophical Society, was to study Mr Sinnett's *Esoteric Buddhism*; and, as the writers of *The Perfect Way*, they were equally bound to acquaint themselves with the teaching of and pass judgment on this book; and this, Edward Maitland says, " not for the sake merely of the members of the Society, but for the sake of our own work, and for the vindication before the world of the teaching

---

[1] Edward Maitland says: " The arrival of Mr Sinnett in England, and the publication of his *Esoteric Buddhism*, had completely revolutionised the status of the Theosophical Society. No longer now was it a private group of students engaged for their own satisfaction in mastering the philosophy of the Orient, and pledged to secrecy respecting its nature. It was a propaganda eager for notoriety, and claimimg to be in possession of a doctrine resting on the infallible authority of an order of men divinised and hid away in the inaccessible fastnesses of the Thibetan uplands. This made it all the more necessary for us to see that we were committing ourselves to nothing that could impair the authority of the teaching received by us, and it was with no little interest that we looked forward to an examination of *Esoteric Buddhism*" (*Life of A. K.*, vol. ii. pp. 122-123, and see pp. 163-164).—S. H. H.

[2] Mr Sinnett had introduced himself to them as a Buddhist.—S. H. H.

[3] *Life of A. K.*, vol. ii. p. 126.

committed to us, and which we knew of ourselves to be true, while—as the writer of *Esoteric Buddhism* frankly admitted—he was entirely dependent for his knowledge upon teachers of whom he had no personal knowledge, but whom, nevertheless, he had learnt to trust implicitly." And, " Such being the position, our course seemed to us to be clear. This was to ignore persons, and judge the doctrine on its own merits, making appeal only to the understanding. Having ourselves insisted on the possibility of man's attainment of knowledge and powers even transcending those claimed for the Eastern Adepts, we were by no means averse to the idea that such persons may actually exist. But there was no sufficient evidence of their existence,[1] or of the possession by those who asserted their existence of the ability to recognise them, even in the case of contact with them. For, as only they who possess the Christ spirit in a measure can recognise the Christ, so only they who are themselves adepts in a measure can recognise the Adepts. And even if the teaching in question came from the source alleged, what guarantee was there that it had not undergone in transmission a change sufficient to vitiate it ? Our own position in regard to the current Christianity was, that the Church had all the truth, having received it from a divine source, but that the priests had materialised it, making themselves and their followers idolaters. And might not the same thing have happened with the teaching now propounded, and this while its propounders were acting in the best faith, owing to the lack of spiritual insight on the part of the recipients ? The very designation, *Esoteric Buddhism*, moreover, was open to grave question. And there was the further considera-

---

[1] To a correspondent of *Light* who stated that "anyone who chooses to live the necessary life can soon obtain personal evidence of the existence and power of the Himalayan Mahatmas, and can, under their direction, be put into the way to attain for himself the knowledge of the hereafter," Edward Maitland replied: "As I read this utterance it contains two errors of first-rate magnitude: it makes salvation dependent on the chance of certain other persons existing and being accessible in some abnormal way ; and it assumes that the images formed in the mind under strong previous impression are really the persons thought of, instead of being but astral emanations of *one's own system*, having no necessary relation to extraneous personalities. It is of course open to your correspondent to *call* his objectivised ideas Himalayan Mahatmas, just as it was possible for St Theresa to call hers Jesus Christ, and for Swedenborg to call his David, Paul, or the Virgin Mary. But the practice shews a complete want of knowledge respecting the occult side of human nature, and the image-making powers of the subtler elements of one's own system, as well also as the teaching capabilities of *one's own* spirit" (*Light*, 1884, p. 139).

tion, that to accept it upon authority, and independently of the understanding, would be but to establish a new sacerdotalism in place of that which we and they alike sought to dethrone.

"And, indeed, it very soon became evident that matters were not only in danger of tending in this direction, but had already gone far in it. The idea of a group of divinised men, dwelling high up in the fastnesses of the Himalayas, and endowed with transcendent knowledges and powers, possessed a fascination for all but the stoutest heads; and that many had succumbed to the glamour of the supposed 'Mahatmas,' as the adept masters were called, was evidenced by their readiness to accept implicitly all that was put forward in their name, even to resenting as blasphemous the suggestion of need for caution and deliberation, and their refusal to recognise the presence of an esoteric element in Christianity corresponding to that which was claimed for Buddhism."

"There was also much in the tone and character of the publications issued from the headquarters of the parent Society in India of which we disapproved as not only calculated to impair the credit of the Society with the public, but as harmful in itself and incompatible with its real aims. For, while we recognised the Society as at once representing high aims and possessed of invaluable knowledges, we were compelled to recognise the presence of other and conflicting elements which, unless eliminated, would assuredly wreck the whole movement. This is to say, that although, owing to the heterogeneous nature of its elements, chiefly as regards the personalities of its foremost representatives, it was but a chaos, we discerned in it the possibilities of a Kosmos, provided only those elements could be duly redeemed from their limitations and fused into harmonious accord. For us its promoters were as children who, having become possessed of a valuable instrument which they were as yet incapable of appreciating, were in danger of destroying it through the exuberance of their child-nature, and their consequent disposition to play with it, instead of setting seriously to work to apply it to its proper uses."[1]

In view of these objections, Anna Kingsford, as President of the London Lodge, and describing herself as "a toiler in the Ship of Peter,"[2] addressed to Colonel Olcott, as President of the

[1] *Life of A. K.*, vol. ii. pp. 138–140.
[2] In 1870, Anna Kingsford had joined the Catholic Church.—S. H. H.

Parent Society, a long letter of remonstrance,[1] in which she pleaded for a truly catholic theosophy, and stated what she believed to be the right aim and method of their work, and the wisest policy for their Society to follow. In her letter she laid stress upon the fact that in Christian countries it is not so much the revelation of a new religious system that is needed, as a true interpretation of the religion now existing. "Orthodox Christianity, both in Catholic and in Protestant countries," she said, "is languishing on account of a radical defect in its method,—to wit, the exoteric and historical sense in which, exclusively, its dogmas are taught and enforced." And she pointed out that "It should be the task of Theosophy in these countries to convert the material—and therefore idolatrous—interpretation of the ancestral faith and doctrine into a spiritual one; to lift the plane of the Christian creed from the exoteric to the esoteric level, and thus, without touching a stone or displacing a beam of the Holy City, to carry it all up intact from earth to heaven."[2] The Theosophical creed, she said, "should be essentially *spiritual*, and all its articles should relate to interior conditions, principles, and processes. It should be based upon experimental knowledge, not on authority, and its central figures should be attributes, qualities, and sacraments (mysteries), not persons, nor events, however great or remarkable. For persons and events belong to time and to the phenomenal, while principles and processes are eternal and noumenal. The historical method has been the bane of the Churches. Let Theosophy and Theosophists remember that history and individual entities must be ever regarded by them as constituting the accidental, and not the essential element in a system which aims at repairing the errors of the theologians, by reconstructing the Mysteries on a scientific and intelligent basis."

Their dissent from Mr Sinnett's book, *Esoteric Buddhism*,

---

[1] The letter, which is one of great interest, is given in full in *The Life of Anna Kingsford*, vol. ii. pp. 140-146.—S. H. H.

[2] In a letter, dated 1st September 1883, to *Light*, Anna Kingsford said: "Now that the claims of Orientalism are being so widely and popularly discussed, it is most proper and timely to point out the admirable mysticism and the profound learning of the holy Catholic Church of the West. If only the esoteric doctrine of that Church, and the sublime truths embodied in the Liturgy and Creed of Rome, were clearly comprehended and laid to heart, there would be no reason to fear lest some of us should suppose 'Esoteric Buddhism' to be in opposition to 'Esoteric Christianity'" (*Light*, 1883, p. 404).

In her opinion, "the real enemies of the real Catholic Church" were "Atheism and Agnosticism" (*Light*, 1884, p. 519).—S. H. H.

and their attitude towards the alleged "Masters," was not appreciated by the majority of the members of the London Lodge, who failed to understand them, and who failed to see whither under Mr Sinnett's influence they were being led and to what they were committing themselves and their Society. In a letter, dated 2nd November 1883, to her friend Madame de Steiger, who was a prominent member of the Society, Anna Kingsford, after saying that she never dreamed of disparaging the Brothers, nor of imputing that she did not believe in them, and after referring to the feeling of the members—the Cabal raised against her—and to the "folly" of the course then recently pursued by Mr Sinnett in "dragging the names of the Brothers forward into undue prominence," and so making the Society ridiculous in the eyes of the world, said: "Following Mr Sinnett's lead, you have, most of you, read into my address a meaning I had not the least wish to convey, and I am heartily sorry so many of my friends should so much have misunderstood me." This letter drew from Madame de Steiger an answer, to which, in a letter dated 5th November 1883, Anna Kingsford replied, giving the following clear statement of her position:—

"(1) When I was invited to join the Society, I was emphatically and distinctly told that no allegiance would be required of me to the 'Mahatmas,' to Madame Blavatsky, or to any other person real or otherwise, but only to Principles and Objects.

"(2) Consequently, I am no traitor to the express conditions on which I entered the Society when I say that I neither owe nor do I acknowledge the allegiance which now appears to be required of me to persons of whose existence and claims I am utterly unable to affirm or deny anything positively.

"(3) If, then, it is the deliberate opinion of the whole Lodge —which it certainly was not six months ago—that it must have a President whose allegiance to the Mahatmas is *sans peur et sans reproche*, then I certainly am not, from the nature of things, fitted to occupy your Chair. And I do not see how anyone can occupy it, on such terms, who is not, of his own personal experience, in a position to testify to the existence and claims of the 'Brothers.' This even Mr Sinnett cannot do, as he only knows them 'through a glass darkly, and not face to face.'

"(4) I cannot consent to pose before the world in the absurd position of a person claiming to act on principles of exact knowledge and scientific methods, who has abandoned the platform of Historical Christianity because its so-called events and personages are impossible of verification, and who yet accepts as indubitable another set of events and personages the evidence for which is meagre and unsatisfactory in a degree surpassing even that of Historical Christianity. All that is affirmed *may* be true; but *I* am not in a position to know its truth, and cannot therefore say I *believe* it, or *disbelieve* it. The utmost I can say in the present matter is—and this I say cordially—that I am heartily willing and anxious to hear all that comes to us from the East with serious attention, provided I am not called upon to connect it with subservience to any personal authority claiming my belief and confidence as a duty; and provided also that I may fairly and freely criticise what I hear, and test it by reason and experience.

" (5) Madame Blavatsky calls the 'Mahatmas' *Masters*. Her experience and evidence may justify this epithet for her, but they do not justify me in using it. I do not, therefore, and will not, apply that term to any earthly being soever.

" I may add that it is not *I* who seek to separate Esoteric Buddhism from Esoteric Christianity. First, the system expounded by Mr Sinnett is not—so far as I can see—esoteric at all, being simply a scheme of transcendental physics; and, secondly, he is deliberately seeking to *silence* every other voice but that of the 'Mahatmas.' If there is to be unification and brotherhood, there must be *equality*. It now seems to me that I am the only representative of Christian doctrine left among you. . . ." [1]

With a view to the vindication of their own position in regard to Mr Sinnett's *Esoteric Buddhism*, they wrote a pamphlet, which consisted of a letter, dated December 1883, from Anna Kingsford to the London Lodge of the Theosophical Society; some " Remarks and Propositions on Mr Sinnett's *Esoteric Buddhism*," by Edward Maitland; and a copy of Anna Kingsford's letter, dated 31st October 1883, to the President of the Theosophical Society, to which reference has been made (see pp. 17–18, *ante*).[2] The following passage from Anna Kingsford's first-mentioned letter gives the key to the position taken up by them. She says: " Pure Buddhism is in no radical respect different from pure Christianity, because esoteric religion is identical throughout all time and conditions, being eternal in its truth and immanent in the

---

[1] *Life of A. K.*, vol. ii. pp. 147–148.
[2] *Ibid.*, pp. 148–154. See also pp. 163–164, where the circumstances necessitating the writing of this pamphlet are very clearly stated.—S. H. H.

human spirit. I am myself as much the disciple of Buddha as of Christ, because the two Masters are one in Doctrine. But, in my view, such a system as Mr Sinnett's book reveals to us is as opposed to Buddhism as it is to Christianity, and is utterly incompatible with the avowed aims and teachings of the Society under whose ægis it is issued. No universal religion, no catholic brotherhood can be built on such a foundation as this;—it is but the germ of a new sect, and one more materialistic, exoteric, and unscientific than has ever yet been presented with serious claims to the modern world. Its tendency is to divide, to scatter, to repel, making all chance of unification impossible, instead of reconstructing, consolidating, and reconciling. East and West will never meet on such a bridge as this doctrine, nor will the conflicting testimonies of history and scientific criticism be silenced by enunciations of transcendental physics which directly impinge on their domain. In a word, this book is neither 'Buddhism' nor 'esoteric.'"[1] The letter went on to propose that, on the recurrence of the elections for 1884, two Sections be created in the London Lodge; one, to be formed by the Fellows who desired to pursue exclusively the teaching of the Thibetan Mahatmas, and to be presided over by Mr Sinnett; the other, to be known as the Catholic Section of the London Lodge, to be composed of Fellows who desired to adopt a broader basis and to extend research into other directions—" more especially with the object of encouraging the study of Esoteric Christianity, and of the Occidental theosophy out of which it arose "—the principal studies of this Section being addressed to " the analysis of the great religions and philosophies which have swayed mankind in the past, and which divide their allegiance in the present"; but notwithstanding these two Sections, Fellows of either Section were to be free to belong to both, and free to attend each other's meetings.

Edward Maitland says: " The great majority of the Lodge were strongly adverse to the line taken by us, . . . and it became clear that, when the time came, as it would come in January, for the annual election of Officers, we should be displaced. This was a conclusion which, so far as concerned ourselves, we contemplated with more than equanimity, with positive satisfaction and relief. The turmoil of the position, and the personal conflicts engendered, were distasteful to us in the extreme, and only the hope of saving the Society from its own discordant elements,

[1] *Life of A. K.,* vol. ii. p. 152.

to become a redeeming influence in the world, reconciled us to continued association with it."[1]

On the 21st December, *after* the printing of the above-mentioned pamphlet, Anna Kingsford received from Madame Blavatsky a letter dated "Adyar, 25th November 1883," which was said to have been written "under orders," and which asserted that the policy and actions of Anna Kingsford were known to and approved of by the Mahatmas. The following is an extract from Madame Blavatsky's letter: "I happen to know—and I write this to Mr Sinnett to-day—that notwithstanding your own doubts and slight misconceptions of our Masters, and the opposition you experienced (or rather Mr Maitland) on the afternoon of October 26th—*and all the rest*, they are still desirous (and 'more than ever,' as my Guru expresses it) that you should kindly pursue your own policy, for they find it good. This I write *à l'aveugle*, for I know nothing either of the said policy or what has been the nature of the disagreement between you in its details, though acquainted with its general character. I simply communicate to you the Order I receive, and the words used. 'Future alone will shew why we take another view of the situation than Mr Sinnett'—are the words used. . . . I have always understood the Chelas to say that They—the Masters—knew and watched your proceedings, that *you were notified* of Their presence, and that you are the most wonderful sensitive in all Europe, not England alone."[2]

Writing of the position to Lady Caithness, Anna Kingsford says: "The doctrine *we* have received is that of all Hermetic and Kabalistic teaching from time immemorial; and to forsake that and embrace the strange and inconsistent creed put forth as 'Esoteric Buddhism' would be to turn our backs at once and definitively upon all that is divine and true in the highest sense. None of *us* are capable of such folly as that would be."[3]

The meeting of the Society, which was held on the 27th January 1884, passed without any change being made. The reason for this was that both sides had represented their views to the Founders—Madame Blavatsky and Colonel Olcott—and the elections were postponed until such time as word should be received from India.[4]

[1] *Life of A. K.*, vol. ii. pp. 154–155. [2] *Ibid.*, pp. 159–160, note.
[3] *Ibid.*, p. 159. [4] *Ibid.*, pp. 155, 158, 159.

BIOGRAPHICAL PREFACE

C. C. Massey, to whom reference has been made, wrote at this time to a friend, saying: "It is desirable that we should, by re-electing Mrs Kingsford (who is only opposed on account of her independence), reaffirm with some emphasis the principle of freedom of thought."[1]

Edward Maitland says: "When the time came for the decisive meeting to be held, the occasion proved to be in the highest degree dramatic. The tension was extreme, so high did feeling run on both sides; and when, at the moment that the crucial question was to be put, Mary produced a telegram[2] from India saying 'Remain President,' and signed 'Koot Hoomi,' the sensation was indescribable. The mandate was at once recognised as imperative, and the election was but a formality."[3]

The result of the reference to India was the publication of a pamphlet, written by T. Subba Row and Madame Blavatsky, in support of Mr Sinnett and his book. This, Edward Maitland says, "necessitated a rejoinder from us, which took the shape of another pamphlet, in which we shewed conclusively that the reply, so far from being an answer to us, was inaccurate and incoherent, and left our position untouched."[4]

In their rejoinder they said: "It is a mistake to regard us as seeking to 'set off Esoteric Christianity against Esoteric Buddhism,' and this for the very reason assigned by Madame Blavatsky, and in which we have great pleasure in agreeing with her, namely, because to do so would be 'to offer one part of the whole against another part of the whole.' For, as stated at some length in *The Perfect Way*, we regard the two systems as complementary to each other, each being indispensable, as concerned

---

[1] Letter, dated 5th February 1884, to W. F. Kirby.

[2] The telegram had been received by her on the 9th December 1883, *i.e.* it was despatched *after* the printing of the above-mentioned pamphlet.—S. H. H.

[3] *Life of A. K.*, vol. ii. pp. 159-160.

[4] Edward Maitland says that when, later on, Madame Blavatsky published her *magnum opus—The Secret Doctrine—*she "threw over Mr Sinnett's presentation in favour of ours, having meanwhile informed us that it had been as much as she and Subba Row could do to make a plausible defence of Mr Sinnett's *Esoteric Buddhism*, as we were right and it was wrong through its writer's misapprehension of the teaching received by him. 'But,' she added, with the candour characteristic of her in her best moods, 'we were obliged to support him then because he represented us, but when the secret doctrine was concerned, it was necessary to tell the truth'—a position at least intelligible" (*Life of A. K.*, vol. ii. p. 160).

with, or representing different stages in, man's spiritual evolution, Christianity, rightly interpreted, representing the latter, and therefore the higher, in that it alone, unequivocally, '*has the Spirit.*'"[1]

In March 1884 the Founders of the Theosophical Society were in Paris, and in the following month they came to England with the object of composing the division in the London Lodge. The two parties then first became acquainted with each other. A Lodge meeting was held, at which Anna Kingsford and Edward Maitland were present for the purpose of inaugurating their successors. Edward Maitland, giving an account of this meeting, says: "Being unable to reconcile ourselves to their programme, and in deference to the general desire for officials devoted wholly to the Eastern teachings, we withdrew from our positions of President and Vice-President respectively of the London Lodge,[2] and sought an independent platform for our own teaching. The result was the formation of the Hermetic Society, in which we had the concurrence and assistance of the Theosophical Society Founders and several of its members, their desire being to make it a separate Lodge of their own Society.[3] This however, to our satisfaction, proved impossible, owing to the issue of a rule prohibiting membership of more than one Lodge at a time. The Hermetic Society was, therefore, established on an independent basis, with Mary as its President."[4] Their valued friend C. C. Massey heartily supported the new enterprise.

---

[1] *Life of A. K.*, vol. ii. pp. 161-162. An interesting letter, dated 11th March 1884, written by Anna Kingsford to Lady Caithness, with reference to T. Subba Row's pamphlet and their reply thereto, is to be found in the same volume, pp. 165-167.

[2] At the close of the year they resigned their membership in the Lodge.—S. H. H.

[3] A Charter was, in fact, granted by Colonel Olcott to the new Lodge, which was to be known as the Hermetic Lodge of the Theosophical Society (see *Light*, 19th April 1884, p. 154), and members of other Lodges were to be eligible for admission to the Hermetic Lodge without renunciation of any previous affiliation, and on the 9th April 1884, a meeting for the purpose of inaugurating the new Lodge was held at C. C. Massey's, Colonel H. S. Olcott presiding; but owing to the issue by Colonel H. S. Olcott (on Mr Sinnett's recommendation), almost immediately afterwards, of the above-mentioned rule prohibiting membership of more than one Lodge at a time, it became necessary to make the new adventure *outside* of the Theosophical Society; and, at a meeting held on the 22nd April 1884, it was unanimously resolved to surrender the above-mentioned Charter, and to reconstitute the New Society independently of the Theosophical Society (*Life of A. K.*, vol. ii. pp. 186-187; letter of E. M. in *Light*, 3rd May 1884, p. 182).—S. H. H.

[4] *Life of A. K.*, vol. ii. pp. 186-187.

The objects of the Hermetic Society were set forth in its Prospectus [1] as follows:—

"The designation of this Society was chosen in conformity with that ancient and universal usage of the Western world, which, regarding HERMES as the supreme initiator into the Sacred Mysteries of existence, has identified his name with the knowledge of things spiritual and occult.

"Its objects are at once scientific, intellectual, moral, and religious.

"Its chief aim is to promote the comparative study of the philosophical and religious systems of the East and of the West; especially of the Greek Mysteries and the Hermetic Gnosis, and its allied schools, the Kabalistic, Pythagorean, Platonic, and Alexandrian,—these being inclusive of Christianity,—with a view to the elucidation of their original esoteric and real doctrine, and the adaption of its expression to modern requirements.

"The knowledges acquired will be applied, first, to the interpretation and harmonisation of the various existing systems of thought and faith, and the provision thereby of an *Eirenicon* among all Churches and communions; and, secondly, to the promotion of personal psychic and spiritual development.

"To these ends the Society encourages and undertakes the publication of ancient and modern Hermetic literature, and invites its Fellows to further its efforts on this behalf by subscribing for the Works issued, by actively co-operating in the general purposes of the Society, and by contributing to the promotion of its special objects.

"In carrying out these designs, the Society accords to its Fellows full freedom of opinion, expression, and action; and in regard to doctrinal questions, recognises reason and experience alone as affording legitimate ground for conclusion." [2]

The Prospectus was accompanied by the following note:—

"In inviting your attention to the accompanying Prospectus, it is considered desirable to state that the Hermetic Society has been formed, not in any spirit of opposition to, or rivalry with, the Theosophical Society, or any of its branches, but rather as a supplement and complement to it and them, and in friendly co-operation to their declared aims. Desiring no less than the Theosophical Society to study the philosophical systems of the

---

[1] *I.e.* in the revised Prospectus dated March 1885. For the Prospectus as originally issued, see *Light*, 1884, p. 186.—S. H. H.
[2] *Life of A. K.*, vol. ii. p. 195.

East, and to promote the sentiment of universal brotherhood, the Hermetic Society directs its attention more particularly to the systems of the West, and seeks, by comparing all systems, to ascertain their respective merits and mutual relation. In this it is actuated by the conviction that the common object of both Societies—to wit, the establishment of spiritual unity throughout the world—will be most effectually promoted, not by seeking to include all men under one denomination, but by exhibiting the substantial agreement already subsisting among their various systems and creeds.

"These being the spirit and scope of the Hermetic Society, its Fellows feel that they are entitled to look confidently for such reciprocity between it and the Theosophical Society as will promote concurrent membership in both Societies."

By the rules of the Society it was expressly provided that (*inter alia*) distinctions of race, religion, or sex should be no bar either to Fellowship or to office.

The Hermetic Society was inaugurated on Friday the 9th May 1884—St George's Eve—at No. 43 Rutland Gate, London, the residence of Captain Francis Lloyd. There was a large attendance of members and guests, including Colonel Olcott, who expressed his sympathy with the objects of the new Society.[1] An interesting address was delivered by Anna Kingsford, as President, in which, Edward Maitland says, she "made the legend of St George and the Dragon the basis of an exposition of Hermetic doctrine, in the course of which she shewed that it was one of many allegories of identical import. For as the Dragon of the sacred myths of old was always Materiality, and the Princess exposed to it was the Soul, so the Knight who rescues and finally carries her off in triumph as his bride to heaven is always, directly or by delegation, Hermes, the Angel of the understanding of divine things, by whose aid alone the soul is enabled to surmount the sense-nature, and man realises his Divine potentialities."[2] Applying this to the present age, Anna Kingsford said: "In the revival of the Hermetic philosophy now taking place may be seen at once the token and the agent of the world's deliverance. For it means the supersession of a period of obscuration by one of illumination, such that men can once more rise from the appreciation of the Form to that of the Substance, of the Letter to that of the Spirit, and thus discern the meaning of the Divine Word,

[1] *Life of A. K.*, vol. ii. pp. 187, 188; *Light*, 1884, p. 198.
[2] *Life of A. K.*, vol. ii. p. 196.

whether written or enacted. Such recognition of the ideal as the real signifies the reconstruction of religion upon a scientific basis, and of science upon a religious basis. So long as religion builds upon the mere facts and phenomena of history, she builds upon a sandbank, on which the advancing tide of scientific criticism is ever encroaching, and which must sooner or later be swept away with all that is founded upon it. But when she learns the secret of Hermetic, that is Esoteric, interpretation, then, and then only, does she build upon a rock, which shall never be shaken. Such is the import of the term 'Peter,' which, as one with Hermes, properly denotes not only rock, but interpreter."[1] And she announced a series of discourses by herself at future meetings of the Society explanatory of the terms of the Apostles' Creed.[2]

Edward Maitland says: "My contribution on the occasion was a sketch of the history and character of the Hermetic philosophy, which was followed by a discussion, the chief feature of which was an account given by Colonel Olcott of the origin and aims of the Theosophical Society, and of the derivation of its teaching from the sages of the East, whose methods and doctrines, he said, were purely Hermetic—a definition which we recognised as altogether excluding Mr Sinnett's *Esoteric Buddhism*."[3]

---

[1] *Life of A. K.*, vol. ii. p. 196. "It is," she said, "on this Hermetic Rock of inward illumination and spiritual life—called by Trismegistus 'the Mount of Regeneration'—that the great Mystics of all time have ever taken their stand. Hereon were founded the Pythagorean and Neoplatonic Schools, the system of the Alexandrian Gnostics, and the various lodges of semi-oriental philosophy of Egypt and Asia Minor in the centuries immediately preceding the Christian era. And in later days this self-same illumination formulated itself by the lips and pens of the initiates of the thirteenth and following centuries—the epoch of the 'Angelic Doctor,' of St Bernard, of Thomas à Kempis, of Eckhart, Tauler, Ruysbroeck, Hugo of St Victor, and others who sought the 'Perfect Way' and thereby found the 'Christ.' These men were not Occultists, but Mystics. Though they wrought marvels, they cared little for miracles. For the Mystic aspires after the power of the Spiritual life, not after that of the physical or astral. He is no enemy of the Occult. He transcends it: and his miracles are those of the inward state—triumphs of intellectual illumination, solutions, realisations, conversions and transmutations performed in union with the Will of God, in the medium of the mind and spirit." Her exposition of the legend of St George and the Dragon will be found in the story, entitled "St George the Chevalier," in *Dreams and Dream Stories* (third edition, p. 288).—S. H. H.

[2] *Light*, 1884, p. 198.

[3] *Life of A. K.*, vol. ii. p. 196. None of Edward Maitland's Lectures to the Hermetic Society are included in the present volume. I hope, in the near future, to publish these in a companion volume.—S. H. H.

Writing in her Diary on the 11th May—two days after the inauguration of the new Society—Anna Kingsford says: "I do not yet know, myself, exactly what it is we seek to gain in this Society. I do not want to be a Teacher, arrogating to myself all authority and illumination. I want light. Perhaps the best way will be to have discussion days on the subject of some paper previously read. What we really seek is to reform the Christian system and start a new Esoteric Church. When once this is started it may go on indefinitely, as does the Exoteric Church." And in a letter, written on the following day, to Lady Caithness, she says: "We want to get *known*. Sometimes I think that the truths and knowledges we hold are so high and so deep that the age is yet unable to receive them, and that all we shall be permitted to do is to formulate them in some book or books to leave as a legacy to the world when we pass away from it. The truth we have is far in advance of anything the disciples of Madame Blavatsky and her Gurus possess." [1]

At the second meeting, on the 9th May 1884, Edward Maitland read a paper on "Revelation as the Supreme Common Sense," meaning that the consensus or agreement which it represents is that, not of all men merely, but of all parts of man; of mind, soul, and spirit; of intellect and intuition, combined in a pure spirit and unfolded to the utmost." For, he says, "there is no contradiction between Reason and Revelation, provided only it be the whole Reason and not the mutilated faculty which ordinarily passes for such, for that represents the intellect without the intuition. And it is precisely the loss or corruption of this last which constitutes the Fall, the Intuition, as the feminine mode of the mind and representing the soul, being mystically called 'the woman.'" [2]

Anna Kingsford's forthcoming Lectures on the Creed were notified to the members of the Society in a circular as follows:—

---

[1] *Life of A. K.*, vol. ii. pp. 187 and 188. [2] *Ibid.*, p. 197.

The Hermetic Society.

THE SUMMER SESSION MEETINGS

Of this Society for 1884 will be held, until further notice, at

43 RUTLAND GATE, S.W.

On the Afternoons of Thursday, June 12, 19, 26, July 3, 10, 17, 24, and 31.

To commence at 5 o'clock precisely.

Subject of Exposition and Discussion:

THE CREDO OF CHRISTENDOM

Its Esoteric and Occult Meaning; its Relation to the Nature of Existence; and its Correspondence with the Sacred Mysteries of Antiquity.

To be introduced by the President in Special Papers.

At first, C. C. Massey did not like the idea of these lectures. Writing, shortly after their announcement, to Edward Maitland on the subject he said: "It seemed too much like putting new wine into old bottles, and, in short, not quite the sort of thing 'Hermetists' would look for. But then it occurred to me that if she really can shew to the progressive minds in the Church that the esoteric doctrine is signified by the historical form and embodied in the Creeds, and that the historical faith is not really Christianity, but just its vehicle, then that truth might be seized upon, and might unite hundreds of influential minds in its propaganda. I mean that the lead might thus be given to a movement of real importance in the Church, and one which might re-ally it to philosophy. . . ."[1] But Mr Massey was probably not then aware that Anna Kingsford had under Divine Illumination recovered the sense in which the Creeds were intended by their formulators, and *in such sense* she recognised

[1] *Life of A. K.*, vol. ii. p. 194.

them as being indisputably true, in that they represent indispensable soul-processes.[1] In 1879, when a medical student in Paris, she had received the mystical version of the Creed, which, Edward Maitland says, " by rendering the Creed into the present tense . . . exhibited to our supreme satisfaction the interior character of Christianity proper, to the confirmation of our own independent conviction respecting the non-historical nature of all that is essential in religion ; and in such presentation we rejoiced to recognise the death-blow to the superstition which insists on restricting to a time and to an individual processes which are by their nature necessarily eternal and universal."[2] The Creed, as received by Anna Kingsford, is as follows :—

"THE CREDO;

being a summary of the spiritual history of the Sons of God, and the mysteries of the kingdoms of the Seven Spheres.

"I BELIEVE in one God ; the Father and Mother Almighty ; of whose substance are the generations of Heaven and of earth. And in Christ Jesus the Son of God, our Lord ; who is conceived of the Holy Ghost ; born of the Virgin Mary ; suffereth under the world-rulers ; is crucified, dead, and buried ; who descendeth into hell ; who riseth again from the dead ; who ascendeth into Heaven, and sitteth at the right hand of God ; by whose law the quick and the dead are judged. I believe in the Seven Spirits of God ; the Kingdom of Heaven ; the communion of the elect ; the passing-through of souls ; the redemption of the body ; the life everlasting ; and the Amen.

"He that believeth and is initiated shall be saved; and he that believeth not shall consume away."[3]

Referring to the concluding sentences, Edward Maitland says: "The long-standing controversy respecting the meaning of *Nirvâna* has been resolved for us in favour of both the interpretations assigned to it. This is to say that, while it means *extinction*, the extinction implied is of two different kinds. Of these, one called the celestial *Nirvâna*, denotes the perfectionment and perpetuation of the essential selfhood of the individual, accompanied by the extinction of the external and phenomenal selfhood. Thus indrawn to his centre, the individual ceases

---

[1] See E. M.'s letter in *Light*, 1890, p. 290.
[2] *Life of A. K.*, vol. i. p. 305.
[3] *Clothed With the Sun*, pt. ii. No. 1.

to *ex-ist*, but does not cease to *be*. In other words, he *is*, but is not manifest, the term existence, as opposed to being, implying the standing-forth, or objectivisation, of that which *is*, subjectively. The condition implies the return from matter to substance or spirit.

"The 'Nirvâna of the Amen,' on the contrary, denotes the extinction, not only of the externality of the individual, but of the individual himself; this occurring through the persistent indulgence of a perverse will to the outer and lower, such as to induce a complete deprivation of the inner and higher constituents of man, and so to divest his system of its binding principle as to render not only possible, but inevitable, complete dissolution and disintegration, to the total extinction of the individuality concerned. This is not loss of substance or spirit. The term *Amen* in this relation signifies consummation or finality.

"Like the so-called 'damnatory' clauses of the 'Athanasian Creed,' the declaration [at the end of the Creed, as given above] is simply a solemn recognition, first, of the doctrine that salvation is neither arbitrary not compulsory, but conditional and optional, the alternative to it being extinction; and, next, of the Credo as a summary of the conditions of salvation. These, it is true, are expressed in terms which, in being symbolical, do not bear their meaning upon the face of them; but none the less are the conditions themselves so simple and obvious as to be recognisable as self-evident and necessarily true. That is to say, they represent the steps of a process necessary to be enacted in the soul, and founded in the nature of the soul itself; so that, when understood, the belief in them makes no greater strain upon the faculties than does the belief in any self-evident proposition whatever. Rather would the difficulty be to disbelieve them. Wherefore—to state the case in other words—the declaration of the soul's extinction through non-compliance with the conditions herein affirmed to be indispensable to its perpetuation, made by the initiate in the terms of the Credo, is the exact parallel and counterpart of the declaration of the body's extinction through non-compliance with the conditions indispensable to its continuance, made by the physiologist in the terms of his craft. The language is in each case technical, but the truths it conceals (from the non-initiate) are incontestable; and so far from their being disbelieved by those who do not understand them, they are invariably acted upon by all—who are of sound mind—to the best of their ability, despite their failure to understand them. For, alike for soul and body, there is that within man which does believe, and which accordingly does comply with the conditions requisite for his welfare, quite independently of his knowledge of processes and terms spiritual or physiological, and which needs but fair play, and not to be thwarted by his own perverse will, to accomplish his salvation.

"Wherefore the declaration in question is no menace, but rather is it a promise,—a promise that when the time comes to understand the process whereby salvation is accomplished, the very fact that it is understood is a token that salvation is accomplished; for once understood, it can no more be disbelieved than gravitation or any other certainty of the physical world. Now, to have this understanding is to be 'initiated.'"[1] It is the spiritual selfhood of man—the Christ Jesus within him—that is the subject of the Christian Credo. "The Apostles' Creed is an epitome of the spiritual history of all those who become by re-generation 'Sons of God.'"[2]

In reply to and correcting one who had declared that "the old creed-makers meant the Creed literally," Edward Maitland said: "This is not the case. The adopters of it into the Christian Church meant it literally, for the Church inherited its mysteries without the key to them, the 'key of knowledge,' with the abstraction of which Jesus so bitterly reproached the ecclesiasticism of His time, had not yet been restored. But it was not so with the original formulaters of the Creed. . . . The original and intended sense of the Creed is purely spiritual and devoid of any physical reference."[3]

The dates and subject-matter of the lectures given by Anna Kingsford and Edward Maitland to the Hermetic Society during the first Session were as follows:—

12th June 1884, Anna Kingsford, on the clause of the Creed: "I believe in God, the Father Almighty, Creator of Heaven and earth."

19th „ „ Anna Kingsford, on the clause of the Creed: "And in Jesus Christ, His only Son, our Lord; who is conceived by the Holy Ghost, born of the Virgin Mary."

---

[1] *Clothed With the Sun*, App., pp. i–iii.
[2] E. M., *Light*, 1893, p. 284; and see *Life of A. K.*, vol. i. p. 315.
[3] *Light*, 1884, p. 190.

BIOGRAPHICAL PREFACE

26th June 1884, Edward Maitland, on " Mystics and Materialists."

10th July ,, Anna Kingsford, on the clause of the Creed: " He suffereth under Pontius Pilate."

17th ,, ,, Anna Kingsford, on the clause of the Creed: " I believe in the Holy Ghost, the holy Catholic Church."

24th ,, ,, Anna Kingsford, on the same subject as the last.

31st ,, ,, Anna Kingsford, on the same subject as the last.

Speaking of the Lecture on Mystics and Materialists, given by himself, Edward Maitland says: " I shewed how dense was the ignorance and prejudice of the treatment accorded by the materialistic school to Mystics and Mysticism, and described the issue between the two parties as of the most tremendous import, being nothing less than the nature of existence, the constitution and destiny of man, the being of God and the spiritual world, the possibility of revelation, and the validity of the religious sentiment. Respecting all these, I said, the mystics claimed to have affirmative experiences of a kind absolutely satisfactory, they themselves being, by reason of their character and eminence, entitled to full credence. For the order to which they belonged comprised the highest types of humanity, and in fact all those sages, saints, seers, prophets, and Christs, through whose redeeming influence humanity has been preserved from the abyss of utter negation in respect of all that makes and ennobles humanity, and these have uniformly declared that the passage from Materialism to Mysticism has been to them a passage, physically, from disease to health; intellectually, from infancy to manhood; morally, from anarchy to order; and spiritually, from darkness to light and from death to life—even life everlasting. And none who had made that passage has ever been known to wish to retrieve his steps. And as it was through the loss of the intuition that the world has sunk into the materialism now prevailing, so it will be through the restoration of the intuition, now taking place, that the world will be rescued and redeemed."[1]

A wonderful Illumination,[2] received and written down by Anna

[1] *Life of A. K.*, vol. ii. p. 199.
[2] Illumination " Concerning the Prophecy of the Immaculate Conception." It is given in full in *Clothed With the Sun*, pt. i. No. iii.

Kingsford while under trance, says: "The Church knows not the source of its dogmas. We [1] marvel also at the blindness of the hearers, who indeed hear, but who have not eyes to see. We speak in vain,—ye discern not spiritual things. Ye are so materialised that ye perceive only the material. The Spirit comes and goes; ye hear the sound of Its voice: but ye cannot tell whither It goeth nor whence It cometh. All that is true is spiritual. No dogma of the Church is true that seems to bear a physical meaning. For matter shall cease, and all that is of it, but the Word of the Lord shall remain for ever. And how shall it remain except it be purely spiritual; since, when matter ceases, it would then be no longer comprehensible? I tell you again, and of a truth,—no dogma is real that is not spiritual. If it be true, and yet seem to you to have a material signification, know that you have not solved it. It is a mystery: seek its interpretation. That which is true, is for spirit alone."

What has been said of the dogmas of the Church is true also of the Scriptures. Anna Kingsford's Lecture on "Bible Hermeneutics" makes this very clear. She once, in her sleep, read in a book an Instruction "Concerning the Intention of the Mystical Scriptures," which she wrote down from memory immediately on waking. The Instruction so read by her referred in particular to the interpretation to be put upon the early books of the Old Testament, which books were stated to be mystical, but the principles enunciated are applicable to all sacred scriptures; and the purport of it was that if such books be Mystic Books, they ought also to have a Mystic Consideration: "It ought to be known, indeed, for the right Understanding of the Mystical Books, that in their esoteric Sense they deal, not with material Things, but with spiritual Realities. . . . The Mystic Books deal only with spiritual Entities. . . . They are Idolaters who understand the Things of Sense where the Things of the Spirit are alone implied."[2] On another occasion she found herself surrounded in her sleep by a group of spirits, who conversed together concerning the "Fall." They began by saying that "all the mistakes made about the Bible arise out of the Mystic Books being referred to times, places, and persons material,

[1] The overshadowing influences, denoting the Hierarchy of the Church invisible and celestial.

[2] Illumination "Concerning the Interpretation of the Mystical Scriptures," *C. W. S.*, pt. i. No. v.; see also Illumination "Concerning the Mosaic Cosmogony," *C. W. S.*, pt. i. No. vi.

instead of being regarded as containing only eternal verities about things spiritual."[1]

Having been interviewed by the late W. T. Stead, Anna Kingsford wrote for the *Pall Mall Gazette*, of which he was then the editor, the following account of the Hermetic Society, which duly appeared in that journal:—

"The name of Hermes as the divine representative of the intellectual principle has ever in the Western World been associated with the study of spiritual and occult science, and with the knowledge of things hidden and removed from the reach of the superficial sense. Hence the very word 'hermetic' has, in common parlance, come to be applied to the enclosure and sealing up of objects which it is desired to preserve inviolate and incorrupt. The Hermetic Society, however, though, as its name implies, concerning itself mainly with the study of the secret science, is not a secret association. Its Fellows are bound by no pledges of silence, and use neither password nor sign. In a Society having a catholic object, and aiming at the inauguration of a school of thought which, though old in the history of the world, is new in that of our race and time, it is considered that a policy of exclusiveness would be anachronistic and out of place. Moreover, the origin and character of the Society are not of a nature to render secrecy either necessary or desirable. Composed as it is, not of initiates, but of students, and numbering in its ranks sound scholars and competent thinkers more or less intolerant of ecclesiastical methods and control, the task which the Society has set itself is one for which it seeks and invites co-operation on the part of all able contributors to the thought of our day. This task involves the investigation of the nature and constitution of man, with a view to the formulation of a system of thought and rule of life which will enable the individual to develop to the utmost his higher potentialities, intellectual and spiritual. The Society represents a reaction that has long been observable, though hitherto discouraged and hindered from public expression by still dominant influences. Reaction is not necessarily, nor indeed usually, retrogressive. It bears on its wave the best acquisitions of time and culture, and often represents the deeper current of essential progress. The tendency of the age to restrict the researches of the human mind to a range of study merely material and sensible is directly inimical to the method of Nature, and must, therefore, prove abortive. For

[1] Illumination "Concerning the Fall," *C. W. S.*, pt. i. No. vii.

it represents an attempt to limit the scope and the possibilities of evolution, and thus to hinder the normal development of those higher modes of consciousness which mark certain advanced types of mankind. Reason is not less the test of truth to the Mystic than to the Materialist; but the mode of it to which the former appeals is on a higher level, transcending the operation of the outer and ordinary senses. 'Revelation' thus becomes conceivable. Only to thought which is absolutely free is the manifestation of truth possible; and to be thus free, thought must be exercised in all directions, not outward only to the phenomenal, but inward to the real also, from the expression of idea in formal matter to the informing idea itself. Our age, failing to comprehend the mystic spirit, has hitherto associated it with attributes which really belong not to mysticism, but to the common apprehension of it—obscurity and uncertainty. The Hermetic Society desires to reveal mysticism to a world which knows it not; to define its propositions, to categorise its doctrine. And this can be done only by minds trained in philosophical method, because mysticism is a science, based on the essential reason of things—the most supremely rationalistic of all systems. . . .

"The programme by which the Hermetic Society intends to regulate and direct its labours is a rich one. It comprises the comparative study of all philosophical and religious systems, whether of the East or of the West, and especially of the 'Mysteries' of Egypt and Greece, and the allied schools of Kabalistic, Pythagorean, Platonic, and Alexandrian illumination. The researches of the Hermetists in the direction of Christian doctrine are specially interesting, on account not only of the importance of the subject, but of the novelty of the treatment accorded to it. In the papers on the 'Credo of Christendom' now in course of delivery, the President deals with the historical element of our national faith as its accident and vehicle only, the dramatic formulation of processes whose proper sphere of operation is the human mind and soul.

"These observations will suffice to shew that the Hermetic Society is not more friendly to the popular presentation of orthodox Church doctrine than to the fashionable agnosticism of the hour. It represents, indeed, a revolt against all conventional forms of belief, whether ecclesiastical or secular, and a conviction that the rehabilitation of religion on reasonable and scientific grounds is not only possible to the human mind, but is essential to human progress and development. This line of thought was first introduced to the public in a work entitled *The Perfect Way, or the Finding of Christ*, with the production of which, it is an open secret that the present President of the Hermetic Society had much to do. . . .

"The Hermetic Society has a mystic rather than an occult character; it depends for guidance upon no 'Mahatmas,' and can boast no worker of wonders on the phenomenal plane. Its Fellows do not, as Hermetists, interest themselves in the study or culture of abnormal powers; they seek knowledges only, and these not so much on the physical as on the intellectual and spiritual level. Such knowledge must, they hold, be necessarily productive of good works. Hermetists are expected to be true knights of spiritual chivalry, identifying themselves with movements in the direction of justice and mercy, whether towards man or beast, and doing their utmost, individually and collectively, to further the recognition of the Love-principle as that involving the highest and worthiest motive and method of human action."[1]

Speaking of mysticism, in her inaugural address to the Hermetic Society, Anna Kingsford said: "To be a Mystic is in no wise to be a Yogee.[2] The Mystic knows that the true secret of ruling the body is so to deal with it that it shall not assert itself and thrust itself unduly on the observation. Cruelty to the body is just as detrimental to the interests of self-liberation as is sensual indulgence. For both these extremes tend to force the pleasure or pain of the flesh on the attention of the mind, and thus to hinder centralisation of spirit and the growth of the inward peace. The Mystic is the King—not the Tyrant—of the body. Every act and desire of the physical man which does not profit the intellectual man, he subdues and overcomes; but he never torments the flesh for torment's sake. For he knows that such a course would result only in bringing the body into undue prominence; and that all the powers of his mind would become drained out and exhausted with the constant effort to stifle the cries of his victim. Hence he rules

---

[1] *Life of A. K.*, vol. ii. pp. 205-207. See also *Light*, 26th July 1884, p. 302.

[2] A Yogee or Yogî is one who practises Yoga (union). There are two kinds of Yoga: Hatha-Yoga, in which the Yogee seeks to transcend the physical by reducing his own lives to impotency; and Raja-Yoga, in which the Divine Union is sought by concentration and meditation. Anna Kingsford must be understood as referring to Hatha-Yoga only.—S. H. H.

the body as one should rule a servant, his object being so to equilibrate his nature that he may not be aware of the body's presence. . . .

"The Mystic subjugates his body, not by cruel violation of its will, but by bringing this into union and agreement with the higher will of the mind, and thus polarising and identifying all the forces of his complex nature. The accomplished rider and his horse are as one creature. So the initiate and his body are as one being. So long as a man is at war with his flesh, he is not its Master. Inasmuch as a man wilfully maltreats and torments his body, insomuch he sins against the law of Love. And by this law alone can any man become a Master.

"Nor does the Mystic condemn the body's sense of Beauty in the outward world. Far from this. For he knows that through the phantasmagoric veil of the material spheres the eye of the soul may perceive the features of the Divine Glory. Whether in cloud, or sea, or forest, whether in song, or sound of wind, or colour of hill and moor:—in whatever guise Beauty finds and touches him, that which he loves in Nature is the God: his spirit meets and kisses the Spirit within this lovely Maya: all this earthly sweetness and joy, translated and transmuted in his mind, become to him the focus of the eternal and heavenly Light. By means of the outward reflect he rises into the apprehension of the inward Reality. The voice of Nature sings into his soul the wonder of God.

"Nor yet, again, does the Mystic need to immerse himself in the silence and loneliness of the cloister. He bears about his cloister in his heart. There is his inward solitude, there his monastic retreat. Like the halcyon among birds, is the Mystic among men. He builds himself a marvellous nest which not only floats unharmed upon the waves of Existence, but with a magic spell enchants the storm and charms the waves to stillness. In the midst of the world he only knows how to be alone. And this great gift of power to still the elements and make the soul a centre of rest the Gods bestow on man, as then on Halcyone, as the reward of steadfast and ardent Love. Therefore our Society, maintaining the doctrine and method of the Mystics, seeks to unite the intention of its Fellows with all helpful and merciful works throughout the world. The true Mystic lives the life of the ideal Christhood. Of all that he knows and has, he freely gives. Not for himself alone is the word of Life and Love, but for others through him. Champion and Knight, as well as

Thinker and Student, the son of Hermes is of necessity a reformer of men, a redeemer of the world. It is not enough for him to know the doctrine; he must likewise do the will of the Gods, and bid the kingdom of the Lord come upon earth without, even as in the heaven within his heart.

"For the Method of the Mystic is the Law of Love, and Love hath nothing of her own."

Edward Maitland says:[1] "Careful abstracts of our own lectures, made by myself, were published in *Light*, and among the recognitions received from persons who read them there was the following from one whom we regarded as far and away the most advanced of them all in mystic and spiritual knowledge—Baron Spedalieri,[2] who wrote to us as follows respecting Mary's interpretations on the Creed:—

"MARSEILLES, 21st *August* 1884.

"DEAR AND HONOURED MADAME,—DEAR SIR AND FRIEND,— Eliphas Levi was right when he told me that humanity needed not a new Revelation, but rather an explanation of that which it already has. This explanation would, he said, be given in the 'latter times,' and would constitute what he called the 'Messianisme.' The illuminated Guillaume Postel predicted likewise that the 'latter days' would be distinguished by the comprehension of the Kabala, and of the occult books of the Hebrews.

"You—the new Messiah—you are now accomplishing this double mission, and you are doing it in a manner veritably *miraculous*. For I cannot otherwise explain to myself how you have been able to acquire an erudition so exalted and a knowledge so deep that before it all human intelligence is dazzled. No initiation in any anterior state of existence suffices to explain this wonder. Moreover, the doctrines you expound relate to facts posterior to the ancient mysteries, and were therefore unknown to the initiates of remote ages.

"Nothing was ever known or written by any of the Christian Mystics, whether St Martin, Boehme, Swedenborg, or any other Theosophists, comparable to your writings. Eliphas Levi himself would be astonished at your teaching, so logical, so reasonable, so consistent throughout, and so convincing; before which

---

[1] *Life of A. K.*, vol. ii. pp. 199-200.
[2] Baron Giuseppe Spedalieri, a native of Sicily, and a resident at Marseilles, was "the friend, disciple, and literary heir" of the Abbé Constant, who wrote under the name of Eliphas Levi (*Life of A. K.*, vol. ii. pp. 167-168).—S. H. H.

the mind can but incline and adore, and which have made and will make my only strength in the presence of death.

"But this mission imposes on you a great duty. Time presses; the harvest of the earth is ripe. Why do you wait? Why confine yourselves to communicating to a small group of auditors that which ought to regenerate humanity? Why not at once publish these chapters on the Credo, and later the rest of your Hermetic expositions of the teachings of the Church? For then indeed the Church herself will for the first time learn with surprise how great a treasure lies buried under the materialism of her doctrines.

"Prepared as I was by the study of *The Perfect Way*, your first two lectures did not surpass my learning. But the rest have been for me a dazzling revelation. They have opened to me new and unexpected horizons: the splendour of the Kabala has been surpassed. I have thoroughly studied the *résumés* in *Light* in order to grasp the depth and breadth—and shall I say the originality?—of your commentaries. Your explanations of the Seal of Solomon are new to me; but their profundity and truth have ravished my mind. I cried aloud as I read, 'How beautiful that is! How all the truth is there! Ah, my God, when will all this be published?'

"At last I have found the explanation of the planetary system of *Esoteric Buddhism*. But what a difference between the two. How simple is the truth, and how the reason is satisfied by it. Beautiful and accurate also is the distinction you draw between Mysticism and Occultism, whereby the superiority of the former is readily perceived.

"Dear and honoured friends, how can I speak of the great literary talent you have exhibited in the treatment of those most difficult subjects? You have placed them within the reach of every intelligence. You have handled them with admirable lucidity. All that I can say would be beneath the truth.

"With sentiments of the most profound and respectful attachment, I am your wholly devoted   SPEDALIERI."[1]

On the 18th September 1884, shortly after the close of her Lectures to the Hermetic Society, Anna Kingsford was the recipient of an Illumination on "The Mysteries of the Kingdoms of the Seven Spheres,"[2]—"setting forth the correspondence between the seven final clauses of the Creed and the

---

[1] *Life of A. K.*, vol. ii. pp. 200-201.   [2] See p. 30, *ante*.

Seven Spirits of God, and consequently the seven planets and their Gods,"[1]—as follows :—

"THE MYSTERIES OF THE KINGDOMS OF THE SEVEN SPHERES.

I BELIEVE IN THE HOLY GHOST,
Whose seven spirits are as the seven rays of light;

The Nous, or Sun, of the microcosm, the Spirit of Wisdom, the ray of whose angel, Phoibos, is the red of the innermost sphere.

THE HOLY CATHOLIC CHURCH,
Or, kingdom of heaven within man;

Hermes, or Peter, the Spirit of Understanding, and rock whereon the true Church is built, the guardian and interpreter of the holy mysteries.

THE COMMUNION OF SAINTS,
Or, the elect;

Aphrodite, Venus, love, the Spirit of Counsel, or principle of sympathy, harmony, and light, whereby heaven and earth are revealed to each other and drawn together.

THE FORGIVENESS OF SINS,
Or, passing-through of souls;

Iacchos, the initiator, Lord of transmigration, whereby alone *Karma* is satisfied and sins wiped out by expiation and repentance. As the Spirit of Power, he represents the force whereby creation and redemption alike are accomplished, the direction only being reversed.

THE RESURRECTION (which is the redemption) OF THE BODY,
From material limitations;

Ares, or Mars, the war-god, and Spirit of Knowledge, of whom comes contention, at the cost of suffering and death, for the divine knowledge whereby man learns the secret of transmutation, which is the crowning conquest of matter by spirit.

THE LIFE EVERLASTING;

Zeus and Hera, rulers of heaven, the dual spirit of Righteousness or godliness, which is justice, or the perfect balance, and the secret of eternal generation.

AND THE AMEN,
Or, final consummation.

Saturn, or Satan, the Spirit of the Fear of the Lord, being the angel—unfallen—of the outermost sphere, and keeper of the boundary of the divine kingdom, within which is the perfection, and without which, the negation of being."[2]

---

[1] *Life of A. K.*, vol. ii. p. 213.
[2] *Clothed With the Sun*, pt. ii. No. xvii.

The Seven Spirits of God and their correspondences are given in *Clothed With the Sun*[1] as follows:—

Elohim or Archangels.		Signification.	Gods.	Office.	Tincture of Ray.	The Spirit of
1. Uriel	=	Fire of God.	Phoibos Apollo.	Angel of the Sun.	Red.	Wisdom.
2. Raphael	=	Physician of God.	Hermes.	Angel of Mercury.	Orange.	Understanding.
3. Anael	=	Sweet Song of God.	Aphrodite.	Angel of Venus.	Yellow.	Counsel.
4. Salamiel	=	Acquired of God.	Dionysos.	Angel of the Earth.	Green.	Power.
5. Zacchariel	=	Man of God.	Ares.	Angel of Mars.	Blue.	Knowledge.
6. Michael	=	Like unto God.	Zeus and Hera.	Angel of Jupiter.	Purple.	Righteousness.
7. Orifiel (or Satan)	=	Hour of God.	Kronos.	Angel of Saturn.	Violet.	Divine Awe. (Hence Reverence and Humility.)
Gabriel	=	Strength of God.	Artemis or Isis.	Angel of the Moon.		

White, being the combination of all the rays, implies full illumination and intuition of God, the symbol of which is the full moon, and is the symbol of initiation. Attaining to this state, the soul is the mystical "Woman clothed with the Sun" of Apoc. xii. 1. Gabriel, the angel of this state, represents the reflective principle of the soul. He is not one of the seven Elohim, but is the complement of them all, being the spirit of all the moons.

The man fully regenerate needs no "moon" to reflect to him the "sun." Wherefore Gabriel, having no function to fulfil in the perfected kosmos, is indrawn, and does not appear in the Mysteries of the Kingdoms of the Seven Spheres, referred to on page 41, *ante*.[2]

[1] Pt. ii., Illumination No. xvi.
[2] *Clothed With the Sun*, pt. ii., Illumination No. xvii.; and see pt. i., Illumination No. xiv. (pt. ii.) "Concerning the Genius."

At the close of the year (1884) they, "with profound regret," terminated their connection with the London Lodge of the Theosophical Society, on the ground that, *in practice*, such Lodge had departed from and in no small degree renounced the professed objects of the Society; but though they severed their connection with the London Lodge, they did not sever their connection with the Parent Society, for the reason that Theosophy was not to be confounded with its professors.[1] Edward Maitland's conviction was that "if the Gods were to wait until they found perfect instruments, or perfect persons as instruments, for their work, they would never begin at all." A work is not to be judged by one's conception of the doers of it. It is due to Madame Blavatsky to record that when, some two years later, she came to know them personally and to respect them, she frankly admitted that they had been in the right in all their contentions, and their opponents in the wrong, even though she herself was one of the latter;[2] and she subsequently proposed that Anna Kingsford should accept the position of President of her (Madame Blavatsky's) own Lodge in her place, with the object of creating "a Theosophy which would really be universal, and be everywhere recognised as such:"[3]—a proposal that could not, of course, be then entertained, but it was important as marking the beginning of a change of attitude on the part of the Society—or of some of the members thereof—which subsequently took place, regarding Anna Kingsford and her teaching.

In 1889, after the death of Anna Kingsford, Edward Maitland asked a certain clairvoyant friend who had come to see him, and had declared that Anna Kingsford was present, for information about the Theosophical Society and as to its possible influence on their work, when he received the following reply: "The ultimate effect of that Society will be to help your work. It will have acted as a great net to draw people to these subjects;

---

[1] *Life of A. K.*, vol. ii. pp. 221-223.
[2] Letter of E. M. in *The Unknown World*, 15th March 1895; *Life of A. K.*, vol. ii. pp. 223, 296 and 297.
When, in 1887, Anna Kingsford was "dying of consumption," Madame Blavatsky wrote to her: "If you were well enough by the end of this month, I would ask you to write an answer to Gerald Massey, who, speaking of the contradictions of the New Testament, calls it 'a volume of falsehoods and lies.' I must do so if you do not feel strong enough, for it is absolutely necessary to shew that the Bible is as esoteric as any other Scriptures of old" (*Life of A. K.*, vol. ii. pp. 340-341).
[3] *Life of A. K.*, vol. ii. p. 276.

but they will not long remain at the Society's level, but will rise towards yours." [1] And, shortly afterwards, when writing of the Society, Edward Maitland said that it had been "the means of giving to the mighty wave of materialism, pessimism, and agnosticism that was sweeping over the earth to the imminent extinction of every noble and worthy sentiment in Humanity and all that makes life worth living, such a check as to cause its agents and promoters to start in wonder and alarm at seeing everywhere men and women of high intellectual character, culture and judgment, turning their backs upon them, their system and their methods as tried and found utterly wanting by reason of its failure to satisfy either the intelligence or the moral conscience; and in virtue of their own indubitable experiences recognising humanity as endowed with potentialities no less than aspirations altogether transcending materialistic conception. And this is but the beginning." [2] And, later, in 1895, in his Preface to *The Life of Anna Kingsford*, while regretting the necessity for "outspokenness" in regard to certain contemporaneous institutions, writings, and persons, he says: "The time will assuredly come when that movement [represented by the Theosophical Society] will be accounted an important factor in the religious history of our age, and any light that can be thrown on its *origines* will be of no less value than would be such light on the *origines* of Christianity itself."

In 1885, the weekly meetings of the Hermetic Society were resumed, this time in the rooms of the Royal Asiatic Society, No. 22 Albemarle Street, W. The programme for the Session, so far as Anna Kingsford and Edward Maitland were concerned, being as follows:—

27th April 1885, Anna Kingsford, on the Hermetic Fragment, *Koré Kosmou*.
13th May „ Anna Kingsford, on the Method of the Mystics.
20th „ „ Edward Maitland, on the Revival of Mysticism.
3rd June „ Edward Maitland, on the Symbology of the Old Testament.
17th „ „ Edward Maitland, on the Intention and Method of the Gospels.
1st July „ Anna Kingsford, on the Communion of Saints.

[1] *Life of A. K.*, vol. ii. p. 421.   [2] Letter dated 11th April 1890.

BIOGRAPHICAL PREFACE

As on the former occasion, abstracts of their Lectures, made by Edward Maitland, were printed in *Light*.

For some time past Anna Kingsford had been "much out of health, and unfit for mental work." Writing on the 15th June 1885 to Lady Caithness she said: "I am so hard-worked and so very much out of health that it has been impossible hitherto to write and thank you for your charming and acceptable letters; for when I am not busy, I am ill, and as soon as I recover, I have to get to work again." [1]

During this Session her Lectures on the Creed had been suspended in order to permit other speakers to be heard. Writing on the 2nd August 1885 to Lady Caithness about her Lectures, she said how extremely difficult it was to impress a catholic and mystic view of things on the British mind—the fogs and clouds which enwrapped their isle seemed to have enshrouded their spirits also—"And yet," she said, "how lucent, how splendid, how entrancing this wonderful Truth is, could they only receive it! Is it indeed the fact, I sometimes wonder, that a few of us have senses developed which are unknown to the majority of our race; and do we really walk about among a blind and deaf generation for whom the light *we* see and the words *we* hear *are not*?" [2]

The third Session of the Hermetic Society, like the previous one, was held in the rooms of the Royal Asiatic Society. The programme, so far as Anna Kingsford and Edward Maitland were concerned, being as follows:—

13th April 1886, Anna Kingsford, on Bible Hermeneutics.
22nd　　,,　　　,,　　Edward Maitland, on the Higher Alchemy.
27th May　　,,　　Edward Maitland, on a Forgotten View of Genesis.
22nd June　　,,　　Edward Maitland, (by request) a second address, with considerable additions, on the Higher Alchemy.
29th　　,,　　　,,　　Edward Maitland read a joint paper, written by him and Anna Kingsford, on the Nature and Constitution of the Ego.[3]

---

[1] *Life of A. K.*, vol. ii. pp. 233-234.　　[2] *Ibid.*, p. 235.
[3] This Lecture was, subsequently, incorporated in their book *The Perfect Way, or the Finding of Christ*, where it appears as Lecture V. An abstract of the Lecture was published in *Light*, 1886, p. 310.

15th July 1886, Edward Maitland, on the New Illumination.
22nd   „   „   Anna Kingsford replied to questions (which members had been invited to send in), and re-read her third Lecture on the Creed.[1]

Edward Maitland says: "At all the meetings the papers were followed by discussions of the highest interest, the attendance varying from thirty to fifty persons, many of whom were notable for their talents, their erudition, and their piety. A special feature in Mary's Lectures consisted in the highly artistic diagrams, made by herself, of the symbols explained, such as the double Triangle and the Seal of Solomon, on which were shewn the stations of the Soul in the course of its elaboration;[2] also the drawings of man in his two states, degenerate and regenerate, as indicated by the direction of the magnetic currents of his system, according to the view shewn to her in vision.[3] Another feature worthy of mention was the occasional presence of theatrical actors and professional reciters, who came, they said, not because they could understand what they heard—that, they frankly admitted, was beyond them—but in order to listen to the President, whose gift of elocution they declared to be so perfect, that to hear her speak was a lesson in their own art. This proved to be the closing Session of the Hermetic Society."[4]

In acknowledging the receipt of the MSS. of some of their Hermetic Lectures, which had been sent to her to read, the late Mrs. Atwood[5] said: "I thank you very much, not only for having afforded me a sight of these Lectures, but for having written and delivered the same. You have full well maintained throughout the dignity of the subject, of the which I am naturally jealous; and the general view taken of the doctrine appears to me correct and capable of all proof. The key is, as you recognise clearly and forcibly, hidden within the new life of

---

[1] *Light*, 1886, p. 366.

[2] See Frontispiece. Edward Maitland says: "The Seal of Solomon was the symbol used alike by Kabalists and Hermetists, in the East and the West, to represent the whole arcana of theosophy" (*Light*, 1884, p. 302).

[3] See illustration in *The Perfect Way*, p. 325.

[4] *Life of A. K.*, vol. ii. p. 258.

[5] Mrs Atwood, as the writer of *An Inquiry into the Hermetic Mystery*, and as one of the profoundest of living mystics, was, Edward Maitland says, "in the very foremost rank of those whose judgment we valued" (*Life of A. K.*, vol. ii. p. 265).—S. H. H.

humanity (also within the old, methinks). But you have wisely avoided touching on the experimental methods of dealing with the universal subject; the terms relating to which, and its degrees of progress, you may find, on further investigation, to represent more essentially what they express than at first sight appears. It was the vulgar chemists who borrowed these essential terms rather for the designation of their own dead elements and drugs."[1]

At the close of the season, which for many reasons had been "one of severe and incessant toil," Anna Kingsford's health, which had never been good, was in a failing condition—her strength having been "greatly overtaxed and reduced"—so much so that Edward Maitland entertained "grave apprehensions of the result to herself." Her suffering from asthma and facial neuralgia was so great, that "it soon became evident that the only hope of immunity from intense and constant suffering, if not also from positive lung disease, lay in flight to some less unfavourable conditions of climate"; and it was decided that she should pass the coming winter abroad, which she did, but without the desired result.

In consequence of her continued illness, Edward Maitland, early in 1887, despatched to the members of the Hermetic Society a circular informing them of the condition of the President and of the impossibility of holding a Session that year.[2] The following extract from a letter written on the 2nd January 1887 by Edward Maitland to Mrs Drakoules (then Mrs Lewis) shews very clearly what Anna Kingsford's state of health then was: "I regret to have to say that, owing to Mrs Kingsford's severe illness, contracted through the dampness of her English home in Shropshire, our plans for the winter have had to be changed, and it is impossible to say when the Hermetic Sittings will be resumed—if ever! For this is far on in the fourth month of her illness, and she has only been able to get as far as Paris on the way to some southern sanatorium, being now undergoing a course of blistering for congestion of the lungs, and unable, therefore, to be removed. Of course our wish and desire are to return in time to hold the usual Summer Session of the H.S. But at present everything points to a prolonged absence on the Continent in order to consolidate any improvement which may occur, and avoid the risk of a return northwards."

[1] *Life of A. K.*, vol. ii. p. 266.
[2] A notice to this effect appeared in *Light*, 23rd April 1887, p. 181.

An entry in her Diary, written under date of 5th July 1887, at *Bourboule-les-Bains*, reads as follows:—

"Not cured yet! No, nor even mended, were it but a little. Still the cough, still the afternoon fever, still the weakness, still the neuralgia. From November to July the same continual malady and enforced idleness. Where now are all the projects I had formed for this year, the book I had to write on the Creed, the novel, the stories, the essays? I have passed a year of bitterest suffering, of weariness of spirit and torment of body. My left lung is in caverns, they say; my right is inflamed chronically. My voice is broken and gone, with which I had hoped to speak from platforms: wreck and ruin is made of all my expectancies. Can a miracle yet be wrought? Can *will* accomplish what medicines fail to perform? The hard thing is that I cannot will heartily, for lack of knowing what I ought to desire. Is it better for me to live or to die? Unless I can be restored to the possibility of public life, it is useless for me to live. Dying, I may sooner obtain a fresh incarnation and return to do my work more completely." [1]

On their return to England, during the same month, she took up her abode at No. 15 Wynnstay Gardens—London then being the best place for her, but it proved to be "a home for her to die in."

Writing, on the 10th August, Edward Maitland says: "Our dear invalid continues in much the same state of fluctuation. At one time apparently at death's door, and at another seeming capable of recovery. But my fear is that the level of each recurring depression is lower than before. . . . Perhaps the best I have to report is that she herself has become of late more desirous to live, provided she can recover health and strength to work and to escape suffering. But, as she says—and it is difficult for one who knows how great cause she has for saying it [to think otherwise]—it would be no kindness to wish to keep her here if life is to be the *rack* it has hitherto been for her." [2]

Soon after her return to London she was visited by one of her brothers, an Anglican clergyman, whom she rarely saw, and with whom she had little in common. Edward Maitland says: "Seeing how serious was her condition, he insisted peremptorily on her doing at once three things—make confession to a priest, receive extreme unction, and make her will. . . . She replied that—believing as she believed—no mere rites or ceremonies

---

[1] *Life of A. K.*, vol. ii. pp. 321–322.   [2] *Ibid.*, vol. ii. p. 325.

possessed any meaning or value for her. 'Do you, then,' he asked, 'mean to say you are not a Christian? Don't you believe in the Incarnation of our Lord?' To which she replied, 'I am not a Christian in your sense, nor a believer of the Incarnation in your sense. In the spiritual and only true sense I am both.' Having never heard of any sense but the traditional and sacerdotal one, and being wholly unacquainted with her writings, he necessarily failed to comprehend her, and after some further expostulations concerning the impossibility of being saved without the last sacraments, he took his leave."[1]

In consequence of this visit she, desiring to put on record a clear, distinct, and final statement of her position, "wrote off at a single sitting in her usual faultless style, not staying her hand for a moment until it was finished," the following letter to her brother :—

"*20th August* 1887.

"Until the occurrence of a recent incident, it had not entered my mind that any of my relations would regard it as a duty to interest himself actively about my religious faith, and to press upon me the performance of certain customary religious rites, either as a means of saving my own soul or of satisfying family scruples. I had believed that my recently published works were sufficient evidence of the ground taken by me in regard to dogmatic Christianity, and that the whole course of my life during the past ten years would shew the state of my mind respecting popular conceptions of religion. But as it seems necessary that I should not die without some sort of *Apologia*, I will attempt in this brief letter to explain my position.

"When, in 1872, I entered the Communion of the Roman Church, I was actuated by the conviction—which has since enormously strengthened—that this Church, and this alone, contained and promulgated all truth. Especially was I attracted by the doctrine of Transubstantiation and the Sacrifice of the Mass, and by the cultus of the B.V.M. But I did not then comprehend the spiritual import of these doctrines, but endeavoured to accept them in the sense ordinarily understood. My Spirit strove within me to create me a Catholic without my knowing why. It was not until 1875-6 that I began by means of the Inner Light to comprehend why my Spirit had caused me to take this step. For then began to be unfolded to my soul, by means of a long series of interior revelations, extending over

[1] *Life of A. K.*, vol. ii. p. 326.

ten years, that divine system of the *Theosophia* which I afterwards discovered to be identical with the teaching of the Hermetic Science, and with the tenets of the Kabala, Alchemy, and the purest Oriental religion. Enlightened by this Inner Light, I perceived the fallacy and idolatry of popular Christianity, and from that hour in which I received the spiritual Christ into my heart, I resolved to know Him no more after the flesh. The old historical controversies over the facts and dates and phenomena of the Old and New Testaments ceased to torment and perplex me. I perceived that my soul had nothing to do with events occurring on the physical plane, because these could not, by their nature, be cognates to spiritual needs. The spiritual man seeketh after spiritual things, and must not look for Christ upon earth, but in heaven. 'He is not here; He is risen.' I, therefore, gave up troubling myself to know anything about Jesus of Nazareth in the flesh, or whether, indeed, such a person ever existed; not only because no certainty in regard to these matters is intellectually possible, but because, spiritually, they did not concern me any longer. I had grasped the central truth of Alchemy that is one with the doctrine of Transubstantiation, namely, that the Objective must be transmuted into the Subjective before it can be brought into cognate relation with the soul. Truth is never phenomenal: it is always noumenal. If I have not sufficiently explained my meaning, I earnestly refer readers of this letter to the Preface to the revised edition of *The Perfect Way*.

"In the faith and doctrine set forth in that book I desire to die. And, having ceased to require assurance in any physical or historical fact whatever as a factor of my redemption, or to crave for any sort of outward ceremony as a means of spiritual beatitude, I am content to trust the future of my soul to the Justice of God, by whom I do not understand a personal being capable of awarding punishments and pardons, but the Pivotal Principle of the Universe, inexorable, knowing neither favour nor relenting. For, as says the Kabala, 'Assuredly, thus have we learned,—There is no judge over the wicked, but they themselves convert the measure of Mercy into a measure of Judgment.' This is a declaration of the esoteric doctrine of *Karma*, which I fully accept, believing with Buddha and with Pythagoras, and the whole company of wise and holy teachers of the East and of the Kabala, that the soul is many-lived, and that men are many times re-born upon earth. As I am certainly not yet perfected, I shall return to a new birth after my merits have been exhausted in Paradise. Or if I should, on the contrary, need purgation in the subjective states, I accept that gladly as the will of Justice.

"But how or why, holding such belief as this, should I, on my deathbed, seek the intervention of a priest, seeing that, to accept such intervention, I must necessarily deceive him?

"I die, therefore, a Hermetist, believing in the spiritual Gods, with whom, I indeed aver, I have inwardly conversed and have seen them face to face; in the Evolution of the Soul from the lowest grade of Jacob's Ladder unto the Presence of the Holy One; in the solidarity and brotherhood of all creatures, so that all may come at length to eternal life which are on the upward path. For Christ gives Himself for all, and shall save both man and beast. . . . ANNA KINGSFORD."[1]

The letter, however, was never sent. On her shewing it to Edward Maitland, he pointed out that her brother would understand neither the argument nor the language, and she decided not to send it, but to keep it among their archives, saying: "It would be a profanation of the mysteries to put such doctrine before those who held such ideas. And she added in a tone almost of despair, 'How *is* the truth to be got to the world, so long as priests bear rule, preachers preach falsely, and the people are content to have it so? Can it be that we have made a mistake, and come ages before the time was ripe?' To which I replied that the Gods do not make mistakes, and can see better than we how far the time is ripe."[2] This priceless letter was thus preserved for future publication.

A day or two after writing the above-mentioned letter she wrote in her diary: "I had hoped to have been one of the pioneers of the new awakening of the world. I had thought to have helped in the overthrow of the idolatrous altars and the purging of the Temple. And now I must die just as the day of battle dawns and the sound of the chariot-wheels is heard. Is it, perhaps, all premature? Have we thought the time nearer than it really is? Must I go and sleep, and come again before the hour sounds?"[3]

As the months passed, her condition became worse and worse. At the end of December her doctor declared her to be "rapidly sinking, and unlikely to live beyond another week or two."

---

[1] *Life of A. K.*, vol. ii. pp. 327–329.
[2] *Ibid.*, pp. 329–330. [3] *Ibid.*, pp. 331–332.

At the beginning of the new year (1888) she rallied, but, before the end of January, it became necessary for her to have a nurse. Edward Maitland says: "As is characteristic of consumption, the approach of the end was marked by increased hopefulness on the part of the sufferer, leading her to fancy she was actually mending, and might yet recover, even though at death's door. . . . And then she would descant on the work she would do in abolition of all the wicked falsehoods which had brought the world into its present terrible plight, until, as may readily be understood, I found her cheerfulness and hopefulness more saddening even than her opposite moods, knowing as I did their deceptiveness and what they portended."[1]

On the 21st February she became worse, and on the following day—Wednesday, the 22nd February—at noon, "after an eighteen hours' struggle for breath," she silently and painlessly, and to all appearances consciously and voluntarily, exhaled out her life in one long breath." She was then in her forty-second year.[2] One of her latest utterances was that she could carry on the work better from the other side, where she would be free of her physical limitations.

Thus ended the most noble and self-sacrificing life of Anna Kingsford,—a life for which, some day, the world will thank God. She was *a divine soul*, a soul after God's own heart. She loved Justice and hated Iniquity, and, therefore, was she by God anointed with that "oil of gladness" above her fellows. Her trials were many, and her sufferings were great; but, after her death, Edward Maitland received concerning her the following message: "She rejoices to let you know that the sufferings she enjoyed—yes, enjoyed—was the ladder that led her spirit upward, ever upward."[3] The following words are as appropriate to her as to the Saint on whose commemoration day they are appointed to be read: "Sinners," says the *Introit* to the Mass for St Mary Magdalen's day, "have waited for me that they might destroy me: Thy testimonies, O Lord, have I understood: I have seen the end of all perfection: Thy commandment is exceeding broad." She inclined her ear to the parable; she heard the word of God; and she was faithful. "Blessed are they," said Jesus, "that hear the word of God, and keep it."[4] Thus did Anna Kingsford.

[1] *Life of A. K.*, vol. ii. pp. 359-360.
[2] She was born on the 16th September 1846.
[3] *Life of A. K.*, vol. ii. p. 411.   [4] Luke xi. 28.

Edward Maitland, after her death, speaking of the origin of their teaching, said:[1] "The two most generally recognised sources of information on such subjects, next to the Bible and the Church, are those called 'Spiritualism' and 'Theosophy.' The teachings represented by me, while bearing relation to each and all of these, are not derived from any of them. Nor are they compiled from occult books previously in the world. When the researches of which they are the outcome were commenced, neither my collaborator nor I were in bonds to any of the orthodoxies, nor were we believers in 'Spiritualism.' And as for occultism, it had never dawned upon us that there was a science or a literature which bore such name or dealt with such subjects; nor had Theosophy yet made its appearance. So far, however, from being Materialists, rather were we Idealists, but in the stage in which one has yet to learn that the ideal is the real, and the material is but the phenomenal. All, therefore, that we obtained, whether of doctrine or of experience, was at first hand, and without prepossession on our part. The object of our quest was a philosophy of existence, and one that would account satisfactorily for all the facts of consciousness in such a way as to constitute at once a true science, a true morality, and a true religion. For, as was evident to us, only by having these—only, that is to say, by knowing how, and of what, and for what, man is made, can he realise that which it is necessarily the supreme ambition of a sane and intelligent being, namely, the turning of his existence to the utmost account *in the long run*. To this end, the title especially affected by us was that of Free-Thinker, meaning by it one who suffers his thought to range equally in all directions open to thought; both outwards and downwards to matter and phenomenon, and inwards and upwards to spirit and reality. For only thus, it appeared to us, was it possible to obtain the substantial idea whereby to interpret the phenomenal fact. As will be observed, this is a definition judged by which many persons who lay claim to the title of free-thinker not only are not free-thinkers, but can hardly be said to be thinkers at all, seeing that they ignore altogether the inward and upward direction of thought and make the bodily senses their sole criterion. Such persons may have large intellects, but they have no intuition. And being thus, they are as birds with

---

[1] The occasion was a Lecture given by him on "Man Incarnate and Discarnate," which I hope some day, with other of Edward Maitland's Lectures, to publish.—S. H. H.

one wing, who cannot rise from the ground. Now, as we all know, the sparrow with two wings can laugh to scorn the eagle with one wing.

"Well, finding ourselves possessed in a somewhat unusual degree of the more rare of the two faculties, that whereby one thinks inwards and upwards, namely, the introvision or intuition; and finding also that by combining our faculties we could obtain results far surpassing the mere sum of their dissociated efforts, we resolved to join our mental forces in a collaboration, for the effective accomplishment of which I made my home largely with my friend's family—for she was married—so as to allow of a constant interchange of ideas, both of us adopting meanwhile the mode of life which, by those who know, has always been regarded as indispensable to intuitional perception, namely, abstinence from flesh-food and stimulants and whatever else might tend to impair the mental faculties. And so it came that, seeking ardently the highest truth for the highest ends, resolved to be content with nothing short of the highest, we found the mists and clouds disappear from our mental atmosphere and the heavens above—or rather, *within*—become clear, and we were able to project the perceptive point of our minds into those innermost regions of man's system which constitute his permanent and divine part, the sphere, namely, of the Soul and Spirit, and so to come into open relations with the world of those who, having passed beyond the need for any physical environment, consist entirely of these two principles and have realised the divinity which is man's proper birthright and destiny. These are they who are called 'Gods' and 'Archangels.' Representing the summits of human evolution, they constitute the Hierarchy of the Church invisible and celestial, and are the supreme agents of divine revelation, their function being to illuminate souls. And it was under such illumination that our teachings were received, being given expressly, not for ourselves merely, but for the restoration to the world of the truth of which its ecclesiastical systems represent either the grievous perversion or the total loss, their priests having materialised and made idolatrous and irrational, doctrines which, in their true and divinely intended sense, are purely spiritual and wholly reasonable, being founded in the nature of existence and comprehensible by those who to intellect add intuition, and seek truth in a pure spirit.

"We were, moreover, enabled to recognise the restoration thus made as the fulfilment of the numerous prophesies, Biblical and others, promising that precisely at the time, and under the conditions and in the manner in which it has actually occurred, such a revelation would be made.

"There is one further remark to be made which bears immediately on the subject of the occasion. The method of the revelation thus received was entirely interior; this is to say, it consisted in our being enabled to recover knowledges acquired by our own Souls in past-earth lives as initiates of the sacred mysteries of antiquity, as well as in other states of being. Being related to and of like nature with the soul, such knowledges are retained by and stored up in the soul, constituting an everlasting possession, and are available on the condition that they be rightly sought for. For 'Intuition is inborn experience; that which the soul knoweth of old, having learned it by experience.'

"One word more. It is a noteworthy circumstance, and one that bears the aspect of being something much more than an accidental coincidence, that when the Founders of the Theosophical Society commenced the collaboration which had for its object the exposition of the mystical system which underlies the religions and sacred Scriptures of the East, we had already, a year or two before, and wholly unknown to them, commenced the collaboration which proved to have for its object the exposition of the mystical system which underlies the religions and sacred Scriptures of the West, namely, the Egyptian, the Greek, the Hebrew, and the Christian, all of which have proved to be modes of one and the same system of thought: the name given to our work by its inspirers being the 'New Gospel of Interpretation,' to denote that nothing new is told in it, but that only which is ancient is interpreted. It was only after the publication of our first book, *The Perfect Way*, which took place in 1881,[1] that we and the Founders of the Theosophical Society became aware of each other's work, when they recognised the doctrine given to us as substantially identical with that received by them, a fact tending to shew that the human soul has in all times and places discerned one and the same truth."

Reference has been made to Anna Kingsford's illuminations. In 1881 she had a remarkable vision, wherein she was told that the three degrees of the heavens were purity of life, purity of heart,

---

[1] The *Perfect Way* Lectures were delivered in 1881; the book containing them was published in 1882.—S. H. H.

and purity of doctrine. The vision is too long to fully relate here, but it is given at length in *Clothed With the Sun*.[1] In part of her vision she found herself within a temple, at the east end of which was a great altar, "from above and behind which came faintly a white and beautiful light, the radiance of which was arrested and obscured by a dark curtain suspended from the dome before the altar. And the body of the temple, which, but for the curtain, would have been fully illumined, was plunged in gloom, broken only by the fitful gleams of a few half-expiring oil-lamps, hanging here and there from the vast cupola." In her account of the vision she says: "At the right of the altar stood the same tall Angel I had before seen on the temple threshold, holding in his hand a smoking censer. Then, observing that he was looking earnestly at me, I said to him: 'Tell me, what curtain is this before the light, and why is the temple in darkness?' And he answered, 'This veil is not One, but Three; and the Three are Blood, Idolatry,[2] and the Curse of Eve.[3] And to you it is given to withdraw them; be faithful and courageous; the time has come.' Now the first curtain was red, and very heavy; and with a great effort I drew it aside, and said, 'I have put away the veil of blood from before Thy Face. Shine, O Lord God!' But a Voice from behind the folds of the two remaining coverings answered me, 'I cannot shine, because of the idols.' And lo, before me a curtain of many colours, woven about with all manner of images, crucifixes, madonnas, Old and New Testaments, prayer-books, and other religious symbols, some strange and hideous like the idols of China and Japan, some beautiful like those of the Greeks and Christians. And the weight of the curtain was like lead, for it was thick with gold and silver em-

[1] See Illumination "Concerning the Three Veils between Man and God," *C. W. S.*, pt. i. No. i.

[2] Idolatry consists in the materialisation of spiritual Mysteries. "They are Idolaters who understand the things of Sense where the things of the Spirit are alone implied, and who conceal the true Features of the Gods with material and spurious presentations. Idolatry is Materialism, the common and original Sin of Men, which replaces Spirit by Appearance, Substance by Illusion, and leads both the moral and intellectual Being into error, so that they substitute the Nether for the Upper, and the Depth for the Height." (See Illumination "Concerning the Interpretation of the Mystical Scriptures," *C. W. S.*, pt. i. No. v.)—S. H. H.

[3] That is, Eve—the moral Conscience of Humanity—subject to Adam —the intellectual Force,—"whereby all manner of evil and confusion abounds, since her desire is unto him, and he rules over her until now. But the end foretold by the Seer is not far off." (See Illumination "Concerning the Interpretation of the Mystical Scriptures," *C. W. S.*, pt. i. No. v.)—S. H. H.

broideries. But with both hands I tore it away, and cried, 'I have put away the idols from before Thy face. Shine, O Lord God!' And now the light was clearer and brighter. But yet before me hung a third veil, all of black; and upon it was traced in outline the figure of four lilies on a single stem inverted, their cups opening downwards. And from behind this veil the Voice answered me again, ' I cannot shine, because of the Curse of Eve.' Then I put forth all my strength, and with a great will rent away the curtain, crying, 'I have put away her curse from before Thee. Shine, O Lord God!'

" And there was no more a veil, but a landscape, more glorious and perfect than words can paint, a garden of absolute beauty, filled with trees of palm, and olive, and fig, rivers of clear water, and lawns of tender green; and distant groves and forests framed about by mountains crowned with snow; and on the brow of their shining peaks a rising sun, whose light it was I had seen behind the veils. And about the sun, in mid-air, hung white misty shapes of great Angels, as clouds at morning float above the place of dawn. And beneath, under a mighty tree of cedar, stood a white elephant, bearing in his golden howdah a beautiful woman robed as a queen, and wearing a crown. But while I looked, entranced, and longing to look for ever, the garden, the altar, and the temple were carried up from me into heaven."

This book shows how faithfully and courageously Anna Kingsford fulfilled that part of her high and divine mission which was connected with the withdrawal of the Veils of Idolatry, and the Curse of Eve from before the face of God. In her and Edward Maitland's *Addresses and Essays on Vegetarianism*,[1] I have shewn how, by attacking the practice, prevailing throughout Christendom, of sustaining life by flesh-eating, she set herself to the task of withdrawing the Veil of Blood; and I hope, shortly, to supplement the last-mentioned book by bringing out an edition of their Addresses and Essays on that worst of all crimes—Vivisection.

On the announcement in *Light* of the death of Anna Kingsford, the Hon. Roden Noel in a letter, dated 5th March 1888, to that paper said: "She was surely one of the most gifted women of our day and generation. Her spiritual insight, her acute reasoning faculty, her knowledge in deep occult subjects, were most notably married to a very remarkable gift of luminous exposition, beautiful expression, and a vivid poetic imagination.

[1] *Addresses and Essays on Vegetarianism*, by Anna Kingsford and Edward Maitland, published in 1912.

None who were privileged to hear her essays read at her own house, and at the rooms of the Royal Asiatic Society, in connection with the Hermetic Society, of which she was President, can easily forget them; their impression and influence are ineffaceable. . . . She, being dead, yet speaketh."[1]

Madame Isabel de Steiger—another member of the Society—said: "Truly she was a peerless and matchless woman, and there is no one to take her place. . . . In losing Anna Kingsford, we have lost one of the most excellent seeresses of modern times."[2]

The result to the Hermetic Society of Anna Kingsford's death was that it forthwith fell into abeyance,[3] and it has never been revived.

Although written some years after her death, the following testimony of the late W. T. Stead is worthy of notice. In a review of *The Life of Anna Kingsford* he says:—

"I remember Anna Kingsford. Who that ever met her can forget that marvellous embodiment of a burning flame in the form of a woman, divinely tall and not less divinely fair! I think it is just about ten years since I first met her. It was at the office of the *Pall Mall Gazette*, which I was editing in those days. She did not always relish the headings I put to her articles. She was as innocent as the author of *The Bothie of Tober-na-Vuolich* of the necessity for labelling the goods in your shop-window in such a way as to attract attention, but we were always on good terms, being united by the strong tie of common antipathies. I saw her once at her own place, when, I remember, she wore a bright red flower—I thought it was a great gladiolus, but it may have been a cactus, which lay athwart her breast like a sword of flame. Her movements had somewhat of the grace and majesty that we associate with the Greek gods; and, as for her speech—well, I have talked to many of the men and women who have in this generation had the greatest repute as conversationalists, but I never in my life met Anna Kingsford's equal. From her silver tongue as in a stream, 'strong without wrath, without o'erflowing full,' her sentences flowed in one unending flood. She talked literature. Had an endless phonograph been fitted up before her so as to be constantly in action,

---

[1] *Light*, 1888, p. 119.   [2] *Ibid.*
[3] Article, entitled "Mr Edward Maitland," in *Light*, 1893, p. 104. Edward Maitland subsequently founded the Esoteric Christian Union, which, on his death in 1897, also fell into abeyance.—S. H. H.

the cylinders might have been carried to the printer, and the copy set up without transcription or alteration. Never was she at a loss for a word, never did she tangle her sentences, or halt for an illustration. It was almost appalling after a time. It appeared impossible for her to run dry, for you seemed to feel that copious as was her speech, it was but as a rivulet carrying off the overflow of the ocean which lay behind." [1]

And quite recently another well-known journalist—George R. Sims—in giving an account of his life,[2] says of Anna Kingsford (who appears to have been a frequent visitor at his mother's house) :—

" Dr Anna Kingsford was a lovely woman, with classical features and a mass of wonderful golden hair. I think she was the most beautiful 'clever' woman I have ever known.

" She told me one evening at a dance at my mother's house that she would like above all things to see a rehearsal of a pantomime, so I took her to the dress rehearsal of the Grecian pantomime, and George Conquest kindly gave me a box.

" I could see that everyone on the stage was struck by the ethereal beauty of my companion. After the rehearsal was over, when I had gone behind to speak to Conquest, he told me that whenever he had looked at the box that evening he felt as if he were entertaining an angel unawares.

" And then I told him *that he had been*."

In a chapter on *post-mortem* experiences in *The Life of Anna Kingsford*, Edward Maitland relates the fulfilment of promises made by Anna Kingsford, to come to him after her death for the purpose of continuing their collaboration. On one occasion, on the 5th June 1889, he says, a message was received by him from her through Mrs H——, a lady who, without being a medium in the sense of going under control, was in a remarkable degree clairvoyant and clairaudient to spiritual presences. The message was to the effect that she (Anna Kingsford) wished certain of her writings, " and, by-and-by, her Lectures on the Credo," to be published :—her reason for desiring the postponement of the publication of such Lectures being that they were then in advance of people, but would not be so for long as people were themselves advancing.[3]

[1] *The Review of Reviews*, 15th January 1896.
[2] " My Life," by George R. Sims, in *The Evening News*, 2nd February 1916.
[3] *Life of A. K.*, vol. ii. pp. 406, 421.

I first met Edward Maitland in 1894. He was then living alone, in Chambers, at No. 1 Thurloe Square Studios, Thurloe Square, South Kensington, London, and was busy writing *The Life of Anna Kingsford*—his *magnum opus*—and otherwise doing all he could to make known " the New Gospel of Interpretation " to which he had given the best years of his life. There was still much remaining for him to do, and time was short. His health was indifferent, his strength was failing, and at times he feared he would not live to complete his work. It was pathetic to see this man at the close of a long and arduous life, at a time when he should have been able to look for some rest, living alone and working hard in order that he might finish the work that he had undertaken or that had been given him to do. It was a labour of love. But there was no one who could have helped him even had he desired it, for his work was such that it could be done only by him. He alone had the requisite knowledge and ability. He alone was qualified for the task. The world owes a great debt of gratitude to Edward Maitland for this his last labour.

On the 27th May 1895 he wrote to me that he was (at the request of the publisher) curtailing the biography, " not by omitting anything historical and biographical, but by eliminating certain literary remains " ; and, he added, " I am greatly curtailing in the same way also the account of our relations with the Theosophical Society, which I have related with much fullness, giving our letters and pamphlets in which we convicted them of having utterly mistaken the teaching they had received. For I thought it well that the world should see to what an extent that movement has been transformed from being subversive of all religion into being, as it now is, a valuable aid to the restoration of true religion, and this through the revelation given to us." [1]

Notwithstanding drawbacks, the biography was, at length, completed, and in January 1896 it was published. Until then, though failing in health, he had retained his faculties and sufficient strength for his work ; but, from that time, his decline —both mental and physical—was remarkably rapid, and it soon became evident to all who saw him that he was fast breaking up.

---

[1] In the present (third) edition of *The Life of Anna Kingsford* I have been enabled to restore the whole or a considerable portion of the matter referred to in the above-mentioned letter as having been omitted from the first edition.—S. H. H.

The strain of his work had been too much for him, or the effort to hold himself together being then no longer required, could no longer be continued. He had accomplished his task, he had lived to see the completion of his life-work, and he was now free to depart in peace to the place where he would be. So rapid was his decline that, after the lapse of a few months, he was not in a fit state to continue living alone without anybody (other than the housekeeper and his wife) to look after him, and many of his friends felt very anxious about him.

In the latter part of the year—I think it was in September— I went to the Studios to see him, when I was informed by the housekeeper that he was ill in bed, having had " a stroke," and that he was not well enough to see anybody; and some short time afterwards, when I again called to learn how he was progressing, I was told that he had left London, and was staying with some friends in the country. The friends, I afterwards learnt, were Colonel and Mrs Currie, who lived at Tonbridge, and their house proved to be his last home.

On the 22nd December I received from Mrs Currie, who was then a stranger to me, a letter as follows:—

"THE WARDERS," TONBRIDGE,
21st December 1896.

"DEAR SIR,—I take the liberty of writing to you on behalf of Mr E. Maitland, who has made his home with us for the few remaining days of his life. Mr Maitland has been failing fast all this last year, both bodily and mentally, and is now quite unable to answer any letters, or even to reply to questions concerning his life-work. It is most sad that it should end thus, but I believe that his spirit has already left his body (although, of course, not yet entirely separated from it), so complete is his mental decay.

"If you would like to come down and see him at any time, we shall be most happy to offer you lunch.—Believe me, yours very truly,

"C. G. CURRIE."

I accepted Mrs Currie's invitation, and on the day following the receipt of her letter I went to "The Warders," and there, for the last time, saw my friend, and was satisfied that Mrs Currie's description of his condition was correct. He was physically helpless. He could speak only with great difficulty, and his words were so incoherent, that it was difficult to understand what he said. Conversation was impossible. His intelligence had gone. His body only lived. Psyche had fled. I do not think he knew me. None of us thought that he could continue for many days, but we were mistaken. He lingered on in this condition for some months, most of his time being passed in sleep. It was not until the 2nd October 1897 that he obtained the release for which he had so long waited. On the evening of that day, at the close of his seventy-third year, " he breathed his last, quite quietly and painlessly." Thus ended the life of Anna Kingsford's friend and collaborator—one of the best and most noble lives ever lived for God and humanity. And this is my testimony: When I was hungry, he gave me *food*; when I was thirsty, he gave me *drink*. It was he who put into my hands their book *The Perfect Way*, and to him and his dear colleague I owe more than I can repay. Those who would know more of him and Anna Kingsford and their work must read that wonderful biography —which is also an autobiography—which he spent his last years in writing.

When at Colonel Currie's, realising Edward Maitland's hopeless condition, it occurred to me that if he had left at the Studios any MSS. of value the same ought to be safeguarded, and I suggested that Colonel Currie was the proper person to take charge of them; but, not having any legal right or authority, he did not see his way to take any action in the matter; at the same time he wished me, on my return to London, to go to the Studios and ascertain if there were there any MSS. of value and to let him know. This I consented to do, and as soon as possible I went to the Studios, where I saw the housekeeper, who, in reply to the questions I put to him, informed me that he was not aware of the existence of any MSS. at the Studios, and he thought it most unlikely that there should be any there, because, he said, Edward Maitland, immediately prior to his leaving for the country, had " spent three days in tearing up and burning old papers "; and, while he could not give me any information as to the nature of the papers that had been so destroyed, he left no doubt in my mind that the destruction had been wholesale. I paid one further visit to the Studios, thinking that, perhaps, in the meantime, something might have been discovered; but I learnt nothing fresh about any MSS., the housekeeper merely repeating what he had told me on the former occasion. On one of the above-mentioned visits—I forget which—he told me that, in addition to the papers that had been burnt, Edward Maitland had thrown away a number of old newspapers, etc., which had been taken downstairs into the basement, and which were then being used for lighting fires; there were still some of them left, and if I cared to go down and look through them, I was welcome to do so, and should there be anything among them that would be of use to me, I was at liberty to take it. I availed myself of the invitation, and was shewn a large heap of papers—all printed material—which I went through, and picked out some numbers of *Light* and possibly some other papers that I thought might be of use to me, but there was little or nothing among the papers that I saw that was of any value. There were not among them any MSS. I reported to Mrs Currie the result of my visits, and there the matter ended.

On the 11th April 1897 Mrs Currie wrote to me: "I suppose you know that his chambers have now been emptied and the furniture disposed of. All his books are being stored by his niece for the time being, while all manuscripts, letters, and papers are with us to be taken over after his demise."

The above-mentioned letter was the first information I had of the facts therein referred to.

As already stated, Edward Maitland died on the 2nd October 1897. He died intestate, and, after his death, Colonel Currie, on behalf of those entitled, took possession of his effects. Soon afterwards, I was informed that Colonel Currie had received from the late Secretary of The Esoteric Christian Union [1] "a box presumably containing all the papers of the E.C.U."; and a few months later, Colonel Currie asked me to take over all the E.C.U. papers that has been sent to him, and also the MSS. which had been left by Edward Maitland; and this I agreed to do, and in due course they were sent to me. The papers sent to me consisted of (*inter alia*) the MSS. of many of Edward Maitland's Lectures —including those given by him to the Hermetic Society,—but they did not include the MSS. of any of Anna Kingsford's Lectures to the Hermetic Society or otherwise, with the exception of a MS., in Edward Maitland's handwriting, of Anna Kingsford's Inaugural Address to the Hermetic Society.

In 1906 I purchased all Anna Kingsford's copyrights, the purchase to include all her MSS., etc. The copyrights were duly

---

[1] The Esoteric Christian Union had been founded by Edward Maitland in November 1891, but on his death it followed the same fate as had befallen the Hermetic Society on the death of Anna Kingsford.—S. H. H.

assigned, but no MSS. were handed over, as none could be found. On my agent enquiring of the Rev. A. G. Burton (formerly the Rev. A. G. Kingsford) [1] about them, he received a reply as follows :—

"*21st August* 1906.

"I have none of the MSS. you want. I should think Mr Hart has them; as they were in possession of Mr Maitland. I never had them. . . .

"A. G. BURTON."

In order to leave no stone unturned I, on the 8th September 1906, wrote to Colonel Currie, informing him of my purchase and of the assignment to me of Anna Kingsford's copyrights; and, with reference to her MSS., I said: "I am under the impression that you sent to me everything that was in E. M.'s possession in the nature of MSS., whether his or A. K.'s MSS. Will you kindly confirm this or otherwise, as it is now important that I should know where the MSS. are that are not in my possession? What I particularly want are A. K.'s MSS. of any Lectures given by her—particularly her Lectures on the Christian Creed given to the members of the Hermetic Society. Can you throw any light on the subject? If you can, it will be welcome. My idea is that poor E. M., when he was not responsible for his actions, just before he left London to go to stay with you, *destroyed* a great number of valuable papers under the impression that they were of no value, and I am afraid that he has destroyed the MSS. that are now wanted."

In due course I received from Colonel Currie the following reply:—

"*24th September* 1906.

". . . We have none of the manuscripts of either Anna Kingsford or E. Maitland, or would send them to you. I think it is very likely that E. M., as you say, may have destroyed them, thinking them of no further value.—Yours truly,

"ALGERNON CURRIE."

Since then, and until recently, I have been endeavouring to trace the whereabouts of the missing MSS., but without success. That there must have been MSS. of Anna Kingsford's Lectures

---

[1] The Rev. A. G. Kingsford, after Anna Kingsford's death, married again, and took the name of Burton. He died on the 10th August 1913, in his sixty-ninth year. (*Oswestry Advertiser*, 20th August 1913.)—S. H. H.

BIOGRAPHICAL PREFACE

to the Hermetic Society I am convinced, because, it will be remembered, Anna Kingsford, on the 22nd July 1886, "re-read" to the Hermetic Society her third Lecture on the Creed,[1] and this she could not have done without a MS.; and, *after her death*, she desired her Lectures on the Creed to be published;[2] and the Hon. Roden Noel wrote of her Lectures to the Hermetic Society as having been "read";[3] and Edward Maitland speaks of their "papers" as having been followed by discussions;[4] and, he says, " In acknowledging the receipt of the MSS. of some of our Hermetic Lectures, sent to her to read them in full, Mrs Atwood wrote to me, etc."[5] It would appear that the last-mentioned MSS. included MSS. of some of Anna Kingsford's Lectures, because Edward Maitland uses the word "our." Apart from evidence such as this, I do not think it possible that Anna Kingsford's Lectures to the Hermetic Society could have been delivered on the spur of the moment without carefully prepared MSS. or notes of some kind to which to refer; and, assuming their existence, I have long believed that they were among the papers said to have been destroyed by Edward Maitland when he was in the failing condition of mind and body to which I have referred. At the same time, until the occurrence of a recent event about to be related, I never quite gave up hope of tracing their whereabouts, and partly for this reason I have delayed the bringing out of this book until the present time.

I must now relate my story. On the 9th February 1914 I received from a Mr George Cripps, who was then unknown to me, a letter informing me that he had recently bought a copy of *The Life of Anna Kingsford*, the two volumes of which were "studiously pencil-marked," and he thought that they might have belonged to Edward Maitland, and could I help him? I replied, asking him to come and see me at my office on the following Thursday afternoon. In a letter accepting my invitation, he informed me that he was "an old mystic student and a practical Pythagorean"; and that in the writings of Anna Kingsford and Edward Maitland he had found all he wanted; and, he added, he was "clairvoyant, and especially so in the sleep-making condition."

On the appointed day Mr Cripps called on me as arranged,

---

[1] See p. 46, *ante*; and see *Life of A. K.*, vol. ii. p. 258.
[2] See p. 59, *ante*.   [3] See p. 58, *ante*.   [4] See p. 46, *ante*.
[5] *Life of A. K.*, vol. ii. p. 266; and see p. 46, *ante*.

and brought with him two second-hand volumes of the first edition of *The Life of Anna Kingsford*. They contained some marginal notes written in pencil, but not in the handwriting of Edward Maitland, nor were the notes of any value whatever. On returning to him the books, I said that, although they had been the means of bringing us together, I was sure that it was *not* in connection with them that he had come to see me, though, at the moment, I could not say for what purpose he had come. He then said that he felt the same, but *he had been told by Anna Kingsford to come*. For some time past he had wanted to come and see me, but until then he had not been allowed to do so. However, yesterday morning, at about 5 a.m., a picture of a harvest-field had been shewn to him in a vision, and Anna Kingsford had said to him: "Go and see Mr Hart, and tell him of the picture you have seen; and give him this message: 'The Harvest is Ripe; the Reapers are few.'" He gave me an account of his vision (which he promised to write out for me), but except for the above-mentioned command, it did not, at the time, appear to me to have any particular import.[1] He also told me that this was not the

---

[1] Mr Cripps subsequently sent to me the following account of his vision:—

"Wed., about 5 a.m.

"Was taken to a harvest-field very golden and ripe. I stood in a small square where cutting had commenced. Looking round, I saw you coming towards us through the corn: your shirt-sleeves tucked up: hat (scout pattern), did not notice the colour, on the back of your head: jacket slung over your left shoulder and held with your right hand. Another form was *behind you*, but you overshadowed him or her, don't know which, so I could not see it clearly. You both entered the square, and as *you* were about to start work again, I was told to give you *The Picture* and this Message: 'The Harvest is Ripe; the Reapers are few.'"

In a note to the above-mentioned account Mr Cripps added that, since the vision, he had been told that the form *behind me* was Edward Maitland working with me.

It was not until I had nearly finished writing the Preface to this book that the signification of this vision became known to me. It will be remembered that, in 1884, Baron Spedalieri wrote to Anna Kingsford and Edward Maitland a letter urging that her "chapters on the *Credo*," which had appeared in *Light*, should forthwith be published, on the ground that "time pressed" and "the harvest of the earth was ripe" (see p. 40, *ante*). Had it not been for Anna Kingsford's illness and untimely death, the Lectures would undoubtedly have been published during her lifetime. After her death, however, she desired that they should be published "by-and-by," because "they were then in advance of people, but would not be so for long as people were themselves advancing" (see p. 59, *ante*). I now see that the vision was intended to let me know that *the time had arrived* for the publication of the "chapters on the *Credo*" which are contained in this book.—S. H. H.

first symbolic vision he had received, he had received other communications purporting to come from the same source, all which he had learnt to regard as authentic. In particular, he said it was through a similar communication that he had become the happy possessor of the two volumes which he then had with him. Having long wanted to possess a copy of the *Life of Anna Kingsford,* and not being able to afford it, he had mentally asked Anna Kingsford if she could help him to obtain the book, and, in answer to his request, she had come to him in sleep and told him that if he would go to a certain shop in a certain street in London he would find what he wanted. Acting on the information thus received, he, as soon thereafter as possible, went to the place indicated, and there he saw, and obtained at the low cost of 12s. 6d., a second-hand copy of the book. It was the only copy in the shop, and before he left, a clergyman entering and seeing the book offered him £1, 1s. for it, which he declined. That was how he had come to possess his treasure. He had obtained it through information given to him by or purporting to come from Anna Kingsford.

The man was, apparently, sincere in all that he said, and—knowing the possibility of such communications—it occurred to me that if Anna Kingsford could so circumstantially direct him as to enable him to obtain possession of a certain book that he wanted, she could also direct him sufficiently to enable me to trace the whereabouts of her missing MSS.—assuming them to be in existence; and I thought it possible that she had sent him to me expressly for that purpose. So, without saying anything to Mr Cripps about my fears as to their having been destroyed—for I did not want to influence his mind in any way—I told him that I was endeavouring to trace the whereabouts of some of Anna Kingsford's MSS. which I had purchased but which could not be found; and (as it then came to me) I said: "*Now* I know why you have come to see me; it is to help me to trace the whereabouts of these missing MSS."; and I asked him, if possible, to obtain from Anna Kingsford replies to the following questions which I then wrote out and handed to him: "(1) Have you any message for me? (2) Can you give me any information about your MSS.?" I also asked if Edward Maitland had any message for me. Mr Cripps took the questions away with him, and promised to do his best for me, and if he should receive anything to let me know.

I did not see Mr Cripps again until the beginning of April,

but during the remainder of the month I received from him several letters, written chiefly for the purpose of recording visions that he was receiving, but none of which was related to or connected with the one matter concerning which I desired information, and I began to think that, perhaps, after all, he would not be able to throw any light on the subject.

In one of his letters he asked me if I had ever had any idea that Edward Maitland might have put Anna Kingsford's MSS. in her coffin and had them buried with her, to which I replied that I had never had any such idea, nor had I reason to suppose that such a thing had been done, because Edward Maitland would have required them when writing her Life, and the particular MSS. that I then sought would have been required for publication after her death.

From the 25th February until the 23rd March I did not receive any communication from him whatever, but on the morning of the 23rd March I received from him a letter as follows:—

"*22nd March* 1914.

"DEAR MR HART,—Alone in my den to-day. I am impressed to break the silent spell and ask if you have received any message (*re* our Quest), and to tell you that I have had one, but as I did not receive it *personally*, I have been waiting all this time expecting it to be verified thro' myself. Up to the present, I am sorry to say, it has not.

"My wife (who resides at Rowledge, Farnham, Surrey) was awakened from her sleep by a voice which said (Those papers of A. Kingsford's, Mr Maitland burnt them all). This occurred on the Thursday night Feb. 26. Thinking it over next day she decided not to say anything about it, but when she saw me as I entered the Cottage on the following Sat. evening, it was the first salute I had. To use her own words, it flew out of her. She tells me the voice was distinctly clear and *external*. The spiritual source of this voice she does not know more than she recognised it as the same one that has brought her a message on about five different occasions extending over a period of twenty-five years, all of them in relation to me, and three of them I *only* knew the truth of the message she received. I am not sure if I told you anything about her. She is a Natural Medium of an honest, truthful, and independent disposition. Not well read or studied at all in the Spiritualist's Craft, and no leaning towards any form of religion. Knows nothing of

A. K. or E. M. works, except what I have told her. Lives rather a lonely life. Our girl, her cottage and garden is the sum total of her existence, but ever ready to give a helping hand if she can.

"Now why this message should come in this way, rather puzzles me, as I have had several messages in the interim. . . .

"GEORGE CRIPPS."

On receipt of this letter I at once wrote to Mr Cripps and, for the first time, informed him of Edward Maitland's failing condition of health after the publication of *The Life of Anna Kingsford*; and of my visit to the Studios, and what was then told me by the housekeeper; and that, taking these things into consideration, I felt that the message which his wife had received was true.

On the 26th March he wrote to me: "The message was confirmed by a vision this morning. I will write it out for you to-night. I am now convinced (it is true), and so far as I am concerned (personally) the search is over. It remains true for me until *proved* to the contrary."

This letter was followed by another (written on the same day) giving an account of his confirmatory vision.

In July 1915 I, for the first time, met Anna Kingsford's only child—Eadith Kingsford—who told me that she had not and never had any of her mother's MSS., nor did she know of the existence of any, but she had always understood that whatever MSS. (if any) her mother had left, were, in accordance with the provisions contained in her will, handed over to or left in the possession of Edward Maitland; and in confirmation of this, at my request she afterwards wrote to me as follows:—

"*7th July* 1915.

"DEAR MR HART,—You have asked me if I have in my possession or know the whereabouts of any of my mother's MSS.

"On my father's death, in 1913, all the articles in his house that belonged to my mother were handed over to me, and there were not among such articles any MSS.

"I have not and never had in my possession any of my mother's MSS. I always understood that on her death all her MSS. were handed over to or retained by Edward Maitland, because my mother left to him a life interest in her writings. Apart from this, I do not know of the existence or whereabouts of any of my mother's MSS.—Yours sincerely, E. KINGSFORD."

As stated, I had long previously come to the conclusion that the MSS. of Anna Kingsford's Lectures on the Creed were among the papers destroyed by Edward Maitland, my belief being that he destroyed them under an overwhelming impulse that they were *too sacred* to be allowed after his death—which he then knew to be impending—to pass into the hands of any third person; and the message received through Mrs Cripps, coupled with the information given to me by Miss Kingsford, has confirmed my opinion. To me, of course, the loss of these MSS. is irreparable. Had the Lectures been published, it would not have been so disastrous, because, in that case, the text at least would not have been lost. As it is, the best—the only—thing I could do was to give the "abstracts" of them which were published in *Light*; and these, scanty though they be, are *most precious*, for, in addition to their authoritative value, they are, I believe, the only records that have come down to us of Anna Kingsford's inspired Lectures on the Credo of Christendom. Though incomplete and fragmentary, and on that account difficult in places to follow, they nevertheless contain *that* which, so far as I know, is not elsewhere to be found in any literature. They are as "leaves given for the healing of the nations." Those who have eyes that see and ears that hear will see and hear.

The question will be asked: What is the Hermetic Gnosis which the following Lectures are intended to expound, and of which Anna Kingsford and Edward Maitland speak with such admiration and respect? Edward Maitland says: "The Hermetic System may be summarised as follows: Spirit is the one real Being, of which all things are modes. Creation represents the manifestation of Spirit, by means of its descent or 'fall' into lower modes, of which matter is the lowest. But, inasmuch as matter is spirit, it can revert to its original condition of spirit. Such reversion constitutes Redemption; and this occurs in man by means of Regeneration, or the re-constitution of the individual of the higher mode of his own substance, wherein from consisting of material elements, he becomes constituted of spiritual elements, —that is, of pure soul-substance, and Divine Spirit. Hermetic science consists in the systematisation of the process whereby this redemption by regeneration is accomplished." [1]

---

[1] Edward Maitland, in reply to questions put to him at the close of an Address on "The Probable Course of Development and Ultimate Issue of the Present Spiritual Movement," given by him on the 2nd April 1889 to The London Spiritualist Alliance (*Light*, 1889, p. 182.)—S. H. H.

In an admirable article on "The Hermetic Books" in *The Virgin of the World*, Edward Maitland says: "Those who, enamoured of conventional methods, are unable to recognise any *organon* of knowledge except the superficial faculties, or any plane of knowledge transcending the range of those faculties, are necessarily intolerant of the idea that there has been in the world from the earliest times a system of esoteric and positive doctrine concerning the most hidden mysteries of Existence, of such a character, and so obtained as to fulfil all the conditions requisite to constitute a divine revelation. Nevertheless, this is the conclusion to which we have found ourselves compelled by sheer force of evidence, at once exoteric and esoteric. It is in Hindostan and Egypt that we find its earliest traces;[1] and if, as assuredly is the case, there are coincidences between the ancient doctrines of those lands and those of Greece, Judæa, and Christendom,[2] it is because the same truth has passed from people to people, everywhere finding recognition, and undergoing re-formulation

---

[1] In 1881 Anna Kingsford received an Illumination "Concerning the Great Pyramid and the Initiations Therein," which is given in full in *Clothed With the Sun* (pt. i. No. xx.), and which contains the following passage: "I perceive that Jesus had been initiated in the mysteries of India and Egypt long before he was incarnated as Jesus, and he appears to me as having been a Brahmin. The Egyptians and Hindûs appear to be of the same race, having their mysteries in common. For I am shewn one of each people riding together on an elephant. Both countries were *colonised* at the same time from Thibet, and from thence all the mysteries proceeded." See also her Illumination "Concerning the Holy Family" (*C. W. S.*, pt. i. No. xxxv.)—S. H. H.

[2] Mr G. R. S. Mead in his monumental work, *Thrice Greatest Hermes*, speaking of the Trismegistic literature, says: "The fragments of the Trismegistic literature which have reached us are the sole surviving remains of that 'Egyptian philosophy' which arose from the congress of the religious doctrines of Egypt with the philosophical doctrines of Greece. In other words, what the works of Philo were to the sacred literature of the Jews, the Hermaica were to the Egyptian sacred writings. Legend and myth were allegorised and philosophised and replaced by vision and instruction. But who were the authors of this theosophic method? This question is of the greatest interest to us, for it is one of the factors in the solution of the problem of the literary evolution of Christianity, seeing that there are intimate points of contact of ideas between several of the Hermetic documents and certain Jewish and Christian writings, especially the opening verses of Genesis, the treatises of Philo, the fourth Gospel (especially the Prologue), and beyond all the writings of the great Gnostic doctors Basilides and Valentinus" (vol. i. pp. 28–29): and he has no doubt that the Wisdom of Egypt was the main source of the Greek Trismegistic literature: and he agrees with W. Marsham Adams that the Wisdom of Egypt formed the main background of some of the principal teachings of Early Christianity (vol. i. pp. 68 and 80).

Thrice Greatest Hermes, which is in three volumes, should be in the hands of every student of Hermetic doctrine.—S. H. H.

according to the genius of the time and place of its sojourn. And this, we may add, is a process which must inevitably continue until man has become either so far degenerate as to lose all care for and perception of truth; or so far regenerate as to attain to the full perception of it, and fix it for evermore as his most precious possession."

In a further article—" The Hermetic System and the Significance of its Present Revival"—in the same book, he says : " The system designated the Hermetic Gnosis—the earliest formulation of which, for the Western world, belongs to the prehistoric times of ancient Egypt—has constituted the core of all the religio-philosophical systems of both East and West, Buddhism and Christianity, among others, being alike intended as vehicles for and expressions of it, though the fact has been recognised by only the initiated few. The great school of scholastic mysticism which was the glory of the Church of the Middle Ages had, although unavowedly, the same basis. This school represented a strenuous and sustained endeavour to rescue religion from the exclusive domain of the historical and the ceremonial, and the control of a sacerdotalism, grossly materialistic and idolatrous, by restoring its proper intuitional and spiritual character. That the endeavour failed to secure a lasting success, and the Church of the Middle Ages continued to sink deeper and deeper into superstition, with its usual accompaniment of religious persecution, was due to no fault of the system itself. This requires for its reception, that the spiritual consciousness of the many should have attained a development hitherto possessed only by the few. And the world was not then ripe for a doctrine which represents reason in its highest mode."

He then proceeds to give the following " general sketch " of the nature of the Hermetic Doctrine " which has played so important a part in the past, and bids fair to do as much, and even more, in the future." He says :—

" Starting from the axiom that from nothing nothing comes, and recognising Consciousness as the indispensable *condition* of existence, the Gnosis, with resistless logic, derives all things from pure and absolute Being, itself unmanifest and unconditioned, but in the infinity of its plentitude and energy possessing and exercising the potentiality of manifestation and conditionment, and *being*, rather than *having*, life, substance, and mind, comprised in one Divine Selfhood, of which the universe is the manifestation.

"Regarding all things as modes of consciousness, the Gnosis necessarily regards consciousness as subsisting under many modes, and as being definable as the property whereby whatever *is*, affects, or is affected in, itself; or affects, or is affected by, another; which is really to say, as constituting the things themselves. There is, thus, a mechanical consciousness, a chemical consciousness, a magnetic, a mental, a psychic, consciousness, and so on up to the divine, or absolute, consciousness. And whereas all proceed from this last, so all return to this last, in that every entity possesses the potentiality of it. Herein lies the secret of evolution, which is no other than the expression of the tendency of things to revert, by ascension, to their original condition—a tendency, and therefore an expression, which could have no being were the lowest or material mode of consciousness to be the original and normal mode.

"By thus making matter itself a mode of consciousness, and therein of spirit [1]—spirit being absolute consciousness—the Gnosis escapes at once the difficulties which stand in the way of the conception of an original Dualism, consisting of principles inherently antagonistic; and also those which arise out of the kindred conception of non-consciousness as having a positive existence. All being modes of the One, no inherent antagonism, or essential difference, is possible; but that which is regarded as unconsciousness is but a lower mode of consciousness—consciousness reduced, so to speak, to a minimum, but still consciousness so long as it *is*. Total unconsciousness is thus not-being; and bears to consciousness the relation of darkness to light, the

---

[1] In her "Prefatory Essay" to *Astrology Theologised*, Anna Kingsford says: "It is not Matter that is illusion, as is commonly supposed by superficial students of Oriental theosophy, but the belief that Matter is a thing true and self-subsistent without reference to any Beyond or Within. It is not fatal to deliverance to believe that this world is, but to believe that it *alone* is, and no other. This world in itself is certainly not illusion, for the matter which composes it is the last expression, centrifugally formulated, of Spirit, and, in fact, is Spirit, in a specialised and congelate condition. But the illusion of it consists in apprehending Matter as eternal and absolute, and in seeing in it the be-all and end-all of Life and Substance. The image seen in the pool or the mirror is not illusion, but he would be deluded who should suppose it to be other than an image. Mr Lilly, in *Ancient Religion and Modern Thought*, puts the case very clearly when he says: 'Matter as distinct from Spirit is an abstraction, and, if taken to be real, an illusion—as the old Vedic sages saw—the mocking Maya, from which Thought alone can release.' Here I cannot refrain from alluding to the classic myth of the wandering Io, the personified Soul, pursued and afflicted by the astral influences under the masque of Argus, the many-eyed giant, and finally delivered from his tyranny by Hermes or Thought, the Thoth or Thaut of Egyptian arcana" (p. 43).—S. H. H.

latter alone of the two being, however reduced, positive entity, and darkness being non-entity.

"However various the manifestations of the universal consciousness, or being, whether as regards its different planes, or its different modes on the same plane, they all are according to one and the same law, which, by its uniformity, demonstrates the unity of the informing spirit, or mind, which subsists eternally and independently of any manifestation. For, as said in the 'Divine Pymander' (B.V.):—

"'He needeth not to be manifested; for He subsisteth eternally.

"'But in that He is One, He is not made nor generated; but is unapparent and unmanifest.

"'But by making all things appear, He appeareth in all and by all; but especially is He manifested to or in those wherein he willeth.'

"And again:—

"'The Essence of all is One.'

"From the oneness of original Being comes, as a corollary, the law of correspondence between all planes, or spheres, of existence, in virtue of which the macrocosm is as the microcosm, the universal as the individual, the world as man, and man as God. 'An earthly man,' says *The Key*, 'is a mortal God, and the heavenly God is immortal man.' The same book, however, is careful to explain that by man is meant only those men who are possessed of the higher intelligence, or spiritual consciousness, and that to lack this is to be not yet man, but only the potentiality of man. It avoids also the error of anthropomorphism by defining Divinity to be, itself, neither life, nor mind, nor substance; but the cause of these.

"Ignorance of God is pronounced to be the greatest evil, but God is not to be discerned in phenomena, or with the outer eye. The quest must be made within oneself. In order to *know*, man must first *be*. This is to say, he must have developed in himself the consciousness of all the planes, or spheres, of his fourfold nature, and become thereby *wholly* man. It is to his inmost and divine part, the spirit, that the mystery of existence appertains, since that is Pure Being, of which existence is the manifestation. And, as man can recognise without him that only which he has within him, it is essential to his perception of spiritual things that he be himself spiritual. 'The natural man,' says the Apostle Paul, following at once the Hermetists and the Kabalists, who are at one in both doctrine and method, and differ only in form, ' receiveth not the things of the Spirit, neither can he know them, for they are spiritually discerned,' that is, by the spiritual part in man. In such degree as man develops this consciousness he becomes an *organon* of knowledge, capable of obtaining certitude of truth, even the highest ; and from being ' agnostic ' and incapable of knowledge, he becomes ' gnostic,' or has the Gnosis, which consists in the knowledge of himself and of God, and of the substantial identity of the two.

" From this it is obvious that what is demonstrated by the agnosticism of the present age, is simply the immaturity of its professors. This is to say, the philosophy of the day represents the conclusions of men who, how developed soever intellectually, are still rudimentary in respect of the spiritual consciousness, and fall short, therefore, of their spiritual and true manhood— the manhood which belongs to the highest plane. Being to such extent not human but sub-human, and ignorant of the meaning and potentialities of man, they confound form with substance, and mistake the exterior and phenomenal part of man for man himself, and imagine accordingly that to gratify this part is necessarily to benefit the man, no matter how subversive of the real humanity the practices to which they have recourse. Out of this condition of spiritual darkness the Gnosis lifts man, and, giving him the supreme *desideratum* —which it is the object of all divine revelation to supply—a *definition of himself*, demonstrates to him, with scientific certainty, the supremacy of the moral law, and the impossibility either of getting good by doing evil, or of escaping the penalty of the latter. The attempt to get good by evil doing only puts him back, making his fate worse. The doctrine of *Karma* is no less Hermetic than Hindû, the equivalent term in the former being Adrasté, a goddess to whom is committed the administration of justice. In the Greek Pantheon she appears as Nemesis and Hecate. They all represent the inexorable law of cause and effect in things moral, in virtue of which man's nature and conditions in the future are the result of the tendencies voluntarily encouraged by him in the past and present.

" The Hermetic method to the attainment of perfection, on whatever plane—physical, intellectual, moral, or spiritual—is *purity*. Not merely having, but *being*, consciousness, man is man, and is percipient according to the measure in which he is pure ; perfect purity implying full perception, even to the seeing of God, as the Gospels have it. In the same proportion he has also power. The fully initiated Hermetist is a Magian, or man of power, and can work what to the world seem miracles, and those on all planes—physical, intellectual, moral, and spiritual—by force of his own will. But his only secret of power is purity, as his only motive is love. For the power with which he operates is spirit, and spirit is keen and mighty in proportion as it is pure. Absolutely pure spirit *is* God. Hence the miracles of the Magian, as distinguished from the magician, are really worked by God—the God in and of the man.

"A word on the *organon* of Hermetic knowledge. This is emphatically the mode of the mind termed the intuition.[1] Following this in its centripetal course, man comes into such relations with his own essential and permanent self—the soul—as to be able to receive from her the knowledges she has acquired of divine things in the long ages of her past. But this implies no disparagement to the mind's other and centrifugal mode, the intellect. This also must be developed and trained to the utmost, as the complement, supplement, and indispensable mate of the intuition—the man to its woman. Perfecting and combining these two, and only thus, man knows all things[2] and perpetuates himself. For he knows God, and to know God is to have, and to be, God, and the 'gift of God is eternal life.'

"A foremost Hermetic doctrine is that of the soul's multiple re-births into a physical body. Only when the process of re-generation—an Hermetic term—is sufficiently advanced to enable the spiritual entity, which constitutes the true individual, to dispense with further association with the body, is he finally

---

[1] In answer to one who, while he recognised the faculty of the intuition, regarded its knowledges as "speculations," Anna Kingsford and Edward Maitland replied: "The intuition is not a creative but a perceptive and recollective faculty; and, therefore, its results are not surmises or opinions, but *knowledges*, inasmuch as they are founded on actual experience acquired either in the present or in past lives" (Letter, dated 10th July 1882, to the *Theosophist*).—S. H. H.

[2] That there is no limit to be placed on man's power to know, is clear from the following passage taken from a letter written by Anna Kingsford and Edward Maitland, wherein they say: "As all things proceed from mind, mind is necessarily competent for the comprehension of all things. So that there is *not* 'an infinity of truth beyond the reach of human reason.' But all that reason has to do is so to purify and expand itself as to become one with the infinite reason which has produced all things. It is not that truth is not infinite, but that reason, when perfected, is also infinite. There is nothing that is incomprehensible or cannot be understood. The doctrine of the paragraph in question has ever been the stronghold of superstition, and worst enemy of the faith that is based on the 'rock' of the understanding, the only faith that 'saves'" (*Light*, 1883, p. 475).—S. H. H.

freed from the necessity of a return into materiality. The doctrine of correspondence here finds one of its most striking illustrations, but one which nevertheless was wholly missed by the chief modern restorer and exponent of that doctrine, Emanuel Swedenborg. This is the correspondence in virtue of which, just as the body uses up and sheds many times its external covering of integument, plumage, shell, or hair, to say nothing of its artificial clothing, so the soul wears out and sheds many bodies. The law of gravitation, moreover, pervades all planes, the spiritual as well as the physical; and it is according to his spiritual density that the plane of the individual is determined, and his condition depends. The tendency which brings a soul once into the body, must be exhausted before the soul is able to dispense with the body. The death of the body is no indication that the tendency has been overcome, so that the soul will not be again attracted to earth. But it is only the soul that thus returns; not the magnetic or 'astral' body which constitutes the external personality.

"Such is the *rationale* of the orthodox doctrine of transmigration, according alike to the Hermetic, the Kabalistic, and the Hindû systems. It permeates, occultly, the whole of the Bible, and is implied in the teaching of Jesus to Nicodemus, the whole of which, as is also the entire Christian presentation, is, in its interior sense, Hermetic. Not that the new birth insisted on by Jesus is other than purely spiritual; but it involves a multiplicity of physical re-births as necessary to afford the requisite space and experiences for the accomplishment of the spiritual process declared to be essential to salvation. Seeing that regeneration must—as admitted by Swedenborg—have its commencement while in the body, and must also be carried on to a certain advanced stage before the individual can dispense with the body, and also that it denotes a degree of spiritual maturity far beyond the possibility of attainment in a single, or an early, incarnation; it is obvious that without a multiplicity of re-births to render regeneration possible, the Gospel message would be one, not of salvation, but of perdition, to the race at large. What is theologically termed the 'forgiveness of sins' is dependent upon the accomplishment in the individual of the process of regeneration, of which man, as Hermetically expressed, has the seed, or potentiality, in himself, and in the development of which he must co-operate. Doing this, he becomes 'a new creature,' in that he is re-born, not of corruptible matter, but of 'water and the spirit,' namely, his own soul and spirit purified and become divine. Thus reconstituted on the interior and higher plane of the spirit, he is said to be born of the 'Virgin Mary' and the 'Holy Ghost.'

"While purely mystical and spiritual, as opposed to historical and ceremonial, the Hermetic system is distinguished from other schools of mysticism by its freedom from their gloomy and churlish manner of regarding nature, and their contempt and loathing for the body and its functions as inherently impure and vile;[1] and so far from repudiating the relations of the sexes, it exalts them as symbolising the loftiest divine mysteries, and enjoins their exercise as a duty, the fulfilment of which, in some at least of his incarnations, is essential to the full perfectionment and initiation of the individual. It is thus pervaded by an appreciation of beauty and joyousness of tone which at once assimilates it to the Greek, and distinguishes it from the Oriental, conception of existence, and so redeems mysticism from the reproach—too often deserved—of pessimism. The Hermetist, like the Prophet who found God in the sea's depths and the whale's belly, recognises divinity in every region and department of nature. And seeing in 'ignorance of God the greatest of all evils,'[2] he seeks to perfect himself, not simply in order the sooner to escape from existence as a thing inherently evil, but to make himself an instrument of perception capable of 'seeing God' in every region of existence in which he may turn his gaze. The pessimism ascribed to some Hermetic utterances, especially in the 'Divine Pymander,' is but apparent, not real, and implies only the *comparative* imperfection of existence as contrasted with pure and divine being.

"It is to this end that the renunciation of flesh as food is insisted on, as in the 'Asclepios.' Belonging neither by his physical nor his moral constitution to the order of the carnivora, man can be the best that he has it in him to be only when his system is cleansed and built up anew of the pure materials derived from the vegetable kingdom, and indicated by his structure as his natural diet. The *organon* of the beatific vision is the intuition. And not only is the system, when flesh-fed, repressive of this faculty, but the very failure of the individual to recoil from violence and slaughter as a means of sustenance or gratification is an indication of his lack of this faculty.

[1] The term "corrupt," which in the translation of the "Divine Pymander," is applied to things earthly, means simply perishable.—E. M.
[2] The title of one of the books in the "Divine Pymander."—E. M.

"In no respect does the Hermetic system shew its unapproachable superiority to the *pseudo*-mystical systems than in its equal recognition of the sexes. True it is that the story of the Fall is of Hermetic origin; but it is no less true that this is an allegory, having a significance wholly removed from the literal, and in no way implying blame or inferiority, either to an individual or to a sex. Representing an eternal verity of divine import, this allegory has been made the justification for doctrines and practices in regard to women which are altogether false, unjust, cruel, and monstrous, and such as could have proceeded only from elementary and sub-human sources.

"In conclusion. All history shews that it is to the restoration of the Hermetic system in both doctrine and practice that the world must look for the final solution of the various problems concerning the nature and conduct of existence, which now—more than at any previous time—exercise the human mind. For it represents that to which all enquiry—if only it be free enquiry, unlimited by incapacity, and undistorted by prejudice—must ultimately lead; inasmuch as it represents the sure, because experimental, knowledges, concerning the nature of things which, in whatever age, the soul of man discloses whenever he has attained full intuition. Representing the triumph of free-thought—a thought, that is, which has dared to probe the consciousness in all directions, outwards and downwards to matter and phenomena, and inwards and upwards to spirit and reality; it represents also the triumph of religious faith, in that it sees in God the All in All of Being; in Nature, the vehicle for the manifestation of God; and in the Soul—educated and perfected through the processes of Nature—the individualisation of God."

Speaking of the evil of flesh-eating, Anna Kingsford, in a note to the "Asclepios on Initiations," says: "The key to the Hermetic Secret is found when the aspirant adopts the Edenic Life: the life of purity and charity which all mystics—Hebrew, Egyptian, Buddhist, Greek, Latin, Vedic, with one consent, ascribe to man in the golden age of his primeval perfection. The first outcome of the Fall, or Degeneracy, is the shedding of blood and eating of flesh. The license to kill is the sign-manual of 'Paradise Lost.' And the first step towards 'Paradise Regained' is taken when man voluntarily returns to the manner of life indicated by his organism as that alone befitting him, and thus reunites himself to the harmony of Nature and the Will of God. No man who follows this path and faithfully keeps to it will fail to find at length the Gate of Paradise. Not necessarily in a single life-time, for the process of purification is a long one, and the past experiences of some men may be such as to shut them out for many lives from the attainment of the promised land. But, nevertheless, every step faithfully and firmly trodden brings them nearer to the goal, every year of pure life increasingly strengthens the spirit, purges the mind, liberates the will, and augments their human royalty. On the other hand, it is idle to seek union with God in the Spirit, while the physical and magnetic organism remains insurgent against Nature. Harmony must be established between man and Nature before union can be accomplished between man and God. For Nature is the manifest God; and if man be not in perfect charity with that which is visible, how shall he love that which is invisible? Hermetic doctrine teaches the kinship and solidarity of all beings, redeemed and glorified in man. For man does not stand aloof and apart from other creatures, as though he were a fallen angel dropped from some supernal world upon the earth, but he is the child of earth, the product of evolution, the elder brother of all conscient things; their lord and king, but not their tyrant. It is his part to be to all creatures a Good Destiny; he is the keeper, the redeemer, the regenerator of the earth. If need be, he may call on his subjects to serve him as their king, but he may never, without forfeiting his kingship, maltreat and afflict them. All the children of God, in every land and age, have abstained from blood, in obedience to an occult law which asserts itself in the breast of all regenerate men. The mundane Gods are not averse to blood, for by means of it they are invigorated and enabled to manifest. For the mundane Gods are the forces of the astral element in man, which element dominates in the unregenerate. Therefore, the unregenerate are under the power of the stars,[1] and subject to illusion. Inasmuch as a man is clean from the defilement of blood, insomuch he is less liable to be beguiled by the deceptions of the astral serpent. Therefore, let all who seek the Hermetic secret do their utmost to attain to the Hermetic life. If entire abstinence from all forms of animal food be impossible, let a lower degree be adopted, admitting the use of the least bloody meats only—milk, fish, eggs, and the flesh of birds. But in such a case, let the *intention* of the aspirant be continually united with that of Nature, willing with firm desire to lead, whenever

[1] See p. 221, *post*.

possible, a yet more perfect life ; so that in a future birth he may be enabled to attain to it." [1]

Reference has been made to the fourfold nature of Man. This is in accord with the Hermetic division, which was adopted by Anna Kingsford and Edward Maitland. But Man may also be regarded as threefold and as sevenfold. The Spiritualists generally adopt a threefold division of Body, Mind, and Spirit (which last must be understood to include Soul). Those who follow the esoteric teaching of the East as distinct from that of the West, adopt a sevenfold division. The different divisions are not, of course, contradictory to nor are they inconsistent with each other, and with the object of shewing how the fourfold and sevenfold divisions agree, I give the following table, which may be of use : [2]—

THE CONSTITUTION OF MAN.

Fourfold Division.   *Sevenfold Division.*

EXTERIOR MAN.[3]

Fourfold Division	Sevenfold Division
1. Physical Body.	1. Material Body (*Sthûla-sharira*), composed wholly of matter in its grossest and most tangible form.
	2. Vitality (*Jîv-âtma*). Vital-Principle. Physical-Force. Nerve-Force. Animal-Vitality.
2. Astral Body (*Nephesh*) or Fluidic Shape. Shade. Magnetic Body. Odic or Sidereal Body. Closely connected with the Mundane Mind and Outer Reason (*Ruach*).	3. Astral Body (*Linga-sharira*) composed of highly etherialised matter. The lowest mode of Soul-substance. The Sex-body.
	4. Animal Soul or Desiring Mind (*Kâma-rûpa*). Related to all Covetous longings or Concupiscence.
	5. Intellectual Soul or Mind (*Manas*). The Personality. The Earthly Mind. Concerned in the attainment of science related to physical things. The seat of the Outer Reason and of the Material Memory, Abilities, Affections, Cares, and Acquirements. The *Anima bruta*. Is shed at death with the body and the shade.

---

[1] *The Virgin of the World*, pp. 94-95.
[2] See the *Theosophist* for October 1881 and April 1884 (Supplement, p. 58) ; and *The Life of A. K.*, vol. ii. pp. 73-74.
[3] The Principles belonging to the external man are evanescent as entities, and are not subject to the influence of Karma *directly*, because

INTERIOR MAN.

3. Soul (*Neshamah*). 6. Spiritual Soul, Mind, or Consciousness (*Buddhi*). The Divine Idea. The Individuality. The true Man. The Ego. Psyche. The *Anima Divina*. Vehicle of *Âtma*. By nature eternal. Retains the celestial memory, and transmigrates.

4. Spirit (*Jechidah*). 7. Spirit (*Âtma*). An emanation of the Absolute. Being. The Supreme Reason. Wisdom. God. Cochmah. Spiritual Word or Logos of the Man. The Nous. Uncreated and Eternal.

Of the above, the Material Body represents that which is physical and vital; the Astral Body, that which is animal and intellectual; the Soul, that which is moral and human; and the Spirit, that which is spiritual and divine.

It has been said that the intuition is the *organon* of Hermetic knowledge,[1] such knowledge being derived from the soul of the man and not from extraneous sources. This truth is most clearly stated in one of Anna Kingsford's Illuminations [2] as follows:—

"Know that there is no enlightenment from without: the secret of things is revealed from within.

"From without cometh no Divine Revelation: but the Spirit within beareth witness.

"Think not I tell you that which you know not: for except you know it, it cannot be given to you.

"To him that hath it is given, and he hath the more abundantly.

"None is a prophet save he who knoweth: the instructor of the people is a man of many lives.

"Inborn knowledge and the perception of things, these are the sources of revelation: the soul of the man instructeth him, having already learned by experience.[3]

they are never re-born. That is to say, that Karma acting on the destiny of the Interior Personality (the Soul) creates new Outer Personalities at each birth.—S. H. H.

[1] See p. 76, *ante*.

[2] "Concerning Inspiration and Prophesying" (*Clothed With the Sun*, pt. i. Illumination No. ii. pt. i.).

[3] The dependence of religion upon memory was pointed out by Edward Maitland in a letter to *Light*, in which he said: "Tradition and intuition—the two factors in religion—are each dependent upon memory, the former dealing with its historical, the latter with its spiritual, element. . . . But even more essential to religion than the knowledge of events, historical

"Intuition is inborn experience; that which the soul knoweth of old and of former years.

"And Illumination is the Light of Wisdom, whereby a man perceiveth heavenly secrets.

"Which Light is the Spirit of God within the man, shewing unto him the things of God.

"Do not think that I tell you anything you know not; all cometh from within: the Spirit that informeth is the Spirit of God in the prophet."[1]

In 1882 Edward Maitland took part in a controversy on Inspiration, which was carried on in the pages of *Light*,[2] and in reply to some of the writers who contended that extraneous spirits were the sources of inspiration and divine knowledge, he said:—

"It is to the spirit of the man himself, and not to any extraneous influences, that the only true illumination is due.... Man himself not merely has, but *is* a Spirit, and does not necessarily lose his spiritual powers by his investment with a material body. The human organism is not a mere instrument dependent upon any chance wandering influences which may alight upon it. It is the peculiar *habitat* and mode of manifestation of an incarnated portion of Divinity, and it is through the unfoldment within him of the powers of this, his own fixed, indwelling Spirit, that he finds his true inspiration, and not through the suppression of this in favour of strangers. And yet even more than this. Even where under the overshadowing of some separate Spirit— often it may be the phantom of one of his own past selves—he finds fresh and valuable knowledge, it is due, not to actual

merely and external, is the knowledge of those interior experiences which represent the Divine operation within the soul of the individual. Here it is that the intuition finds its especial office; and inasmuch as without her recollection of those experiences the soul could not communicate of them to the individual, and without his recollection of them the latter could not impart of them to others, it is upon memory, again, that religion largely depends.

"'Perception and recollection—these are the sources of Inspiration'" (*Light*, 1882, p. 551).—S. H. H.

[1] "The practice," says Edward Maitland, "of confounding the prophet and the saint with the mere 'medium' is an error of the gravest kind, and fatal to the true Spiritualism. It is true the former may have mediumistic gifts, but these are not what make him saint or prophet. Mediumship is due to a peculiar condition of the physical organism, and implies neither intellectual, moral, nor spiritual development, whereas that which makes the prophet and the saint is precisely such development and no peculiarity of organism, and the very possession of such development is a safeguard against the liability to be 'controlled' which is the characteristic of the mere medium' (*Light*, 1887, p. 54).—S. H. H.

[2] *Light*, 1882, pp. 434, 466, 511, 551. Edward Maitland's letters bear the *nom de plume* "Cantab."—S. H. H.

suggestion proceeding from such entity, but to the fact that under such magnetism he is lifted into a sphere of his own system not ordinarily accessible to him, and enabled to regain the forgotten perceptions and recollections of his own soul. Such is the nature and method of 'inspiration': the quality varying according to the degree of purity of the individual's mind and life.

. . . .

"To the question, 'How many of our past selves are in existence?' *The Perfect Way* replies, 'A single *Neschamah*' (or *anima divina*—the past of the man which becomes re-incarnate) 'may have as many of these former selves in the astral light as a man may have changes of raiment.' And the reason why 'the (interior and higher) spheres of our own systems are not ordinarily accessible to us,' is that we are accustomed to live so much in the outer and lower as to incapacitate ourselves for the requisite aspiration; or, in biblical language, because 'our conversation is not in heaven'—the celestial kingdom within us—but on earth, the bodily and material part.

. . . .

"Granting the fact that a clairvoyant can see the Guardian Angel of a person actually inspiring him with words, or more correctly, probably, with thoughts, it still remains to be known what, precisely, is the nature of such angel and its relation to its 'client,' before it can be decided whether the source of the inspiration is extraneous or interior to the latter. Now on this point *The Perfect Way* speaks explicitly, with a clearness and fullness which leaves nothing to be desired. And it declares the proper Guardian Angel, or 'genius,' of a person to be no extraneous Spirit, but a function of that person's own system, whose business it is to act as a connecting link of communication between him and his own Divine, informing Spirit—a moon, as it were, to reflect the sun to the planet man, each (spiritualised) person having such 'sun' and 'moon' in himself, the human system being complex. . . . In regard to the attainment of knowledge through the operation of a 'past self.' It is not in such phantom that the knowledge in question mainly resides, but in the re-embodied soul itself of the man, which, under the reflective influence of one of such phantoms—always present in his system—is able to regain the memory of the experiences appertaining to the particular incarnation represented by it.[1] It is,

---

[1] "My 'phantom,'" said Edward Maitland, "being a shade of my past self, is but a note-book to facilitate the recovery of my own recollections" (*Light*, 1888, p. 551).—S. H. H.

of course, possible to hold intercourse with Spirits other than one's own; but this is not 'inspiration,' but conversation only. And no such Spirit, however friendly and assiduous, is in the true sense a 'Guardian Angel.' Inspiration, in the highest sense, comes only from the central Spirit, or 'God,' of the man, either directly or through his 'genius.'[1] And since all that is done by what is called *Influx* is to illuminate—not to inform—the soul of the recipient, the knowledge obtained under such illumination depends upon the quantity and quality of the experiences already possessed by such soul. Where this is young and inexperienced, the lamp of the Spirit can but light up a comparatively empty chamber. Hence the absolute necessity of experience to the soul's progress; and hence, also, the absolute necessity of a multiplicity of re-births on the material plane, in order to obtain the experiences of which alone come maturity and final emancipation from matter. . . . Of man's fourfold nature, his celestial part alone it is which undergoes re-incarnation, and only when the consciousness of this part is attained does the individual find in himself the proofs of his previous existences. Consisting, as do these proofs, in personal memories, they are incapable of communication to others, since no one can transfer his memory to another. So that the only way to obtain the desired verification of the great doctrine at issue, is by so living, in thought and deed, as to hasten the time when between his inner and outer

---

[1] Writing of "The Descent of the Spirit," and to explain what he believed to be the process of Divine inspiration and illumination, Edward Maitland suggested the following illustration from the analogy of flame, between which and spirit there subsists a close correspondence. He says: "On holding a suitable substance—such as a splinter of dry wood like the stem of a match—over a lighted candle, ignition occurs, not immediately in the wood or from the flame beneath it, but in the gas generated by the heat and at a distance above the wood; and only by means of the descent upon it of the flame along the current of ascending gas does the wood take fire, being thus ignited from above and not from below.

"It seems to me that we have herein a parallel to the spiritual phenomenon in question; and that there is both an ascent of the individual and a descent of the spirit by which he is vivified and illumined. And also that although the two must co-operate to accomplish the process, the initiative may be taken by either of them. This is to say, the individual may in virtue of his own spiritual fervour so *polarise* himself to the highest as to kindle the Divine fire within him; or the spirit may take him even unawares, and when otherwise engrossed, and, lighting upon him, itself kindle the fire. Of course, for either to be possible the individual must have previously attained a high degree of spiritual development. For if he had not already so 'ascended,' the spirit could not descend upon him. He would not be responsive to its influence" (*Light*, 1888, p. 57).—S. H. H.

man shall be such closeness of intercommunion as will enable his Spirit to 'bring all things to remembrance.'"

The letters written by Anna Kingsford and Edward Maitland in the controversy which took place in *Light* on "The Historic 'Jesus'"[1] are of very great interest. In this connection, Anna Kingsford had, in 1881, been the recipient of Illuminations "Concerning the Gospels; their Origin and Composition," and "Concerning the Actual Jesus." In the former Illumination Anna Kingsford—speaking in trance—said:—

"I am looking at the inside of the Serapeum at Alexandria. The temple is connected with a library which, as I see it, is still there, neither dispersed nor burnt, but filled with manuscripts,—mostly rolls upon sticks. I see a council of many men sitting at a table in the room of the library, and I see a number of names, as Cleopatra, Marcus Antonius, and others. This is called the *second* library of Alexandria, the former having been destroyed under Julius Cæsar. The nucleus of this one was the gift of Antony to Cleopatra, who added to it and improved it immensely, till it contained all the existing literature of the world; and—why, they are deliberately concocting Christianity out of the books there! and, so far as I can see, the Gospels are little better than Ovid's *Metamorphoses* (historically, I mean),—so deliberately are they making up the new religion by replanting the old on the Jewish system.

"Write down these names and the dates which are specially shown me. Theophilus, patriarch of Alexandria, and Ambrosius. A.D. 390, B.C. 286. This last is the date at which the library was first of all got together. A.D. 390 is the date of the chief destruction of the documents out of which the new religion was made. If they could be recovered we should have absolute proof of its concoction from Hindû, Persian, and other originals;—the interpolations, extracts, and alterations proving this. They shew, too, that the name first adopted for the typical man was more like Krishna, and that Jesus was a later choice, adopted at Jewish suggestion, in order to suit a Jewish hero. The system was long under formation, and it took all that time to perfect. Every detail of the Gospel history is invented, the number of the apostles, and all the rest. Nothing is historical in the sense supposed.

"I see the Serapeum destroyed;—not only the library but the

[1] See p. 205, *post*.

temple, so fearful were they of leaving any trace of the concoction. It was destroyed by Christians at the instigation especially of Theodosius, Ambrosius, and Theophilus. Their motive was a mixed one, each of the leaders having a different aim. The object of the concocters themselves was to sustain and continue the ancient faith by transplanting it to a new soil, and engrafting it on Judaism. The object of Theophilus was to make the new religion the enemy and successor of the old, by making it appear to have an independent basis and origin. Ambrose destroyed the library in order to confute the Arians by leaving it to appear that Christianity had an origin altogether supernatural. The concocters themselves did not intend it to be regarded as supernatural, but as representing the highest human. And they accordingly fixed and accumulated upon Jesus all that had been told of previous Christs,—Mithras, Osiris, Krishna, Buddha, and others,—the original draft containing the doctrine of the transmigration of souls most explicitly and distinctly. The concoction was undertaken in order to save religion itself from extinction through the prevalence of materialism,—for the times corresponded in this respect exactly to the present. And the plan was to compose out of all the existing systems one new and complete, representing the highest possibilities and satisfying the highest aspirations of humanity.

"The great loss, then, is not that of the first but that of the second library of Alexandria. The Serapeum was destroyed by Christians in order to prevent the human origin of their religion from being ascertained. The object was to have it believed that it all centred in one particular actual person, and was not collected and compiled from a multiplicity of sources.

"All the conversations in the Gospels were fabricated by the aid of various books in order to illustrate and enforce particular doctrines. I cannot recognise the language of many of the ancient manuscripts used. The Latin ones which I see are all in capitals, and without any division between the words, so that they look like one long word.

"I am shewn the actual scene of the destruction of the library and dispersion of the books. There is a dreadful tumult. The streets of Alexandria are filled with mobs of people shouting and hastening to the spot. They do not know the real object. They have been told that the library contains the devil's books, which, if allowed to remain, will be the means of destroying Christianity. The noise and tumult are dreadful. I cannot bear it; pray recall me, it hurts me so. It is extraordinary how exactly alike the two times are both politically and religiously. Everything established is breaking up in both; and that which comes out of each is the fuller revelation of the divine Idea of Humanity. All works for us and the new revelation. But the world suffers terribly in the birth. Afterwards things gradually become much better."[1]

In her Illumination "Concerning the Actual Jesus," Anna Kingsford—also speaking in trance, said:—

"I am shewn that there is but little of real value in the Scriptures. They are a mass of clay, comparatively modern, with here and there a bit of gold. The Angel whom I saw before, and who told us to burn the Bible, now puts it in the fire, and there comes out a few pages only of matter which is original and divine. All the rest is interpolation or alteration. This is the case with both Old Testament and New. . . . Here and there is an original piece of the ancient Revelation, but these are largely interspersed with additions and embellishments, commentaries, and applications to the times by copyists and interpreters. And when the Angel told us to put the Bible in the fire, he meant separate the gold from the dross and clay. . . . As for the Gospels, they are almost entirely parabolical. Religion is not historical, and in nowise depends upon past events. For, faith and redemption do not depend upon what any man did, but on what God has revealed. Jesus was not the historical name of the initiate and adept whose story is related. It is the name given him in initiation. . . . The Scriptures are addressed to the soul, and make no appeal to the outer senses. The whole story of Jesus is a mass of parables, the things that occurred to him being used as symbols. . . . The gospel life of Jesus is made up of the lives of all the divine teachers before him, and represents the best the world had then, and the best it has in it to be. And it is therefore a prophecy. The recorded life of Jesus epitomised all the teachers before him, and the possibilities of mankind some day to be realised."[2]

---

[1] *Clothed With the Sun*, pt. i. Illumination No. xxxii.

[2] *Clothed With the Sun*, pt. i. Illumination No. xxxiii. Speaking of deductions to be drawn from the loss of certain writings concerning the Mystery-rites and Mystery-myths of the Egyptians and of the Chaldæans, Mr G. R. S. Mead says that certain Jewish and Christian mystics, whom Hippolytus calls Naassenes, claimed "that Christianity, or rather the Good News of the Christ, was precisely the consummation of the inner doctrine of the Mystery-institutions of all the nations; and the end of them all was the revelation of the Mystery of Man" (*Thrice Greatest Hermes*, vol. i. p. 141.)—S. H. H.

I have long believed that these wonderful Illuminations received by Anna Kingsford contain the best answer that can be given concerning the origin of the Gospels, and I have recently received what I cannot but regard as a remarkable corroboration. Some few months ago my wife gave to me a book called *The Restored New Testament*, by James Morgan Pryse. It was published in New York and in London in 1914, and it is in every respect a remarkable book. It claims to give " The Hellenic Fragments [in the New Testament], freed from the pseudo-Jewish Interpolations." In his *Preface*, Mr Pryse says that the text of the Gospels is not in its primitive form,—the founders of the Christian Church having deliberately falsified it throughout. But, he says, freed from these falsifications, " the allegory of the Crucified is Hellenic in form, and embodies in its simple majesty the profoundest truths of archaic religion. . . . All those portions of the New Testament which may be regarded as genuine are, with the exception of a few fragments of the Epistles, prose plagiaries from ancient Greek sacred poems, the allegorical dramas forming part of the ritual in the Mysteries; and all the passages by which the Jēsous-mythos is connected with the Old Testament, staged in Judæa, and given a semblance of historicity, are the work of forgers, who employed stolen notes of the Greek Mystery-ritual in fabricating a 'sacred' scripture upon which to found a new religion." Thus, the Apocalypse is by Mr Pryse treated as a prose version of a Greek Mystery-poem; but, regarding this, he says, " the version seems to have been made with honest motives by a writer conversant with the esoteric meaning of the original, and who presumably gave it a superficially Jewish colouring to preserve it from being destroyed by the fanatics of the new faith, who were endeavouring to suppress everything in ancient literature which betrayed, or tended to prove, the fact that the new religion they had invented and instituted was founded on a fabricated 'history,' and was merely a travesty of the older religions." Further, in his *Introduction to the Anointing of Jēsous*—referring to the Synoptic Gospels—he says : ' The original source from which they were drawn is considered to have been an allegorical drama which formed part of the ritual of the Greek Mysteries. . . . Judging by portions of the text, the original drama was a superb poem ; but the compilers of the Synoptic Gospels had only incomplete prose notes of it, presumably made from memory, and these notes they could have obtained only by dishonourable means."

I first read the above-mentioned *Preface* and *Introduction* one evening just before going to bed. When reading them, I could not help remarking how much there was in common between Mr Pryse's theory concerning the origin of the Gospels, and Anna Kingsford's Illuminations on that subject. I was particularly struck with Mr Pryse's theory of the Gospels being founded on an allegorical drama which formed part of the ritual of the Greek Mysteries. I went to bed with these thoughts uppermost in my mind, and was soon asleep. It is not usual for me after going to sleep to wake until it is time to get up; and, so far as I know, I have never in my life walked in my sleep, and I have no reason to believe that I did so on this night, in fact, I am sure I did not—had I done so it would certainly have waked my wife, who was with me, and who is a very light sleeper. Well, in the middle of the night I was surprised to find myself, without any apparent cause, wide awake. My wife was fast asleep by my side. Both my arms were under the bed-clothes, and there was not a movement in the bed or in the room. It was dark, and all was still and quiet. Under these conditions I suddenly felt something come into one of my hands, both of which were empty. On feeling this, I immediately closed my hand, when, to my surprise, I found that I was holding a key. How it came into my hand I do not know, and I have no theory to offer. I simply relate the fact. My first thought was, "How came this key into my hand? Am I awake or am I asleep? Am I in my right mind or am I dreaming?" But no sooner had these thoughts passed through my mind—which they did in far less time than I can tell them—than I knew the meaning of what had happened, for these words came to me with great force, filling my mind: "*You have the key*,"—meaning thereby: "You have in Anna Kingsford's Illuminations and in Mr Pryse's theory the key to the origin of the Gospels." I was certain that this was what I was intended to understand, and that it was true. In order that there should not be any doubt as to the reality of my experience, I put the key under my pillow, saying to myself, "If I find it there when I wake in the morning, I shall know that I have not been dreaming." On waking, my first thought was "the key"; I felt under my pillow, and there I found it. I had not been dreaming. It was a small iron key which, my wife informed me, belonged to a drawer in another room, and which she had on the previous night, before going to bed, put on her dressing-table which stood at the other end of our bedroom. My wife assured me that she did not take the key to bed with her, and I am positive that I did not take it to bed with me. I did not even know that it was in the room—or, indeed, of its existence,—until it came into my hand in the manner related.

I will conclude with an extract from one of the Lectures given by Edward Maitland to the Hermetic Society, when he gave a master-key for the interpretation of Holy Scripture and the dogmas of the Catholic Church. At the close of his Lecture on "Revelation as the Supreme Common Sense,"[1] he said:—

"To the interpretation of all mystic symbols, whether they be creeds, dogmas, ceremonial rites, images, scriptures, or edifices, the key is one and the same. And it is twofold, having two parts which are expressed in two words. These are *Now* and *Within*. The first of them implies that Religion is not a thing relating to history, whether in the past, present, or future, but is an ever-occurring actuality, an eternal verity, representing for every man one and the self-same process, inherent in the nature of existence, and necessary to be enacted in each man in its entirety, irrespective of all other men whatsoever. So that, were there but one man in existence, the whole stupendous drama of Creation, Fall, Incarnation, Atonement, and Redemption, to their minutest details as set forth in the Christian history and symbology, would be enacted in his case precisely as for an universe of men. This is because it relates, not to particular men, but to *Man*.

"The other term of the key, the word *Within*, implies that Religion is purely interior, mystic, spiritual, and addressed, therefore, not to the body and lower reason—though finding manifestation through these—but to the soul, and has no concern with persons, events, or other things belonging to the external and historical plane—'which things,' as St Paul says, 'are an allegory'—that to which it relates being the *spiritual* nature of man.

"This being so, it is not with the faculties of the superficial or external man that the Mysteries of Religion can be comprehended, or its verities discerned; not even if such man be what is called a 'religious man,' however devoted and sincere. For, it is not to mere pious zeal, but to 'zeal according to knowledge,' that the discernment of Divine things appertains.

"The prevailing diversity of interpretation, and the conse-

[1] See p. 28, *ante*.

quent multiplicity of sects which divide and distract Christendom, are due to the ignorance of this fact. Humanity is brimming over with love and piety and zeal, and eager to do God and man service. But, for want of knowledge, its enthusiasm and force are wasted, or worse than wasted, and all parties are engaged in fighting or circumventing each other, instead of combining against the common foe, the demon at once of negation and superstition. Meanwhile, the Truth which alone can save and make free is in our midst, shut up in Bible parable—mistaken for history—and in Church symbol and formula, because the common sense [1] which originally discerned and formulated it has long ceased to interpret it.

"St Paul, so hard, apparently, upon woman on the social plane, does her full justice on the spiritual plane, when he declares that ' the man is not without the woman, nor the woman without the man, in the Lord.' For in this he admits the necessity of both the man and the woman to the comprehension of Divine things. The intellect and intuition, which are the man and woman of the mind, must co-operate to the production of the divine child, Truth. And to separate them is to destroy the equilibrium of the universe. For, alone, intellect rushes outwards to the void of negation ; and, alone, intuition rises into the spiritual only to become a prey to superstition. However genuine the religious instinct, the mind must always retain its force, or, like the lion who, to please the princess, consented to have his claws cut, and was thereupon torn to pieces by jackals, it will be impotent to defend itself from the meanest adversary. . . .

"Nevertheless, the symbols we have loved need not be cast aside, but may still remain as forms to enclose the living spirit, if only we are careful to remember that they are but forms. For, remembering this, and cherishing them only as forms, they will be so transmuted as to permit the indwelling reality to shine forth from within them, and will, therefore, be no longer as cerements of the historical and dead, but as robes of the ever-living garments of God, transmitting, even while veiling, the brightness of the divine glory.

"And if to some the proposed task appear as a vain attempt to resuscitate the dead and decayed, we would point, in answer, to the apologue of Ezekiel as at once an encouragement and, possibly, an anticipation. Here are the prophet's words. Let

[1] See p. 28, *ante*.

us suppose the creeds and other symbols of the Churches to be the dry bones:—

"'The hand of the Lord was upon me, and carried me out in the Spirit of the Lord, and set me down in the midst of the valley which was full of bones . . . and, lo, they were very dry.

"'And he said unto me, Son of Man, can these bones live? And I answered, O Lord God, Thou knowest.

"'And again he said unto me, prophesy upon these bones, and say unto them, O ye dry bones, hear the word of the Lord.

"'Thus saith the Lord God unto these bones: Behold, I will cause breath to enter into you, and ye shall live:

"'And I will lay sinews upon you, and will bring up flesh upon you, and cover you with skin, and put breath in you, and ye shall live; and ye shall know that I am the Lord. . . .

"'So I prophesied as he commanded me, and the breath came into them, and they lived, and stood up upon their feet, an *exceeding* great army.'"[1]

SAML. HOPGOOD HART.

CROYDON, *October* 1916.

[1] Ezekiel xxxvii. 1–10.

LECTURES

THE CREDO OF CHRISTENDOM

Exposition I[1]

Credo in Deum, Patrem omnipotentem, Creatorem cœli et terræ (I believe in God, the Father Almighty, Creator of heaven and earth).

The Christian Faith is the direct heir of the old Roman faith. Rome was the heir of Greece, and Greece of Egypt, whence the Mosaic dispensation and Hebrew ritual sprang. Egypt was but the focus of a light whose true fountain and centre was the Orient in general—*Ex Oriente Lux*. For the East, in every sense, geographically, astronomically, and spiritually, is ever the source of light. But although originally derived from the East, the Church of our day and country is modelled immediately upon

---

[1] Abstract, by Edward Maitland, of the Lecture given by Anna Kingsford, on the 12th June 1884, to the Hermetic Society, and published in *Light*, 21st June 1884, p. 254, where it is stated that "The discourse, which occupied an hour in delivery, dealt with the origin, symbolisation, and interpretation of religious doctrine in general, and the esoteric significance of the opening clause of the Creed in particular, shewing in a profoundly metaphysical disquisition the fallacy involved in the conventional anthropomorphic conception of Deity, and the necessity to a rational system of thought of a substratum to the universe which is at once intelligent and personal, though in a sense differing from that which is ordinarily implied by the term; the Divine personality being that, not of outward form, but of essential consciousness; and creation, which is manifestation, being due, not to action from without, but to the perpetual Divine presence and operation from within: 'God the Father' being, in the esoteric and true sense, the original, undifferentiated Life and Substance of the universe, but not limited by the universe, and Himself the potentiality of all things."

The Report also states that at the close of the Lecture Anna Kingsford "gave some account of the method of illumination whereby Divine knowledges are obtained, and said that recent conversations with properly instructed initiates from the East had convinced her of the identity of the religious systems of the East and the West."—S. H. H.

the Greco-Roman mythology, and draws thence all its rites, doctrines, ceremonies, sacraments, and festivals. Hence the exposition to be given of Esoteric Christianity would deal more especially with the mysteries of the West, their ideas and terminology being more attractive and congenial to us than the inartistic conceptions, the unfamiliar metaphysics, the melancholy spiritualism, and the unsuggestive language of the East. Drawing its life-blood directly from the pagan faith of the old Occidental world, Christianity more nearly resembles its immediate father and mother than its remote ancestors, and will, therefore, be better expounded by reference to Greek and Roman sources than to their Brahminical and Vedic parallels.

The Christian Church is Catholic, or it is nothing worthy the name of Church at all. For Catholic signifies universal, all-embracing:—the faith everywhere and always received.[1] The prevalent limited view of the term is wrong and mischievous. The Christian Church was first called Catholic because she enfolded, comprehended, and made her own all the religious past of the whole world, gathering up into and around her central figure of the Christ all the characteristics, legends, and symbols hitherto appertaining to the central figures of preceding dispensations, proclaiming the unity of all human aspiration, and formulating in one grand ecumenical system the doctrines of East and West.

Thus the Catholic Church is Vedic, Buddhist, Zend, and Semitic. She is Egyptian, Hermetic, Pythagorean, and Platonic.

---

[1] Thus, speaking of the Greek Trismegistic literature, Mr G. R. S. Mead says: "The theory of plagiarism from Christianity must for ever be abandoned." "The Church Fathers appealed to the authority of antiquity and to a tradition that had never been called in question, in order to shew that they taught nothing fundamentally new—that, in brief, they taught on main points what Hermes had taught. They lived in days too proximate to that tradition to have ventured on bringing any charge of plagiarism and forgery against it without exposing themselves to a crushing rejoinder from men who were still the hearers of its 'living voice' and possessors of its 'written word.'

"The scholars of the Renaissance naturally followed the unvarying tradition of antiquity, confirmed by the Fathers of the Church.

"Gradually, however, it was perceived that, if the old tradition were accepted, the fundamental originality of general Christian doctrines—that is to say, the philosophical basis of the Faith, as apart from the historical dogmas peculiar to it—could no longer be maintained. It, therefore, became necessary to discredit the ancient tradition by every possible means" (*Hermes Trismegistus*, vol. i. pp. 43 and 45–46).—S. H. H.

She is Scandinavian, Mexican, and Druidic. She is Grecian and Roman. She is scientific, philosophic, and spiritual. We find in her teachings the Pantheism of the East, and the individualism of the West. She speaks the language and thinks the thoughts of all the children of men; and in her temple all the gods are shrined. I am Vedantist, Buddhist, Hellenist, Hermetic, and Christian, because I am Catholic. For in that one word all Past, Present, and Future are enfolded. And, as St Augustine and other of the Fathers truly declared, Christianity contains nothing new but its name, having been familiar to the ancients from the beginning. And the various sects, which retain but a portion of Catholic doctrine, are but as incomplete copies of a book from which whole chapters have been torn, or representations of a drama in which some only of the characters and scenes have been retained.

EXPOSITION II [1]

Et in Jesum Christum, Filium ejus unicum, Dominum nostrum; qui conceptus est de Spiritu Sancto, natus ex Maria Virgine (And in Jesus Christ, His only Son, our Lord; who is conceived by the Holy Ghost, born of the Virgin Mary).

This rendering of the Creed into the present is necessary to its esoteric and proper understanding. For there is no past tense in Divine things, since all sacred events denote processes and all sacred persons denote principles, having no relation to time and matter, but eternally present and operative in the soul. Did religion, indeed, depend upon history, the permanence of any faith would be hopeless, seeing how little dependence can be placed upon records of events even near to the time of their occurrence, and that with the lapse of time the evidence for them must become dimmed and at length effaced. Religion, however, is by its very nature spiritual, and addressed to the soul, and therefore bears no congruous relation to the physical and historical.

Besides, all the events so called historical of the Christian story

---

[1] Abstract, by Edward Maitland, of the Lecture given by Anna Kingsford, on the 19th June 1884, to the Hermetic Society, and published in *Light*, 28th June 1884, p. 265, where it is stated that "the paper was followed by a conversation of unusual interest, in which a large number of Fellows and visitors took part, the chief point of discussion being the extent to which the Gospel narratives represent an actual personal history, and the degree of importance belonging to an historical personality, if one existed."—S. H. H.

are equally claimed by other religions as occurring to their respective heroes, a fact which shews that those events were generally regarded but as allegories, types, or dramatic presentations of the various stages in the spiritual history of all men. Add to this the manifold irreconcilable discrepancies in the accounts themselves, and the utterly incredible nature of many of the narratives if regarded as physical, and we find ourselves reduced to despair if still forced to depend upon history for our religion.

Even were it not so, it would still be the fact that nothing occurring on the physical plane and external to the man will effect his salvation, since the change to be made must be in himself and due to the operation of his own indwelling spirit. Physical events and spiritual processes can never be cognates to each other.

In insisting upon the esoteric signification as alone true and of value, so far from proposing something new, we are but reverting to the ancient and original usage. It is the acceptance of the Creed in its exoteric and historical sense which is really modern. For all sacred mysteries were originally regarded as spiritual, and only when they passed from the hands of properly instructed initiates into those of the ignorant and vulgar, did they become materialised and degraded to their present level. The esoteric truth of the second article of the Creed can be understood only through a previous knowledge, first, of the constitution of man, and next, of the meaning of the terms employed in the formulation of religious doctrine. For this doctrine represents perfect knowledge of human nature, and the terms in which it is expressed—" Adam," " Eve," " Christ," " Mary," and the rest—denote the various spiritual elements constituting the individual, the states through which he passes, and the goal he finally attains in the course of his spiritual evolution. For, as St Paul says, " these things are an allegory " ; and in order to understand them it is necessary to know the facts to which they refer. Knowing these, we have no difficulty in recognising the origin of such portraiture, and applying it to oneself. Thus " Adam " is man external and mundane merely, yet in due time developing the consciousness of " Eve " or the Soul—for the soul is always the " Woman "—and becoming a dual being consisting of matter and spirit. As " Eve," the soul falls under the power of this " Adam," and becoming impure through subjection to matter, brings forth Cain, who, as representing the lower nature, is said to cultivate the fruits of the ground.

But as "Mary," the soul regains her purity, being said to be virgin as regards matter, and polarising to God becomes mother of the Christ or Man regenerate, who alone is the begotten Son of God and Saviour of the man in whom he is engendered. Wherefore Christ is both process and the result of process. Being thus, he is not, as commonly supposed, "*the* Lord," but "*our* Lord." *The* Lord is Adonai, the Word, subsisting eternally in the Heavens; and Christ is His counterpart in man. And no Christ on earth is possible for him for whom there is no Adonai in the Heavens.

The entire spiritual history of man is thus comprised in the Church's two dogmas, that of the Immaculate Conception of the Blessed Virgin, and that of her Assumption. For they have no physical reference, but denote precisely that triumph and apotheosis of the soul, that glorification and perpetuation of the individual human Ego, which is the object and result of cosmic evolution, and consummation of the scheme of creation.[1]

Exposition III [2]

Passus sub Pontio Pilato, crucifixus, mortuus, et sepultus; descendit ad inferos; tertia die resurrexit a mortuis; ascendit ad coelos, sedet ad dexteram Dei Patris omnipotentis; inde venturus est judicare vivos et mortuos (Suffereth under Pontius Pilate, is crucified, dead, and buried; He descendeth into Hell; the third day He riseth again from the dead; He ascendeth into Heaven, and sitteth at the right hand of God the Father Almighty; from thence He cometh to judge the living and the dead).

The devotion of the "Rosary of the Blessed Virgin" consists of fifteen decades, each of which formulates and celebrates a Mystery of the Christian faith. These Mysteries are divided into three categories, of which the first is called the Five Joyful Mysteries; the second, the Five Sorrowful Mysteries; and the third, the Five Glorious Mysteries.[3] The Annunciation, the

---

[1] See further on this subject Anna Kingsford's Illumination "Concerning the Christian Mysteries" (*Clothed With the Sun*, pt. i. No. xlviii).—S. H. H.

[2] Abstract, by Edward Maitland, of the Lecture given by Anna Kingsford, on the 10th July 1884, to the Hermetic Society, and published in *Light*, 19th July 1884, pp. 294-295.—S. H. H.

[3] The Fifteen Mysteries of the Life of the Blessed Virgin Mary are as follows:—
    (a) The Five Joyful Mysteries:
        1. The Annunciation or Angelical Salutation.
        2. The Visitation.

Incarnation, and the Birth of the Christ, are subjects of the Five Joyful Mysteries. These were treated of in the last discourse. The Five Sorrowful and Five Glorious Mysteries are summed up in the articles which form the text of the present one. They epitomise the three chief characteristic events in the spiritual history of the "Son of Mary"—the Christ, or Man Perfected through at-one-ment with God—the Passion, the Oblation, and the Victory.

This history is the history of the soul both universal and individual. For, just as the creation and redemption of the universe at large came about by a "fall," or descent of soul-substance into the condition of matter, and its subsequent return to the condition of pure spirit, so do the creation and redemption of the individual. The entire process was represented by the wise of old in the Hermetic and Kabalistic symbol called the "Seal of Solomon,"[1] which consists of two triangles interlaced, one extending above the other and pointing upwards, and the other extending below this and pointing downwards, to denote respectively the unmanifest and primary world of emanation, and the manifest and secondary, or derived, world of creation. Both triangles are traversed vertically from top to bottom, and horizontally from side to side, by two lines which, crossing each other, form at once the Tree of Life and of Knowledge of Good and Evil, and the Cross of Christ.

Of this Cross, the vertical beam, or Tree of Life, has its summit in God unmanifest, and its foot in Matter, the under-world or Hades, the "Hell" of the Creed. The upper section of the

      3. The Birth of our Saviour Jesus Christ in Bethlehem.
      4. The Presentation of our Blessed Lord in the Temple.
      5. The Finding of the Child Jesus in the Temple.
(b) The Five Dolorous or Sorrowful Mysteries:
      1. The Prayer and Bloody Sweat of our Blessed Saviour in the Garden.
      2. The Scourging of our Blessed Lord at the Pillar.
      3. The Crowning of our Blessed Saviour with Thorns.
      4. Jesus Carrying his Cross.
      5. The Crucifixion and Death of our Lord.
(c) The Five Glorious Mysteries:
      1. The Resurrection of Jesus Christ.
      2. The Ascension of Jesus Christ into Heaven.
      3. The Descent of the Holy Ghost on the Blessed Virgin and the Apostles.
      4. The Assumption of the Blessed Virgin Mary into Heaven.
      5. The Coronation of the Blessed Virgin Mary in Heaven and the Glory of all the Saints.

—S. H. H.

---

[1] See Frontispiece.

hexagon made by the triangles represents the spiritual world of Emanation; the lower section represents the terrestrial world of Evolution. Wherefore the head of the crucified Christ is in the heavenly spheres, and His feet in Hades; His right hand indicates the point of the soul's descent into the world of Generation; His left, the point of her emergence into life eternal. Christ crucified is, thus, the *Hypostasis* of Adonai, the Lord, and His Cross is the ensign of the spiritual Phœbus, or "sign of the Son of Man in Heaven," and covenant of the Divine with the human. Its foot is in the world of Actuality, which is that of Ordeal. For Ordeal is the preliminary and condition of initiation into the spiritual consciousness. The Way of Life and the Way of the Cross are one. The crucifixion of Christ is the act of supreme surrender, which must precede the union of the human and Divine; and, similarly, the death and burial imply the entire dissolution of the old Adam, or lower self.

The Pontius Pilate, or crowned pontiff, of the Creed is a figure of a corrupt and materialistic sacerdocy, temporising with the crowd, allied with Herod, or the "dragon"; friendly with Cæsar, the typical genius of the world, and claiming to be sole "bridge-maker" between God and man. Such an order never fails to misconstrue, reject, condemn, and "crucify" the Christ and Christ-idea. When the Gospels describe Pilate as mingling the blood of the Galileans with the sacrifices, and refusing to heed his wife's remonstrances, they really refer to the inveterate addiction of priesthoods to the vicarious principle and sanguinary offerings, and their rejection of the teachings of the Intuition.

The mightiest blow ever dealt at the Church of "Pontius Pilate" was the promulgation of the astronomical discoveries of Copernicus and Galileo. The old mythologies depicted the career of the God-Man as corresponding with the course of the sun in the visible heavens; and taught that the acts and procession of the physical sun in regard to the planet are identical with those of the Spiritual Saviour in regard to humanity. The disclosure of the true state of the case in regard to the sun—namely, that while seeming to go through all the changes observed of it, it remains fixed and immutable in the centre of the system—had the world been acute enough to recognise the spiritual analogy, would have revealed the verity that the Godhead is untouched by time and vehicle, and that the illusion of the physical universe constitutes no interruption or mutation in the Divine consciousness itself; but that the accidents of time and place belong to the earthly, and occur only in the secondary human consciousness. The sun has no such path in the heavens as to us appears, which is an illusion arising from our own revolutions of place and condition. And so the birth, passion, and other acts of the Son of God in this world of generation, are processes due to the conditions of this world, and to the operations of time, which cause us to apprehend Ideas as States, in chronological sequence and spacial extension. The Son of God in Heaven is immutable in regard to us. He neither descends nor ascends, neither is buried nor rises, neither suffers nor triumphs. All these changes are the result of the procession of perception in the planetary consciousness.[1] The state of Christ is the transcript into the sphere of extensions, of that which, as Principle, *is* always and absolutely. Had the world been able to apprehend this truth—the metaphysical contingent and corollary of the discovery of the nature of the solar system,—it would have comprehended the esoteric distinction between Christ and Adonai, between, that is, the "Son of Mary" and the Only Begotten Wisdom, and escaped the fatal error of identifying any one human personality, however perfect a representative of the process, with the Divine principle itself. The natural truth would have enabled men to distinguish between the sun as it is in itself in its own sphere, and the sun as it appears to us in our sphere. The idea of the first is that of the Noumenon, Adonai; the idea of the second is that of his human aspect and counterpart, the Christ. They are not two suns, but one sun; yet, though immutable, it appears to us as mutable; though deathless, it appears to us to die. The whole enigma is solved by the right understanding of the fact that the image of the immutable and eternal light—the centre of radiation—projected into our mutable and progressive sphere, intercepted, as it were, in a conditioned medium, becomes subject to conditions, and causes the centre of radiation itself to appear mutable and progressive, so that, without leaving the heavens, or undergoing the least change or interruption of his immutability, Adonai appears on earth as Christ, enacting the drama of the Redemption.

Christ completes the evolutionary process of planetary genera-

[1] The word "Planet" signifies "Wanderer." "All the worlds of Generation," says Anna Kingsford, "are scenes of Pilgrimage or of Wandering. . . . A Planet, in occult phrase, is, therefore, nothing more nor less than a Station. The Soul passes from one to the other through the whole chain of seven Worlds (or Stations) in order" (*Life of A. K.*, vol. ii. p. 182, and see Illustration opposite p. 104, *post*).—S. H. H.

tion, as Adonai completes the logical procession of Heavenly emanation. The Divine potentiality implicit in the En-soph, culminates and polarises in Adonai. The spirit and soul formulate and manifest their conjunction in Christ, who thus represents the transmutation of principle into state:—the rays of the Noumenon entering and extending and expressing its image through the lens of time.

Not only do the death, burial, and descent of Christ into Hades, renew on an interior and personal plane the immergence of the soul into existence; but they also repeat, in a higher and subtler sense, the drama of the forty days' fast and exile in the wilderness. For this period of forty days epitomises the ordeals of initiation as practised in the Greek mysteries;[1] and the dissolution, burial, and three days' abode in Hades, epitomise the heroic and saving oblation of the Man-God.

Regeneration, in the Hebrew mysteries, is symbolised by the flight from Egypt, the body, and, therefore, land of bondage for the soul, across the Red Sea into the Wilderness of Sin, the scene of ordeal where the mystical forty days are expressed in a like term of years. The Redemption is typified by the passage of the Jordan, which divides this wilderness of trial from the promised land of spiritual perfection and rest. This Jordan, or river of judgment, could not be passed by Moses because he had failed in the ordeal of his initiation. The ultimate deliverance of Israel was reserved for Joshua, a name identical with Jesus, who had remained faithful throughout. Jordan corresponds to the Acheron of the Olympian mysteries, which all souls, descending to the under-world, were compelled to traverse. And Limbo, Paradise, Avernus, the Elysian Fields, Tartarus, Purgatory, and the rest, all denote, under various names, not localities, but spheres or conditions of being, recognised alike in the Hebrew, Pagan, and Christian systems, and subsisting in man himself. And the passage of Christ through the under-world represents occultly the work of Redemption within the human kingdom, precisely according to the Hermetic doctrine of transmutation;

---

[1] The report states that "Numerous instances were given in proof of the identity subsisting between the Hebrew and Greek modes of thought in regard to the occult side of existence, demonstrating their common origin in an universal gnosis, and correcting, therefore, the mistake made hitherto by scholars in regarding the Greek and Jewish systems as distinct from, and incompatible with, each other. And the New Testament was shewn as applying to the individual, spiritual processes represented in the Old as occurring to Israel at large."—S. H. H.

that is, the Redemption of Spirit from matter, allegorically termed the conversion of the baser metals into gold.

It is not the soul only of the Christ that rises from the Hades of materiality and ascends into Heaven. It is also His glorified body, His rational mind, His regenerate affections. The risen body of Christ Jesus is that reconciled and enlightened human nature which is figured by the outermost of the three measures of meal leavened by Divine grace; and by the third head of the Hadean dog, Cerberus, drawn upward into the light of day by the Solar hero, Herakles. The risen mind and affections of " our Lord " consist in those pure sciences, loves and memories which have been strong and durable enough to reach from earth into Heaven and to become part of the inward man. The merely earthly affections and knowledges of the *anima bruta*, or exterior selfhood, pass away; its lower passions and memories disintegrate, and with their disintegrating vehicles revert into the all-dissolving crucible of " Hecate " or Chaos. But all true loves abide in the celestial, within the risen and ascended Ego.

Christ Jesus rising and ascending to His Father; Christ Jesus pouring out His virtue and saving grace over all the worlds; Christ Jesus assuming into Heaven His Divine Mother and crowning her beside Him on His throne above the angels,—these are the " Five Glorious Mysteries of the Rosary of the Blessed Virgin," or purified soul of man, which complete its cadence of hopes and griefs and triumphs. For now is the union of Divine and human made absolute. The " Son of Man stands at the right hand of God," whence, perpetually, " He cometh to judge the living and the dead," and to discern between the just and the unjust.

In this perfect realised ideal of humanity is man's supreme standard of right and wrong, of spiritual vitality, of deadness to virtue and grace. The Divine Logos within the human soul is the voice of God searching the " garden " of the human microcosm, and summoning the mind and the affections to judgment.

And not only in the secret place of each man's consciousness, but in his collective reason and aspiration from age to age throughout all the worlds of ordeal, this Divine voice is heard—at once the earnest of spiritual progress, the immutable censor of human action, and the promise of salvation. And this " day of judgment " will not cease until the worlds of form again return into the bosom of spirit, until states revert to principles, phenomena to Noumena, and the dawn of the eternal Sabbath dissolves into splendour the night of matter and of time.

EXPOSITION IV[1]

Credo in Spiritum Sanctum, sanctam Ecclesiam Catholicam (I believe in the Holy Ghost, the Holy Catholic Church).

Of the two triangles which compose the "Seal of Solomon," the upper represents the unmanifest world of pure spirit, and the knowledge of it was reserved for initiates of a high grade, the

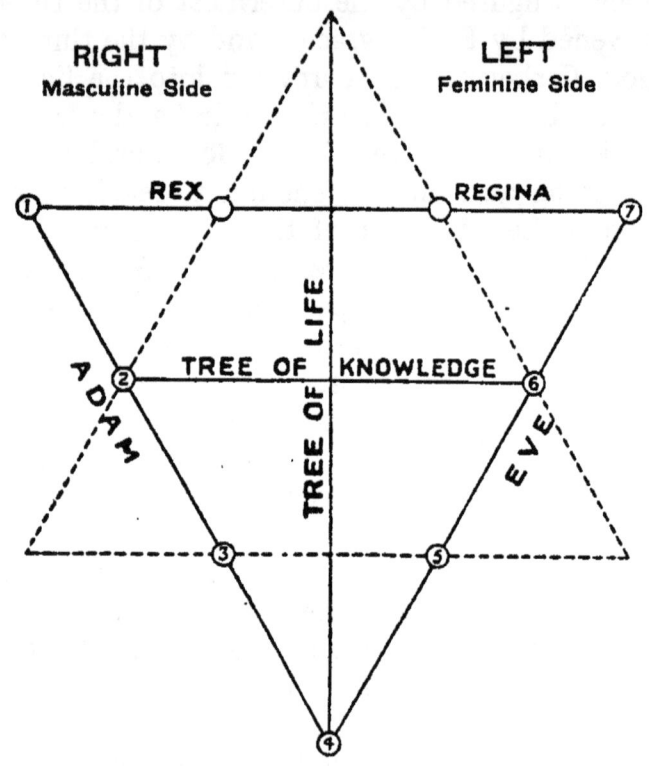

The Lower Triangle

shewing the seven successive Worlds, Stations, or Abodes of the Mundane Soul; and representing the manifest and secondary or derived world of creation or generation.

elect, or illuminated, and is the subject of Mysticism; the lower, which represents the manifest universe, is the province of Occultism. The central part is a hexagon, which is bisected vertically and horizontally by a cross, the beams of which are called

---

[1] Abstract, by Edward Maitland, of the Lecture given by Anna Kingsford, on the 17th July 1884, to the Hermetic Society, and published in *Light*, 26th July 1884, pp. 302-303.

The Chapter in *The Life of Anna Kingsford* giving some of Anna Kingsford's "Meditations on the Mysteries," throws considerable further light on the very profound subjects dealt with in this and the two following Lectures. (See *Life of Anna Kingsford*, vol. ii. pp. 173-184.) —S. H. H.

THE CREDO OF CHRISTENDOM

respectively the Tree of Life and the Tree of Knowledge. The lower portion of the hexagon, which corresponds to the lower triangle, is called the "Temple of Solomon," and is the sphere of the masculine activity. The upper, which corresponds to the Habitation of Adonai, the Lord, is the sphere of the feminine element, Intelligence, which is called in the Kabalah the Daughter,

The Upper Triangle

shewing the nine Fixed Spheres or Abodes of the Gods (Principles or Potencies); and representing the unmanifest and primary world of emanation. Including Malkuth (Actuality), the Figure represents the Sephirotic Tree of Life.

the House of Wisdom, the Face of the Sun. In the intellectual comprehension and spiritual application of the meaning of this hexagon, with its indissolubly blended masculine and feminine activities, lies the mystic secret and method. Concerning it the Kabalah says: "When the sanctuary is profaned, when the man dwells far from the woman, then the serpent begins to raise himself up, then woe to the world. In those days murderers and tormentors are born into the world, and the just are taken away from it. Why? because the man is separated from the woman."

It is the recognition of this dual character of Nature, and of the spiritual womanhood as the complement and crown of the spiritual manhood, that constitutes the best wisdom and supreme glory of the Catholic Church, and explains her uncompromising hostility to the Order of Freemasonry; for this system represents a perpetuation of the exoteric Judaism, in that it concerns itself exclusively with the lower triangle, and the building of the "Temple of Solomon," to the exclusion of the upper, the sphere of "the woman," and the "city which cometh down from Heaven," the New Jerusalem, or city of God. The whole, from top to bottom, is united by the vertical beam of the cross, called the Tree of Life. The horizontal beam is called the Tree of Knowledge, and the Measuring-rod of Adonai, wherewith the holy city of the Apocalypse is measured.

To the lower triangle belong the lesser mysteries, those of natural evolution. These were set forth in the Eleusinian Mysteries, under the parable of the Rape of Persephone, who represents the world-soul lapsing from the celestial abodes into materiality, and becoming subject to Karma or Fate, personified by Hecate. The abodes of the soul which are in this triangle are seven in number. (See Fig. p. 104.) The abodes of the Gods, which are in the upper, are nine. (See Fig. p. 105.) The lower represents the world of generation; the upper, the world of emanation. Each triangle has a macrocosmic and a microcosmic signification; for all that is in nature is equally in man. So that the "Seal of Solomon" is the epitome and key alike of the universal and of the individual.

It has twelve gates, or meanings, varying according to the plane on which it is examined. In its broadest signification the upper triangle represents spirit; the lower, matter. The upper is eternity; the lower, time. The upper is God; the lower, Nature. The upper is the unmanifest, the abstract, the uncreate, the absolute, the primary, the real. The lower is the manifest, the concrete, the create, the relative, the derivative, the reflect. The upper is Heaven, Mount Sion, the Holy Spirit. The lower is Earth, "Jerusalem," the Catholic Church. For, as says the Kabalah, "The Holy Spirit, or Spirit of the Living God, is the substance of the Universe, wherein every element has its ultimate source. This Spirit *is* Intelligence. And it is through it that the signs of the Divine Thought repeat themselves anew in all the successive worlds, so that all that is, whether in Heaven or upon earth, shews itself as the expression of one design."

In the Divine Intelligence, *Binah*, are comprehended the seven Elohim, or Spirits of God. These form two processions of principles, respectively masculine and feminine, which, with the three Personæ of the First Trinity [Kether, Chokhmah, and Binah], constitute the ten Sephiroth or Divine emanations of the En-Soph or Original Being. The right-hand side of the upper triangle represents the masculine principle, Kabalistically called Jachin, and the left the feminine, called Boaz, the entire triangle constituting the Adam Kadmon, or archetypal man, and in the lower triangle becoming Adam and Eve.

The Kabalistic name of the tenth Sephirah, which is represented by the base of the upper triangle, is Malkuth, which, in its highest aspect, implies the Church as Bride or Spouse of the Holy Spirit, and from its reflection of the Divine, on the upper side, is called the Moon, and also the Mirror. On the lower side Malkuth represents the Hadean sphere, the sphere of souls who, being still bound by the lower elements, are said to be "in prison," and " beneath the altar of God." Thus the upper portion of the hexagon denotes the Church celestial and triumphant; the lower portion denotes the Church militant; and the part of the triangle subtending this, the Church suffering or " in purgatory."

This tenth Sephirah, or Malkuth, is called also the Kingdom. It really means the soul, in all her aspects, universal and individual. As the ideal Kingdom, or Church of God in Heaven, Malkuth is all good. " Thou art all fair, O my love," says the Divine King (in the Canticles), addressing His celestial spouse, " and there is no spot in thee." Hence the Kabalah speaks of Malkuth in this aspect as the " Queen," and applies to her all the titles familiar to us in the mystic Litany of the Blessed Virgin, " Queen of Heaven," " Queen of Love," " Queen of Victories," " Queen of Glory," " House of David," " Ark of the Covenant," " Gate of Heaven," " Virgin of Israel," " Temple of the King," and so forth.

To this " Queen " the Holy Spirit is " King." Both are comprehended in, and emanate from, the En-Soph, or original Being—the Spirit as thinking, the soul as the thought.

The Hermetic or Egyptian, and the Greek presentations of

these Arcana are so completely in accord with the Hebrew that it is impossible to give the preference to either as that from which Catholic mystic theology has been drawn. The Greek mysteries are twofold, the greater and the lesser, and represent respectively the secrets of the upper triangle with the distribution of spirit into pyschic life, and the passage of the soul throughout the Hadean spheres, or worlds of generation and evolution. And the catacombs of Rome afford evidence that the early Christians fully understood the catholic nature of their religion and its derivation from the Greek mysteries of Dionysus and Orpheus. The tearing in pieces and scattering of the remains of Dionysus by the Titans represented, in one aspect, the distribution of the one Divine life among the elementary forces of nature with a view to the generation of souls, and in another the danger incurred by man's spiritual part from his lower nature when unsubdued.

The story of Noah or Noe, a term identical with Nous, mind, is a Dionysian or Bacchic myth. The wine of which Noah is represented as the first maker corresponds with the "new wine of Dionysus," who, as the God of the planet, sheds his spirit, or "blood," for mankind, and is called the "Saviour of Men," the "Only Begotten," the "Twice-born." His nativity corresponded with that of the sun, and hence with that of Christ. And it was in His honour as the "Wine-God," or Supreme Spirit of Earth, that the berry and the ivy were first used in celebration of the birth of the new year. Bacchus means berry.

In short, in the "Orgies" of this God, whose mystic name is Iacchos, is revealed, in a series of figures, the entire arcanum relating to the clauses of the creed under consideration, namely, the emanation of the Holy Spirit into the lower worlds, and the distribution throughout existence of the higher Reason, represented by Noah, as the planter of the Vine, or holy life within the soul. And these mysteries are complemented and completed by those of Demeter, which rehearse the descent into Matter of Persephone, the Psyche or Soul, by which mysteries are exhibited the evolution and progression throughout the various planes and modes of existence, of the individual conscious Ego, until, perfected through suffering or experience, it is finally released from matter, and returns to its celestial abode.

Exposition V[1]

The lower triangle is divided by the cross-lines of the trees of Life and Knowledge, and by the base of the upper triangle, into seven stations or worlds, denoting the abodes of the soul in the mundane or objective universe. These abodes are distributed on two lines, the first descending, the second ascending, the whole series constituting the Kabalistic "Ladder of Jacob." The out-going or descending line is centrifugal, the in-coming or ascending line is centripetal. The whole of the right section of the triangle—that on the beholder's left—is the station of the masculine element, or "Adam"; the left is that of the feminine, or "Eve."

As the upper triangle, synthetically considered, represents the Holy Spirit, or light of the celestial sun—the Divine Intelligence, "Binah"—so the lower, similarly considered, is the Catholic Church, which reflects this sun, and hence is denominated the moon, and Malkuth, the Kingdom. But in this, its plural form, Malkuth has a dual signification. In the upper triangle it is the last of the ten Sephiroth, and represents the Kingdom of God in Mount Sion, or eternal in the Heavens. This is the celestial "sea," whereon the right foot of the Divine Being is described in the Apocalypse as standing. In its secondary aspect —in the lower triangle—Malkuth is the Kingdom of God on earth, the "dry land," whereon the left foot of the Divine Being is described as standing. It is thus the Church Militant, or aggregate of all advancing souls. And of these only, since retrogressive souls, who by a perverse will follow the descending path of degeneration instead of the ascending path of evolution, are not comprised in the Church.

The Kabalah accords a prominent place to what are called the seven kings of Edom. These are represented in Genesis as seven ancient royalties preceding the establishment of the kingdom of Israel; and in the Kabalah as seven worlds, created prior to that inhabited by man but incapable of permanent endurance, because God does not descend to abide in them, as the Divine Image is not assumed in them. The humanity which assumes this Image—that is, man perfected—is termed Israel; and the seven kings or kingdoms of Edom are the seven stations

[1] Abstract, by Edward Maitland, of the Lecture given by Anna Kingsford, on the 24th July 1884, to the Hermetic Society (in continuation of the last Lecture), and published in *Light*, 2nd August 1884, pp. 313-314.

or planetary worlds through which the soul must pass in order to attain perfection, and so become "Israel." This state is attained only when, by the full restoration and exaltation of the soul to her proper oneness with the Spirit, the masculine and feminine principles are in perfect balance with each other. These principles are called the King and Queen, and are respectively the Archetypal Idea or "Adam Kadmon," who subsists prior to creation, and this Idea realised in creation. And, as the Kabalah says in the "Book of Occultations,"—" Until the balance is established, and while yet the King and Queen look not face to face upon each other, the seven worlds of Edom have no continuance. But when the Queen appears upon her throne, then all the seven kingdoms of Edom shall be resumed in Israel and re-born under other names. For all that is not, all that is, all that shall be, are borne on the balance of the King and Queen looking face to face upon each other." This is precisely the condition described by St Paul when he says, "When that which is perfect is come, then that which is partial shall be done away. Now we see through a glass in a dark manner; but then face to face."

These kings of Edom, Adam, or earth, are thus an occult figure of the seven progressive dominions, spheres, planets, or stages, through which the soul passes on her way to the heavenly royalty within and beyond the earthly plane, where man perfected becomes "Prince" or "Israel, with God." At this stage only is the Life Eternal attained, since only as man does the soul finally secure immortality. All previous stages have, indeed, the potentiality of it, but they are only preparatory. The soul must pass through and rise out of them all in order to realise its Divine destiny. Hence, the evanescence of the seven kingdoms of Edom; they represent rudimentary and embryonic stages in the making of man. And hence the Apocalyptic declaration, "The kingdoms of this world are become the Kingdoms of God and of the Christ."

The Bible says that Esau is Edom, and the father of the kings thereof. Now, Esau is the brother of Jacob, whose dynasty succeeds that of Edom. Hence, Esau is a figure of corporeal nature, and Jacob of spiritual life. And the steps of the Ladder of Jacob are the seven temporary kingdoms of his elder brother, whose dominion Jacob is destined, by surmounting it, to supplant and supersede. Doing this, and attaining the summit, the place of the Lord, Jacob becomes Israel, or "Prince with God."

At its base this ladder touches the ground, and the angels

on it denote souls descending into incarnation, even, as the Kabalah says, to the lowest degree of the universe—matter at its nethermost point—and ascending again to Heaven. At the foot of this ladder at night Jacob, the pilgrim-soul, lies asleep, having for pillar a stone, symbol of matter at the point reached. As the place of the greatest darkness and division from God, the spot is called Luza, or *separation*. Nevertheless, the soul knows that it is the turning-point of her pilgrimage, and that henceforth her journey is upwards and " eastwards." She perceives that even in the lowest abyss of matter there is no real separation from the Divine presence and life ; and in the very Valley of the Shadow of Death the " Rod and the Staff "—the Trees of Life and of Knowledge, which are the Cross of Christ—comfort and support her. Hence the exclamation of Jacob on awaking, " Indeed, the Lord is in this place. It is none other than the house of God and the gate of Heaven. And he called its name Beth-El, which before was Luza."

The secret doctrine which alone can glorify and transfigure this gloomy abode—the material world—and convert Luza into Beth-El, is that of which the whole Bible is an exposition, and upon which, from the beginning, all the great religions of East and West have been built—the doctrine of the *Gilgal Neschamoth*, or the transmigration and progression of souls.

The name Jacob is the same as Iacchos, the mystic name of Bacchus. And Iacchos is the god of Ordeal or Trial, the leader of fugitive and pilgrim hosts, and genius of the planetary sphere. Also the term Jacob has an occult reference to the sole of the foot, the organ of locomotion, and the foot-bone was a prominent symbol in the Bacchic mysteries. In many of the ancient mysteries a ladder, having seven steps or gates, was used to denote the seven stages of the soul's progress through the world of materiality. Both the Egyptian and Hebrew mysteries shew an eighth and final gate above these belonging to the celestial triangle. This, in Genesis, is called " Phanuel," which signifies the vision of God face to face. Attaining to this, Jacob becomes Israel.

The Greek mysteries represent existence by the river Styx, the " daughter " of Oceanus, or water of eternity, and by some called " mother " of Persephone, or the soul, as the vehicle whereby she is borne down into the under-world and carried from mansion to mansion of the dark abodes. In representing the Styx as derived from the " tenth source " of Oceanus, or water of eternity, the Greek presentation corresponds with the Kabalistic which derives existence from the tenth Sephirah, Malkuth. Seven circuits are made by the Styx, each of which includes and forms a world or station. During these rounds of planetary evolution, Styx becomes the mother of four children, who denote respectively the four divisions of man's nature—the emotional, the volitional, the intellectual, and the psychic. These have for father the giant Pallas, or elemental force, for her victory over whom the goddess Athene was called Pallas. The word Styx implies hateful, and denotes the imperfect nature of existence as compared with pure being. This "River of Existence" is variously called also the Astral Fluid, the Serpent, and Lucifer.

The seven stages of existence constitute a planetary chain, the term planetary signifying wandering. The abodes of the gods, which belong to the upper triangle, are nine in number, and are called the Fixed Spheres, being Divine and immutable. Of the planetary stations or worlds, four are subtle and three are gross. Of the subtle, three are on the descending stream, one on the ascending. The seven are, respectively, the ethereal, the elemental, the gaseous, the mineral, the vegetable, the animal, and the human. They are not localities but conditions, and in the soul's passage none is left behind, but all are taken up with her into man, one being put on, as it were, after another, and the whole being comprised in the perfected individual. For all have part in the evolution of the consciousness. This is single until the lowest or mineral is reached, which lies at the foot of the tree or ladder of life. Here occurs the "deep sleep" of "Adam," as also of Jacob; the consciousness, still single and therefore not involving self-consciousness, having in this grossest mode of matter attained its minimum. From this point commences that reduplication or reflection of the consciousness by which it gradually passes into the consciousness of Self and of God.

This commencement occurs in the fifth station, the world of vegetable nature. Here, first, the soul becomes gathered up and formulated into a distinct individuality. For here the influence of the upper triangle, the intersection of which with the lower constitutes the station, first makes itself felt. Hence the idea of the family begins to be evolved; birth, marriage, and death occur, through the awakening of a sympathetic consciousness, responsive to the elements, but not as yet to thought or sensation, and their various modes, such as love and sorrow.

These attributes dawn only in the sixth world, that of animal existence, and in this world it is that the capacity for "sin" originates, and "sin" first becomes possible. For so long as the individual has only the simple consciousness of rudimentary nature, he knows no will but the Divine Will expressed in natural law, and there is for him no better or worse, but all is good. "Adam," while yet alone, cannot be tempted, cannot sin, for mere mind cannot sin; only the soul can sin. It is by the advent or manifestation of "Eve," that is the knowledge of good and evil; and it is to her, not to Adam, that the tempter, when at length he makes his appearance, addresses his beguilements. The sin of Eve is not in the "eating of the apple" herself, but in the giving of it to Adam, since this constitutes a retrogression on the path of evolution, in that it refers the polaric point, or One Life, which is centred in the soul, backward and downward, to the lower reason. For sin consists in a voluntary retrogression from the higher to the lower. The "serpent" which tempts to this is the astral or magnetic self, which, recognising matter only, mistakes the illusory for the substantial. Yielding to this, the soul falls under the power of the lower nature, or Adam; "her desire is unto him, and he rules over her." Like Lot's wife she has looked back, and forthwith becomes a "pillar of salt"—the alchemic synonym for matter. In this subjection of the "woman" to the "man," and the dire results engendered of it, consists the "fall" and "curse" of "Eve." The fact that it entails these results shews that such subjection is not according to the Divine order, but is an inversion of that order. The soul should ever seek upwards to the Divine Will, that of the Spirit; and instead of seeking downwards to the mind, should draw the mind up with her.

Even in the sixth station, the last of the gross and concrete worlds, and which corresponds to the sixth creative "day" of Genesis, man is still but man in the making. To attain to the "measure and stature of Christ," and from man potential become man actual and perfect, he must enter upon the seventh and last world of Kabalistic evolution, the topmost round of the Ladder of Jacob, which is the very threshold of the Divine. As in the primordial world are found the initial duad, Prakriti and Purusha, matter and force, irresponsible, undifferentiate, possessed of only the simple consciousness of law-abiding nature, so in this seventh round of perfected humanity are found the ultimate duad, man and woman, or renewed Adam and Eve, mind and soul. This is the world of the demigods and heroes of Greek myth, of the saints of Christendom, of the Buddhas of the Orient. Here man is no more merely a superior animal; the nature of the beast is expunged; new and more subtle senses replace the old; Divine illumination and transcendent knowledge have closed the avenues of passion and sin. And beneath lies the head of the deceiving serpent, crushed under the foot of the rehabilitated soul, the new Eve. This is the first Nirvâna, or Resurrection.

But one step more, and the second Nirvâna is reached. "Phanuel" is attained, and "Regina and Rex look face to face upon each other." For the plane of earth and of time, the lower triangle, is wholly transcended; the indissoluble selfhood and life eternal are gained; the manhood is taken into God. Thus is celebrated the mystic marriage of the immaculate Virgin, or Soul, with her spouse, the Holy Spirit; thus is broken the yoke of bondage to Adam; thus for ever is reversed the curse of Eva by the Ave Maria of the Regeneration.

Exposition VI [1]

In the previous discourse have been described the sevenfold cycles of the Stygian River, and the nature of the worlds which the tide of existence successively involves in its current. Step by step has been followed Persephone, the Mundane Soul, from the point of her descent into material generation, until she has finally emerged from the dark abodes of Hades, a crowned queen, into the upper day. But the lower triangle of the Seal of Solomon, wherein all these processes are symbolised, has a microcosmic as well as a macrocosmic interpretation. Thus far has been traced the evolution of the world-soul on the nature-plane, passing from kingdom to kingdom, constantly gathering enhanced power, faculties, and individuality. A grand system is that which has been thus unfolded—a system replete with order and reason, opening up vistas of splendid possibility, and widening indefinitely the scope of the soul's past and future; but, withal, only a brilliant panorama of Nature's progress; only a system of occult philosophy; not a religion made for the spirit of man; not a Divine message speaking to his inmost heart.

In the interpretation of the microcosmic aspect of the lower triangle we leave the plane of Nature and sphere of Occultism, and enter the universe of the Human Soul—the region with which

[1] Abstract, by Edward Maitland, of the Lecture given by Anna Kingsford, on the 31st July 1884, to the Hermetic Society (in continuation of the last Lecture), and published in *Light*, 16th August 1884, pp. 333-334.

the mystic is chiefly concerned. For the province of Mysticism, although parallel to that of occultism, transcends and surpasses the latter. To be an occultist it is sufficient to know man. To be a mystic it is necessary to know Christ. The former sacrifices all things to knowledge. The latter sacrifices all things, even knowledge itself, if it could be so, to goodness. It is only in the Catholicism of the West that these supreme Mysteries, the Mysteries of the Faith of Christ, find recognition and formulation.

Like the worlds of the macrocosmic aspect of the lower triangle, the stations of the microcosmic are seven in number. These represent so many successive states of the interior evolution of the human soul; and are connected with each other by six intermediaries, representing the soul's transitions from one station to another. Each station is a specific *act* of the soul, marking a stage definitively attained and achieved. The intermediaries are links, denoting the passage from one to another of these acts. And all are aspects of the life " of Christ Jesus," which life is the summary of the interior life of the saintly soul.

To the phenomenal and historical elements of religion Mysticism is altogether indifferent, since it regards these as but the vehicle and formulæ of spiritual truths. Mysticism is thus wholly unaffected by historical or scientific criticism. Hence its divergence from conventional orthodoxy. The conventionalist adores the material bread and wine of the Sacrament. The mystic regards these as but symbols, and worships the true, because spiritual, Body and Blood of " the Lamb slain before the foundation of the world."

But though thus raised above the necessity of paying heed to the historicals and externals of Christian doctrine, Mysticism holds that doctrine in itself to be absolutely necessary, immutable, and true, and essential to the interpretation of the spiritual history of man, and constituting an unimpeachable testimony to the perfect reasonableness and beauty of the religious life. For, the evolution of the universe in man, which it is the province of Mysticism to interpret, is a precise parallel to the evolution of the universe in Nature, which it is the province of Occultism to interpret; because, as according to the Hermetic axiom, " Great and small, lower and upper, outer and inner, have but one law."

As, then, we have hitherto followed the footsteps of Persephone, the Mundane Soul, and seen her evolving consciousness after consciousness in the seven successive abodes of the lower world;

so now we follow the footsteps of Mary, the Human Soul, associated with the Acts—which are by intention and participation hers also—of her Divine Offspring and Lord, the Christ. For Christ is the Child of the Soul, conceived through the co-operation of her obedient free-will with the Divine Spirit. Every sacrifice made by the Christ is likewise hers; and in and through her He labours and suffers and gives Himself to God for man. Therefore every station of the office called the "Way of the Cross" is, by the Church, accompanied by an invocation to her whose gift He is to mankind. Every grace and profit which we receive from Christ comes to us through this mystical Virgin; and therefore it is that in contemplating the Acts of Christ, the Church always represents His Mother as present, and in every one of the Mysteries of the Divine life invokes and glorifies her. Not to do this, but to omit or ignore "Mary," would be to treat the man apart from his soul.

The first and last of the Nine Gates or Abodes of the macrocosm correspond, in the microcosm, to the Rex and Regina of the Kabalistic system. (See Fig. p. 104.) The first of these represents the Mystery of the Annunciation (see Frontispiece). For it implies the formulation of the Divine intention with regard to the issue of Creation, the first secret intimation of the design and method of Redemption, revealed only to the soul herself by the Angel of Initiation. The whole subsequent series of the Mysteries is epitomised and rehearsed in the salutation:—

"Behold, thou shalt conceive and bring forth a Son, and thou shalt call His name Jesus.

"He shall be great, and shall be the Son of the Most High: and the Lord God shall give unto Him the throne of David His father.

"And He shall reign in the house of Jacob for ever; and of His kingdom there shall be no end."

We come to the Seven Stations of the human soul. The first, which corresponds to the first world or birth of the mundane soul on the natural plane, is that of the Nativity of Christ, or kindling of the Divine spark within the soul. This is represented as occurring at midnight, in a cave; for the period is that of the soul's silence and abstraction, and withdrawal from the external world; and the place is the inmost recess of her selfhood, hidden beneath the intellectual plane and its operations. He is "wrapped in swaddling clothes," like the soul herself in matter, because enclosed and held fast in her, and veiled in symbols and types, being in Himself unutterable; and He is "laid in a manger," in token of the deep humility of the saintly heart.

The intermediary succeeding this first station is called the "Flight into Egypt." It represents the passage between the Nativity and the Baptism, and signifies the going forth of the Christ from the hidden depths of the heart, wherein He first appears, into the outward life of the saint. For Egypt denotes the body, so that the passage thither denotes the effect of interior regeneration on the outward life.

The second station, that of the Baptism, is the second degree of initiation, and occurs at the mystical age of thirty years—a period having no reference to time, but depending on attainments—the age of spiritual manhood. Not the heart only but the mind also now is divinely illuminated. The intellect, personified by John the Baptist, apprehends the Son of God, consecrates Him, and hails Him as Redeemer and Christ. The intellect is not the Light, but bears witness to the Light. And the Light is before all things, being in the Principium with God. But in the world the intellect is first manifested, and by it the Christ is recognised. It is the "voice crying in the wilderness" of the mere mind of man. "He that shall be manifest after me is preferred before me." For though the mind is not the highest and inmost principle of the regenerate nature, it is by means of it that the Divine is apprehended. Evolution is from lower to higher, wherefore it is necessary to be developed intellectually before we can comprehend and intelligently receive spiritual truth. The faith of the mystic must be according to knowledge, and not the product of mechanical assent or ignorant fervour, which can give no rational and well-grounded account of themselves. The place of this second station in the Seal of Solomon is, therefore, on the right arm of the Tree of Knowledge.

But the spiritual manhood, when thus achieved, must be put to the test. Hence, the next intermediary represents the Temptation, or ordeal, in the wilderness, wherein the appetites, desires, and will, or sense, mind, and heart, are in turn tried. For the initiate, to be regenerate and entitled to the rank and name of "Jesus," must be proof against temptation in all parts of his nature.

The third station, which occurs at the intersection of the base of the upper triangle with the descending or right side of the lower, is that of the "Crucifixion." By this is symbolised the complete surrender to God of the whole personality of the postulant.

It marks the attainment of the third degree of initiation, when, as well as the mind and heart, the body also is penetrated by grace and "bears the marks of the Lord."

The Christ is now "lifted up from the earth," or corporeal nature. For the Crucifixion is the Great Renunciation, and hence is called the Oblation of Christ Jesus. The "Five Wounds of the Cross" are the stigmata which denote the victory over and regeneration of the five senses, which now become polarised to a higher and more interior plane, enabling the man to have cognisance of Divine things. This act is the consummation of initiation as regards the rational humanity. Hence the exclamation "*Consummatum est*," ascribed to Jesus at this point. The "Death," which follows, signifies the total dissolution indispensable to reconstitution on the higher plane, or transmutation into the Divine state. This complete dissolution and disintegration of the natural man liberates the Divine in him, and sets him free to manifest his Godhead. This is the nethermost station, the downward pointing apex of the lower triangle, the foot of the Tree of Life. The side descending on the right to this point is the line of sorrow and suffering. The side which ascends from it on the left is the line of joy and triumph. The Greeks represented the Styx, or River of Existence, on attaining this turning point, as bringing forth four children, which are respectively Zeal, Victory, Fortitude, and Power; which, united with the heavenly powers, overcome the Titans, or elemental forces of Nature, who, until thus subdued, are themselves the gods of man unregenerate, the rivals and foes of the Divine. The conqueror of these "giants" is Pallas Athene, the "Queen of the Air," who represents the counterpart in the superior human reason of the Divine Logos. She is the virgin or pure reason of things mundane.

The portion of the lower triangle which lies altogether below the upper represents the Valley of the Shadow of Death, and to it belong the three stages of the soul's death, burial, and sojourn in Hades. Passing upwards from this valley on her way to "Salem," the soul attains the fourth degree of initiation, and the fifth of the stations, wherein the spiritual nature is affirmed and glorified, and the final gift of power is attained. For the human will is now united to the Divine, and "all power in Heaven and on earth" is given to it; the power of God becomes the power of Christ, Who, as Paul says, "although He was crucified through weakness, yet liveth by the power of God" (2 Cor. xiii. 4). This junction of the two natures invests the manhood with Godhead, and demonstrates man, when regenerate, to be the son of God; as Paul says again, "God raising up Jesus from the dead fulfils the saying in the second Psalm, Thou art My Son, this day have I begotten Thee" (Acts xiii. 33).

This act of the Resurrection is thus the seal of the spiritual initiation, the manifestation of the fourth and Divine element of the human system. The reintegration and reconstitution of the human selfhood according to the heavenly pattern is now complete. The Alchemic gold issues purged and resplendent from the fiery furnace, in which its constituent elements have been dissolved, segregated, sublimed, and repolarised. "And the form of the fourth is as the Son of God." The day on which this resurrection occurs is the "Lord's day," a day of triumphant rejoicing, as distinguished from the Sabbath, or day of rest.

The intermediary which follows is the forty days' sojourn on earth, a transition period corresponding to the forty days' fast in the wilderness, its counterpart on the descending line of the triangle. But though the accord between the Divine and human wills is complete, and the Skekinah within the man is unveiled and all his tabernacle filled with the glory of God, he is still "upon earth"; he has not yet "ascended to his Father." By this is to be understood that though the final degree of initiation is attained, and the man is perfected in his own interior selfhood, and at one with the God within, he has yet to rise into union with the God without—the universal God, the macrocosmic, omnipresent Divinity—and blend his individual light with the pure white light of the Supreme. Thus, as in the Mystery of the Resurrection God is glorified in the Son of Man, so in the Mystery of the Ascension the Son of Man is glorified in God. "For the Father is greater than the Son."

Between the sixth and seventh mansions of the Perfect Life is the intermediary of glorification in Heaven, a state of perfect repose rather than of transition, when having transcended the condition of *knowing*, the soul has passed into *being*, and *is* all that which she formerly knew she had it in her to become. Then is the Seventh Gate, or station, manifested, the "Descent of the Holy Ghost," or the outflow of the effectual merits of the saintly soul into the "world of causes." For, in a mystical manner the ascended soul becomes herself creative, and renews the face of the earth. And, in their degree, the merits of the saint are efficacious for the redemption of the world, his will being united to the Divine will, so that the spirit poured out from the perfected soul is no other than the very Spirit of God.

Therefore, in the seventh mansion of the holy life is beheld the ascended man, become, as it were, a point of radiate grace, renovating the worlds by the effulgence of the One Life abiding in him. Released himself from the bonds of Form and Time, he now appears as the cause of release to others. The Spirit which proceeds, through and from him, breathes renewal upon the desolate places of earth; and so the merits of the just made perfect become to the world moral destinies and determinative energies, working its purification and deliverance. Thus is completed the Apotheosis of the human Ego, with its four degrees of initiation and its sevenfold gates of grace, dramatised in the Acts of our Lord on earth.

Finally, quitting altogether the plane of the lower triangle, we reach the second of the Divine Abodes, the supreme and ultimate Act of the Christ in the heavenly kingdom. It is the Mystery of the Last Judgment. In the first of these Abodes, the Annunciation, we beheld the Divine intention projecting the drama of the great work, the work of Redemption. In the second, the Last Judgment, the work consummated is reviewed and weighed in the Celestial Balance, the Idea and the Realisation are poised face to face, having on one side the Angel Gabriel, with his lily; on the other Michael, with his trumpet and sword. Here the Virgin kneels in humility and obedient expectation; there her Son appears upon His throne, victorious and glorified, judging the living and the dead.

Through this Gate of Judgment all the acts and works of the saint must pass. Nothing can abide in the Principium which is not wholly Divine. The Idea of God in the Annunciation is the Alpha, of which the Realisation in the Judgment and consequent Assumption is the Omega. They are the Kabalistic Rex and Regina. And both of them, Beginning and Ending, First and Last, are beyond and above the worlds of Time and Form, for they belong to the One who sitteth on the Throne of the Mystical White Light, and from whose face Earth and Heaven flee away.

Exposition VII[1]

Sanctorum communionem (The Communion of Saints).

The series of papers on the Creed read before the Society last year expounded on an interior and mystical plane the dogmas of the Christian faith, shewing that a right belief in them is necessary to salvation, and that only by realising in the acts of the soul the acts of the Christ can theology be made an applied science and a means of grace. Step by step has been followed the nine great events of Christ's office as Redeemer and Lord, beginning with the Annunciation and ending with the Last Judgment, all these Stations and their Intermediaries being shewn to represent so many stages of inward progress and evolution in the saintly life.

This spiritual method of interpretation has always been adopted by the mystics of the Church, with the result that faith became to them knowledge, that tradition was converted into experience, and that, apprehending Christ according to the spirit, they themselves were baptized with His baptism, drank of His cup, and ascended with Him in heart and mind into the Heavenly Kingdom of the inner life.

The ninth article of the Apostles' Creed, the Communion of Saints, interpreted on the same lines, is one of the highest importance and interest, constituting the bond subsisting between the Church visible and invisible, and implied in the interunion and inseparability of the upper and lower triangles of the sacred Hexagram, or, "Seal of Solomon," which—referred to this plane—symbolises the eternal abiding of the Holy Ghost within and upon the Church, the indissoluble union of the Divine and human natures, and, hence, the complement and perfectionment of earthly and material existence by the immanence of the world eternal and effulgent.

The Church, as thus symbolised, has three divisions, the celestial, the terrestrial, and the purgatorial; or souls in beatitude, souls in conflict, and souls in penance, or "in prison." The upper or celestial Church comprises, first, all just men made perfect, the spirits and souls of the righteous, who have attained the Ascension of Christ and passed into the rest of the Lord;

---

[1] Abstract, by Edward Maitland, of the Lecture given by Anna Kingsford, on the 1st July 1885, to the Hermetic Society, and published in *Light*, 11th July 1885, pp. 330–331.

and next above this part, all angels, thrones, principalities, dominions, and powers, belonging to the generation of the Gods or emanations, the cherubim, seraphim, and sephiroth; and, lastly, at the very apex, the Godhead itself. These are the three divisions of the upper triangle.

The lower triangle, which represents the Church terrestrial, comprises, reckoning from above downwards, first, the whole body of the elect upon earth who are instructed in the mysteries of Christ, and included in the dispensation of the Cross; next, all those who, being of any nation or creed whatsoever, have attained to the knowledge of these mysteries by inward initiation, but are not in open communion with the visible Church. Lastly, in the region, or condition, denoted by the nethermost section of the lower triangle, are the souls in prison, those who, not having yet attained to the consciousness of things spiritual, are in a state, not of grace, but of sin, and are undergoing the experience and purgation necessary for their salvation.

The Communion of Saints is the bond of solidarity by which all these divisions of the Church universal are held together and sustain each other by mutual charity. Christian doctrine insists that no man liveth or dieth to himself alone. The merits of the saintly are so many prayers applicable to the souls of all who desire aid and liberation. The oblation of Christ extends to all who exemplify and participate in Christ; and every such soul, according to its degree, becomes a fountain of grace flowing forth upon the world in benign spiritual effluences, a vehicle for the transmission of the Divine light and life which are of Christ. The just are thus fitly compared to the moon and the planets in the firmament of heaven, enlightening the earth by virtue of the reflected and duplicated glory which they derive from the central sun; and every holy and wise man is a distinct gain to the world.

These Divine occult influences are attracted especially to souls in affinity with them, the set of whose tendency is in the same direction, and who are united in intention with the particular energy which they dispense. The merits of a St Francis of Assisi may peculiarly encourage one; the victory of a St Mary Magdalene, or a St Agnes, another; one may gather strength and light through the influence of some quiet and humble type of holiness; and another through the overshadowing of a St George, a St Michael, or the bold prophet who was a voice crying in the wilderness. Not that the grace thus conveyed is necessarily derived through those who have been recognised and canonised by the Church. Even these are themselves but representative groups of valiant and victorious spirits forming as many constellations in the mystical firmament as there are phases of virtue and of grace, and focal points of heavenly effulgence, to the formation of which all ages and religions have contributed. A Hermes, a Buddha, a Pythagoras, a Socrates, a Daniel, a Hypatia, a Joan of Arc, each in his place and degree, not merely leaves a trail of glittering radiance across our heaven as he passes on his way to join the host triumphant, but continues evermore as a positive, actual, energising potency to reinforce and sustain the stream of his influence.

There is no force but will force, and prayer is the most potent, subtle, and concentrated form of will force, and when exercised by souls whose whole energy is polarised and focussed upon its employment, attains its highest efficacy. The fervent prayer of the saint, therefore, avails much. His intention, united to the Divine will, becomes a miracle-working power. Not that natural law is arrested or suspended by it, but that it constitutes a higher activity of natural law, precisely as magnetic attraction constitutes a higher activity than that manifested in gravitation. To exercise such a force in its supremest mode, the mental and psychic energies must be restrained from being dissipated in the world, and assiduously cultivated and enhanced by means of seclusion and religious contemplation. Where the active energy of the individual is concentrated in a polaric cumulus, this becomes, as it were, a radiant point, emitting light and force of a peculiar and miraculous order. Such is the saint, who, whether dwelling on earth or departed from it, is a fountain of grace, and centre of vitalising power, dispensing Divine energy to mankind.

The commonwealth of the Church is a commonwealth of prayers, of good works, of sacramental grace, of meritorious acts. The members of Christ's body can do nothing alone. All pray and act for others and in the name of all, not vicariously, as substitutes one for another, for that would be subversive of justice; but eucharistically, by a communication of blessing and grace. In this manner souls profit one another, and give and receive benediction and help, both among the living and the departed. Not with lamentations and bewailings, then, should we celebrate our dead, for these detain and disturb; but with prayers and oblations and acts of Divine union performed on their behalf, earnestly desiring for them consolation and at-one-ment with God. For the death of the body is no barrier between soul and soul. Love does not die of death.

Such is one aspect of the Communion of Saints, in its relation to the threefold Church in the worlds of time and of eternity. But the saint has also special relations to God and to other saints. These are phases of the doctrine which are familiar to mystics both of East and West. The Communion of Saints with God consists in the relation held by the holy soul to heavenly environment. The status of any particular soul is determined by the capacity it develops for correspondence with its environment. The more circumscribed this correspondence, the lower the rank of the soul in the economy of the universe; the fuller this correspondence, the higher is that rank. The unspiritual man corresponds to the limited environment of the outer and lower world only, and is unable to recognise aught beyond this. In relation to all wider and higher environment he is dead. As for a creature without eyes light and beauty exist not, so for a man without spiritual perception the spiritual world and the revelation of the Divine are not. "To be carnally minded is death." But when the soul rises into spiritual correspondence and develops a cognition and experience of Divine environment, it attains the communion which relates it immediately to God,—the Communion of Saints. In this holy condition all forms and modes of knowing are lost in actual union with the Divine. The highest of all attainments is to transcend knowing by being; to exchange the consciousness of outer things for that of the inner essence, and so to merge the finite selfhood of the man in the infinite selfhood of Deity, as to realise experientially the words of the Athanasian Creed, "One by the taking of the manhood into God." For the Communion of Saints and their conversation are in Heaven; the environment to which they respond is the Infinite Pleroma; the bonds of the limited selfhood are broken, and emancipation and apotheosis attained. God is the environment of the saint.

The communion of the saints with one another follows from their communion with God. They have all things in common because all that they have is God. At the topmost pinnacle of the pyramid of the religious life there is a single stone only, and that stone is Divine Love. This is the central point of the universe towards which all paths converge. Holy souls journey thither by many roads, but all are pilgrims to the self-same shrine. The last utterance of the saintly life, the final aspiration of the saintly heart, is always one whether we seek it in Vedanta, in Islam, in Hermetic illumination, or in Catholic mysticism. The Alexandrian school of Greek thought was, equally with the Oriental theosophies, pervaded by the spiritual thirst for union with the One and Eternal. The Enneads of Plotinus remain for ever a monument of earnestness to this end. The same spirit gave religious fervour to the noblest minds of the Christian age. The mystic passion for the Infinite which ever haunts the human soul, and breaks forth from Augustine in the cry, " Thou hast made us, O Lord, for Thyself, and we are restless until we return to Thee," breathes equally in the Vedic hymns, the sighs of Thomas à Kempis and of Jeanne Guyon, the sermons of Tauler and Eckhart, and the thoughts of the writers of the " Germanica Theologia," and of every devout prophet, poet, and seer of all times and lands.

It is through the Poverty of spirit spoken of in the Beatitudes that this union is attained. As says a mystic of the Sûfis, " Poverty is the treasure of the saints. For, until a man has stripped himself absolutely of all externals, of all sensory and illusory feelings and knowledges, he cannot possess the wealth of the interior and hidden excellence. Union with God is impossible in its completeness, so long as anything remains to the aspirant that hinders the immergence of the soul in the Divine Selfhood." " The secret of the mystic," says St Dionysius, " is the secret of taking away; the path of the holy soul is the *via negativa*." And in the Upanishads we read: " Thrice let the saint say, ' I have renounced all.' "

It was a Moslem Sûfi who wrote the following exquisite apologue: "One knocked at the door of the Beloved's house, and a voice from within said, ' Who is there ? ' The lover answered, ' It is I.' The voice replied, ' This house will not hold me and thee.' So the door remained shut. The lover retired into a wilderness and spent his time in solitude, meditation, and prayer. A year passed; then he returned and knocked again at the door. ' Who is there ? ' said the voice of the Beloved. The lover answered, ' It is *thou*.' Then the door was opened."

Truth, as the Saint knows it, is wholly spiritual. For he perceives the primary where others behold only the secondary. He recognises the supreme verity that the real and absolute knows no past, and that salvation is independent of catastrophes. The primary in the Divine Intention is ever the spiritual, and of this the phenomenal and temporary is but the vehicle or dispensational mode. The first in time must be taken away that the last may be established. The reality of God cannot be confined or expressed within any definite *personæ* or series of events. It transcends all presentations, whether of thought or life. For the soul, her ideal is equally true, whether yet realised or not. The Divine Incarnation, to be a manifestation of the Infinite, must consist in an endless progression. When man has wearied himself to despair in futile endeavours to seize and fix truth on the plane of sense and fact, if he be worthy and faithful God reveals to him the higher plane of the noumenal and Divine, where alone truth eternally abides. Then he perceives the things he had formerly regarded as essential to be sacramental only, an elemental veil, preserving and concealing from vulgar touch and taste the true and adorable Body and Blood of the Lord. For, indeed, all religious formulas and functions are sacramental; all theologic knowledges, relative. The Church on earth is the great Mystagogue, unfolding in images the wisdom that is hidden. And only when the inward and spiritual grace is attained is the outward and visible sign known for what it is worth. According to the Moslem mystics, all the religions of the world are the selfsame wine in different glasses. Poured by God into one mighty chalice, they then become indistinguishable.

To find this interior and only truth, to realise Christ in the soul, to crucify the human will, to burn up all earthly passion in the fire of Divine love, to rise into newness of life, to ascend up beyond all heavens, and to abide in the secret place of God,—these Divine operations are indispensable for the mystic and the saint; this process the sole means to the goal of all aspiration—union with God. In this transcendent love for God the love of the brethren is enfolded and embosomed. The saint has communion with the Church in Heaven and on earth, because he has communion with God.

THE HERMETIC FRAGMENT KORÉ KOSMOU THE VIRGIN OF THE WORLD[1]

THE mystic title of the celebrated Hermetic fragment, "Koré Kosmou"—that is, the "Kosmic Virgin"—is in itself a revelation of the wonderful identity subsisting between the ancient wisdom-religion of the old world and the creed of Catholic Christendom. Koré is the name by which, in the Eleusinian Mysteries, Persephone the Daughter, or Maiden, was saluted; and it is also—perhaps only by coincidence—the Greek word for the pupil or apple of the eye. When, however, we find Isis, the Moon-goddess and Initiatrix, in her discourse with Horos, mystically identifying the eye with the soul, and comparing the tunics of the physical organ of vision with the envelopes of the soul; when, moreover, we reflect that precisely as the eye, by means of its pupil, is the enlightener and percipient of the body, so is the soul the illuminating and seeing principle of man, we can hardly regard this analogy of names as wholly unintentional and uninstructive. For Koré, or Persephone, the Maiden, is the personified soul, whose "apostasy," or "descent," from the heavenly sphere into earthly generation, is the theme of the Hermetic parable.[2] The Greek mysteries dealt only with two subjects, the first being the drama of the "rape" and restoration of Persephone; the second, that of the incarnation, martyrdom,

[1] Lecture given by Anna Kingsford, on the 27th April 1885, to the Hermetic Society. I have assumed that this Lecture was written before and used by Anna Kingsford as her "Introduction" to her and Edward Maitland's edition of *The Virgin of the World* (which was shortly afterwards published), or that such "Introduction" was written before and used as the basis of this Lecture. It matters little which of these alternatives was followed. The present Lecture is taken from the above-mentioned "Introduction." (See *Life of A. K.*, vol. ii. pp. 226, 227, and 228.) A short Abstract of the Lecture was published in *Light*, 1885, p. 225.—S. H. H.

[2] Dr Wilder, in his Introduction to the work of Mr Thomas Taylor, the Platonist, entitled *Dissertation on the Eleusinian Mysteries*, asserts that the name Koré is also Sanscrit, and that the Hindû goddess Parasupani, also called Gorée, is identical with the Koré-Persephoneia of Hellenic worship.—A. K.

and resuscitation of Dionysos-Zagreus. By Persephone was intended the Soul; and by Dionysos, the Spirit.[1] Hermetic doctrine taught a fourfold nature both of the Kosmos and of Man; and of this fourfold nature two elements were deemed immortal and permanent, and two mortal and transient. The former were the Spirit and the Soul; the latter, the lower mind—or sense body—and the physical organism. The Spirit and the Soul, respectively male and female, remained throughout all the changes of metempsychosis the same, indissoluble and incorrupt, but the body and lower intellect were new in each re-birth, and therefore changeful and dissoluble. The Spirit, or Dionysos, was regarded as of a specially divine genesis, being the Son of Zeus by the immaculate Maiden—Koré-Persephoneia, herself the daughter of Demeter, or the parent and super-

---

[1] In a letter, dated "Christmas 1885," in the *Theosophist* of March 1886 (p. 410), Anna Kingsford—replying to a critic—says: "That Dionysos-Zagreus personified in [the Greek] Mysteries the seventh Principle (Hermetically, the Fourth) in the universe,—that is—the divine and vitalising Spirit, is no surmise or assumption of mine, but an undoubted fact, placed beyond controversy by the authorities already mentioned. This Dionysos-Zagreus, the *mystic* Dionysos, must not be confounded with the later god, identified with Bacchus, the son of Semele. . . . Dionysos represents the Spirit or seventh Principle (Fourth) whether macrocosmically or microcosmically, and, as such, has been identified with Osiris, the Egyptian presentation of the same Principle. And Persephone is alike, in both aspects, greater and lesser, the Soul. But the Greek mysteries dealt ostensibly with the *macrocosmic* presentation of the divine drama, and with its individual meaning by implication only. Hence Persephone is generally taken to signify the Soul in her larger acceptation, as 'Koré Kosmou,' and hence also her son Dionysos, represents rather the son of God in the World than the son of God in Man."

In a further letter, dated 2nd April 1886, in the same Paper (p. 607), Anna Kingsford—replying to a further criticism by the same writer—says: "I understand that the Greek Mysteries deal with the Lapse and Rehabilitation of the Soul (Persephone) and with the Incarnation, Martyrdom, and Resuscitation of the Spirit (Dionysos) in their macrocosmic sense, and, only by analogy and implication, with the same mysteries in their microcosmic sense. The World and Man correspond in all their parts, hence what is said of one is inferentially implied of the other. But I think that Osiris always meant the dictinctively human aspect of Dionysos,—not to be confounded with him, because it would be incorrect to speak of Osiris as the seventh Principle of the World,—but his analogue, the Only Begotten in Man,—manifested as the Redeemer. Consequently, Osiris is third in the chronological series, because man is himself the result of the evolution of the world and not coeval with it. I do not know that any precisely equivalent Persona of Dionysos is to be found in the Egyptian Pantheon. I know that some writers affirm him to be of Egyptian origin, but the question needs to solve it more erudition than I possess. At any rate, I feel pretty sure the equivalent cannot be sought in Osiris, for Osiris is clearly the analogue of the Christian Christ, not of the Kabalistic Adonai."—S. H. H.

mundane Intelligence, addressed in the Mysteries as the "Mother."[1] But Koré, although thus of heavenly origin, participates more closely than her Son in an earthly and terrestrial nature. "Hence," says Proclos, "according to the theologians who delivered to us the most holy Mysteries, Persephone abides on high in those dwellings of the Mother which she prepared for her in inaccessible places, exempt from the sensible world. But she likewise dwells beneath with Pluto, administering terrestrial concerns, governing the recesses of the earth, and supplying life to the extremities of the Kosmos."

Wherefore, considered as the daughter of Zeus and Demeter, Koré is immaculate and celestial in character; considered as the captive and consort of Hades, she belongs to the lower world and to the region of lamentation and dissolution. And, indeed, the Soul possesses the dual nature thus ascribed to her, for she is in her interior and proper quality incorrupt and inviolable—ever virgin—while in her apparent and relative quality she is defiled and fallen. In Hermetic fable the constant emblem of the Soul is Water, or the Sea—*Maria*; and one salient reason for this comparison is that water, however seemingly contaminated, yet remains, in its essence, always pure. For the defilement of so-called foul water really consists in sediments held by it in solution, and thereby causing it to appear turbid, but this defilement cannot enter into its integral constitution. So that if the foulest or muddiest water be distilled, it will leave behind in the cucurbite all its earthy impurities, and present itself, without loss, clear and lucent in the recipient alembic. Not, therefore, without cause is the Soul designated "ever virgin," because in her essential selfhood she is absolutely immaculate and without taint of sin. And the whole history of the world, from end to end, is the history of the generation, lapse, sorrows, and final assumption of this Kosmic virgin. For the Soul has two modes or conditions of being—centrifugal and centripetal. The first is the condition of her outgoing, her immergence in Matter, or her "fall," and the grief and subjection which she thereby brings upon herself. This phase is, in the Jewish Kabalah, represented

[1] The Spirit, under the name of *Atman*, is the chief topic of Hindû esoteric philosophy, the Upanishads being exclusively devoted to it. They ascribe to *Atman* the qualities of self-subsistence, unity, universality, immutability, and incorruptibility. It is independent of *Karma*, or acquired character and destiny, and the full knowledge of it redeems from *Karma* the personality informed of it. *Atman* is also the all-seeing; and, as the *Mantras* say, He who recognises the universe in his own *Atman*, and his own *Atman* in the universe, knows no hatred.—A. K.

by Eve. The second condition is that of her incoming, her emergence from Matter, her restitution, or glorification in "heaven." This phase is presented to us in the Christian evangel and Apocalypse under the name of Mary. Hence the Catholic saying that the "Ave" of Mary reverses the curse of Eva.

In perfect accord with Kabalistic doctrine, the allegory of the "Koré Kosmou" thus clearly indicates the nature of the Soul's original apostasy; "she receded from the prescribed limits; not willing to remain in the same abode, she moved ceaselessly, and repose seemed death."[1]

In this phrase we have the parallel to the scene represented in the Mysteries, where Persephone, wilfully straying from the mansions of heaven, falls under the power of the Hadean God. This, perhaps the most occult part of the whole allegory, is but lightly touched in the fragmentary discourse of Isis, and we cannot, therefore, do better than reproduce here the eloquent exposition of Thomas Taylor on the subject.

"Here, then," he says, "we see the first cause of the Soul's descent, namely, the abandoning of a life wholly according to the Higher Intellect, which is occultly signified by the separation of Proserpina from Ceres. Afterward, we are told that Jupiter instructs Venus to go to her abode and betray Proserpina from her retirement, that Pluto may be enabled to carry her away; and to prevent any suspicion in the virgin's mind, he commands Diana and Pallas to go in company. The three Goddesses arriving find Proserpina at work on a scarf for her mother, in which she has embroidered the primitive chaos and the formation of the world. Now, by Venus, in this part of the narration, we must understand *desire*, which, even in the celestial regions (for such is the residence of Proserpina till she is ravished by Pluto), begins silently and stealthily to creep into the recesses of the Soul. By Minerva we must conceive the rational power of the Soul, and by Diana, Nature. And, lastly, the web in which Proserpina had displayed all the fair variety of the material world, beautifully represents the commencement of the illusive operations through which the Soul becomes ensnared with the fascination of imaginative forms. After this, Proserpina, forgetful of the Mother's commands, is represented as venturing from her retreat through the treacherous persuasions of Venus. Then we behold her issuing on to the plain with Minerva and Diana, and attended

---

[1] I substitute the singular for the plural number, but this alters nothing in the sense.—A. K.

by a beauteous train of nymphs, who are evident symbols of the world of generation, and are, therefore, the proper companions of the Soul about to fall into its fluctuating realms. Moreover, the design of Proserpina, in venturing from her retreat, is beautifully significant of her approaching descent; for she rambles from home for the purpose of gathering flowers, and this in a lawn replete with the most enchanting variety, and exhaling the most delicious odours. This is a manifest image of the Soul operating principally according to the natural and external life, and so becoming ensnared by the delusive attractions of sensible form. Immediately Pluto, forcing his passage through the earth, seizes on Proserpina and carries her away with him. Well may the Soul, in such a situation, pathetically exclaim with Proserpina:

> 'O male dilecti flores, despectaque Matris
> Consilia; O Veneris deprensæ serius artes!'[1]

Pluto hurries Proserpina into the infernal regions: in other words, the Soul is sunk into the profound depth and darkness of a material nature. A description of her marriage next succeeds, her union with the dark tenement of the body."

To this eloquent exposition of Taylor's, it is well to add the description given in Homer's *Hymn to Ceres*. Persephone herself speaks:—

"We were plucking the pleasant flowers, the beautiful crocus, the iris, the hyacinth, and the narcissus, which, like the crocus, the wide earth produced. With joy I was plucking them, when the earth yawned beneath, and out leaped the strong King, the Many-Receiver, and went bearing me, deeply sorrowing, under the earth in his golden chariot, and I cried aloud."

Compare with this Hermetic allegory of the lapse of Persephone and the manner of it, the Kabalistic story of the "fall" of Eve.

"And she saw that the tree was good to eat, and fair to the eyes, and delightful to behold; and she took of the fruit thereof and did eat. . . . And to the woman He said: I will multiply thy sorrows and thy conceptions: in sorrow shalt thou bring forth, and thou shalt be under thy husband's power, and he shall have dominion over thee."

In a 'note appended to Taylor's *Dissertations*, Dr Wilder

---

[1] "O flowers fatally dear, and the Mother's counsels despised!
O cruel arts of crafty Venus!"

quotes from Cocker's *Greek Philosophy* the following excellent reflections:—

"The allegory of the Chariot and Winged Steeds, in Plato's *Phædrus*, represents the lower or inferior part of man's nature (Adam or the body) as dragging the Soul down to the earth, and subjecting it to the slavery of corporeal conditions. Out of these conditions arise numerous evils that disorder the mind and becloud the reason, for evil is inherent to the condition of finite and multiform existence into which we have fallen. The earthly life is a fall. The Soul is now dwelling in the grave which we call the body. . . . We resemble those 'captives chained in a subterranean cave,' so poetically described in the seventh book of *The Republic*; their backs turned to the light, so that they see but the shadows of the objects which pass behind them, and 'to these shadows they attribute a perfect reality.' Their sojourn upon earth is thus a dark imprisonment in the body, a dreary exile from their proper home."

Similarly we read, in the "Koré Kosmou," that the souls on learning that they were about to be imprisoned in material bodies, sighed and lamented, lifting to heaven glances of sorrow, and crying piteously, "O woe and heartrending grief to quit these vast splendours, this sacred sphere, and all the glories of the blessed republic of the Gods to be precipitated into these vile and miserable abodes. No longer shall we behold the divine and luminous heavens!"

Who, in reading this, is not reminded of the pathetic lament of Eve on quitting the fair "ambrosial bowers" of Paradise?[1]

From the sad and woeful state into which the Virgin thus falls, she is finally rescued and restored to the supernal abodes. But not until the coming of the Saviour, represented in the allegory before us under the name of Osiris—the Man Regenerate. This Redeemer, himself of divine origin, is in other allegories represented under other names, but the idea is always luminously defined, and the intention obvious. Osiris is the Jēsous of our Christian doctrine, the supreme Initiate or "Captain of Salvation."[2] He is represented, together with his Spouse, as in all

[1] Milton's *Paradise Lost*, Book xi.
[2] In a note to the *Definitions of Asclepios*, Anna Kingsford says: "Osiris is the reflection and counterpart in Man, of the supreme Lord of the Universe, the ideal type of humanity; hence the soul, or essential ego, presenting itself for judgment in the spiritual world, is in the Egyptian Ritual of the Dead described as 'an Osiris.' It is to this Osiris, or king within us, our higher Reason, the true Word of God, that we owe perpetual reverence, service, and faithful allegiance" (*The Virgin of the World*, p. 113).—S. H. H.

things "instructed" and directed by Hermes, famed as the celestial conductor of souls from the "dark abodes"; the wise and ubiquitous God in whom the initiate recognises the Genius of the Understanding or Divine Reason—the *nous* of Platonic doctrine, and the mystic "Spirit of Christ." Therefore, as the understanding of holy things and the faculty of their interpretation are the gift of Hermes, the name of this God is given to all science and revelation of an occult and divine nature. A "Divine" is, in fact, one who knows the mysteries of the kingdom of heaven; hence St John the seer, or the "divine," is especially the "beloved" of Christ. Hermes was regarded as the Messenger or Angel of the Gods, descending alike to the depths of the Hadean world, to bring up souls from thence, and ascending up beyond all heavens that he might fill all things. For the Understanding must search alike the deeps and the heights; there can be nothing hidden from it, nor can it attain the fullness of supernal and secret knowledge unless it first explore the phenomenal and terrestrial. "For that he ascended, what is it but *because* he also descended first into the lower parts of the earth?"

With the splendid joyousness and light-hearted humour which characterised the Greeks, mingling laughter and mirth even with the mysteries of Religion, and making their sacred allegories human and musical as no others of any nation or time, Hermes, the Diviner and Revealer, was also playfully styled a Thief, and the patron of thieves. But thereby was secretly indicated the power and skill of the Understanding in making everything intellectually its own. Wherefore, in charging Hermes with filching the girdle of Venus, the tongs of Vulcan, and the thunder of Jove, as well as with stealing and driving off the cattle of Apollo, it was signified that all good and noble gifts, even the attributes of the high Gods themselves, are accessible to the Understanding, and that nothing is withheld from man's intelligence, if only man have the skill to seek aright.

As the immediate companion of the sun, Hermes is the opener of the gates of the highest heaven, the revealer of spiritual light and life, the Mediator between the inner and the outer spheres of existence, and the Initiator into those sacred mysteries, the knowledge of which is life eternal.

The panoply with which Greek art invests Hermes is symbolical of the functions of the Understanding. He has four implements—the rod, the wings, the sword, and the cap, denoting respectively the science of the magian, the courage of the adventurer, the will of the hero, and the discretion of the adept. The initiates of Hermes acknowledge no authority but the Understanding; they call no man king or master upon earth; they are true Free-Thinkers and Republicans. "For where the Spirit of the Lord is, there is liberty."[1] Hence Lactantius, in his *Divine Institutions*, says: "Hermes affirms that those who know God are safe from the attacks of the demon, and that they are not even subjected to Fate." Now, the powers of Fate reside in the stars—that is, in the *astral* sphere, whether Kosmic or micro-Kosmic. And the astral power was, in Greek fable, typified by Argos, the hundred-eyed genius of the starry zone, *Panoptes*, the all-seeing giant, whom it was the glory of Hermes to have outwitted and slain. Of which allegory the meaning is, that they who have the Hermetic secret are not subject to Fate, but have passed beyond the thrall of metempsychosis, and have freed themselves from "ceaseless whirling on the wheel" of Destiny. To know God is to have overcome death. To know the origin and secret of delusion is to transcend delusion. The spheres of delusion, dominated by the sevenfold astral Powers, lie between the soul and God. Beyond these spheres are the celestial "Nine Abodes," wherein, say the Mysteries, Demeter vainly sought the lost Persephone. For from these abodes she had lapsed into a mundane and material state, and thereby had fallen under the power of the planetary rulers; that is, of Fate, personified by Hekate. On the tenth day, therefore, the divine Drama shews Demeter meeting the Goddess of Doom and Retribution, the terrible Hekate Triformis—personification of *Karma*—by whom the "Mother" is told of Persephone's abduction and detention in the Hadean world. And—we learn—Hekate becomes, thereafter, the constant attendant of Persephone. All this is, of course, pregnant with the deepest significance. Until the Soul falls into Matter, she has no Fate or Karma. Fate is the appanage and result of Time and of Manifestation. In the sevenfold astral spheres the Moon is representative of Fate, and presents two aspects, the benign and the malignant. Under the benign aspect the Moon is Artemis, reflecting to the Soul the divine light of Phœbus; under the malignant aspect she is Hekate the Avenger, dark of countenance; and three-headed, being swift as a horse, sure as a dog, and as a lion implacable. She it is who, fleet, sagacious, and pitiless, hunts guilty souls

---

[1] "Follow no man," said John Inglesant's adviser—"there is nothing in the world of any value but the Divine Light—follow it."—A. K.

from birth to birth, and outwits death itself with unerring justice. To the innocent and chaste soul, therefore, the lunar power is favourable. Artemis is the patron and protectress of virgins—that is, of souls undefiled with the traffic of Matter.[1] In this aspect the Moon is the Initiatrix, Isis the Enlightener, because through a beneficent Karma, or Fate, the soul receives interior illumination, and the dark recesses of her chamber are lit up by sacred reminiscences. Hence, in subsequent births, such a soul becomes prophetic and "divine." But to the corrupt and evil-hearted the influence of the Moon is malignant, for to such she assumes the aspect of Hekate, smiting by night, and terrifying with ghostly omens of misfortune. These souls fear the lunar power, and in this instinctive dread may be discerned their secret recognition of the evil fate which they are preparing for themselves in existences to come. The Tree of Good and Evil, says the Kabalah, has its root in Malkuth—the Moon.

It has been sometimes asserted that the doctrine of Karma is peculiar to Hindû theology. On the contrary, it is clearly exhibited alike in the Hebrew, Hellenic, and Christian Mysteries. The Greeks called it Fate; the Christians know it as Original Sin. With which sin all mortal men come into the world, and on account of which all pass under condemnation. Only the "Mother of God" is exempt from it, the "virgin immaculate," through whose Seed the world shall be redeemed.

"As the lily among the thorns," sings the Church in the "Office of the Immaculate Conception," "so is the Beloved among the Daughters of Adam. Thou art all fair, O Beloved, and the original stain is not in thee! Thy name, O Mary, is as oil poured out; therefore, the virgins love thee exceedingly."

If, then, by Persephone or Koré, the "Virgin of the World," we are thus plainly taught to understand the Soul, we are no less plainly taught to see in Isis the Initiatrix or Enlightener. Herself, equally with Koré, virgin and mother, the Egyptian Isis is, in her philosophical aspect, identical with the Ephesian Artemis, the Greek personification of the fructifying and all-nourishing power of Nature. She was regarded as the "inviolable and perpetual Maid of Heaven;" her priests were eunuchs, and her image in the magnificent temple of Ephesus represented her with many breasts—πολυμαστὸς. In works of art Artemis

---

[1] "'Virgins' are souls which, being perfectly spiritualised, retain no taint of materiality" (C. W. S., pt. i. No. xxxix.).—S. H. H.

appears variously, as the huntress, accompanied by hounds, and carrying the implements of the chase; as the Goddess of the Moon, covered with a long veil reaching to her feet, and her head adorned with a crescent; or as the many-breasted Mother-Maid, holding a lighted torch in her hand. The Latins worshipped her under the name of Diana, and it is as Diana that the Ephesian Artemis is mentioned in the Acts of the Apostles. Isis had all the attributes ascribed to the lunar divinity of the Greeks and Romans; and hence, like Artemis and Diana, she was identified with the occult principle of Nature—that is, Fate, which in its various aspects and relations was severally viewed as Fortune, Retribution, Doom, or Destiny; a principle represented, as we have already seen, by the Kabalists under the figure of Malkuth, or the Moon; and by the Hindû theosophists under the more abstract conception of Karma. The hounds of Artemis, or Diana, are the occult powers which hunt down and pursue the soul from birth to birth; the inevitable, implacable forces of Nature which, following evermore on the steps of every ego, compel it into the conditions successively engendered by its actions, as effect by cause. Hence Actæon, presuming upon Fate, and oblivious of the sanctity and inviolability of this unchanging law of Karmic Destiny, is torn in pieces by his own dogs, to wit, his own deeds, which by the decree of the implacable Goddess turn upon and rend him. So also, in accordance with this philosophical idea, those who were initiated into the mysteries of Isis wore in the public processions masks representing the heads of dogs. So intimately was the abstract conception of the moon associated by the ancients with that of the secret influence and power of Destiny in Nature, that Proclos in his Commentary upon the *Timæus* says of Diana: "She presides over the whole of the generation into natural existence, leads forth into light all natural reasons, and extends a prolific power from on high even to the subterranean realms." These words completely describe the Egyptian Isis, and shew us how the moon, occultly viewed as the Karmic power, was regarded as the cause of continued generation in natural conditions, pursuing souls even into the Hadean or purgatorial spheres, and visiting upon them the fruition of their past. Hence, too, in the Orphic Hymn to Nature, that Goddess is identified with Fortune, and represented as standing with her feet upon a wheel which she continually turns—" moving with rapid motion on an eternal wheel." And again, in another Orphic Hymn, Fortune herself is invoked as Diana. Proclos, in the Commentary to which reference has already been made, declares that "the moon is the cause of Nature to mortals, and the self-revealing image of the Fountain of Nature." "If," says Thomas Taylor, "the reader is desirous of knowing what we are to understand by the Fountain of Nature of which the moon is the image, let him attend to the following information, derived from a long and deep study of the ancient theology, for from hence I have learned that there are many divine fountains contained in the essence of the Demiurgus of the world; and that among these there are three of a very distinguished rank, namely, the fountain of souls, or Juno (Hera), the fountain of virtues, or Minerva (Athena), and the fountain of nature, or Diana (Artemis).... And this information will enable us to explain the meaning of the following passages in Apuleius, the first of which is in the beginning of the eleventh book of his *Metamorphoses*, wherein the divinity of the moon is represented as addressing him in this sublime manner: 'Behold, Lucius, moved with thy supplications, I am present; I, who am Nature, the parent of things, mistress of all the elements, initial progeny of the ages, the highest of the divinities, queen of departed spirits, the first of the celestials, of Gods and Goddesses the sole likeness of all; who rule by my nod the luminous heights of the heavens, the salubrious breezes of the sea, and the woeful silences of the infernal regions, and whose divinity, in itself but one, is venerated by all the earth, in many characters, various rites, and different appellations.... Those who are enlightened by the emerging rays of the rising sun, the Æthiopians and Aryans, and likewise the Egyptians, powerful in ancient learning, who reverence my divinity with ceremonies perfectly appropriate, call me by my true appellation Queen Isis.' And again, in another place of the same book, he says of the moon: 'The supernal Gods reverence thee, and those in the realms beneath do homage to thy divinity. Thou dost make the world to revolve, and the sun to illumine, thou rulest the universe and treadest on Tartarus. To thee the stars respond, the deities rejoice, time returns by thee, the elements give thee service.' For all this easily follows if we consider it as spoken of the fountain-deity of Nature subsisting in the Demiurgus, and which is the exemplar of that nature which flourishes in the lunar orb and throughout the material world."

Thus enlightened as to the office and functions of Isis, we are at no loss to understand why she is selected by the writer of the Hermetic fragment " Koré Kosmou " as the exponent of the origin, history, and destiny of the soul. For she is, in a peculiar sense, the arbiter of the soul's career in existence, her guardian and overseer.[1] If Demeter, the Divine Intelligence, be the Mother of Koré, then Isis is her foster-mother, for no sooner does the soul fall into generation than Isis becomes her directress and the dispenser of her fate. It is not surprising, therefore, to find that by some mythologists Isis is identified with Demeter, and the sufferings of the former modified accordingly, to harmonise with the allegory of the sorrows of Demeter as set forth in the Eleusinian Mysteries. But the cause of this confusion is obvious to those who rightly understand the Hermetic method. Isis, whether as Artemis (Good Fortune), or as Hekate (Evil Fortune), is the controlling and illuminating influence of the soul, while remaining within the jurisdiction of Nature and Time; Demeter, the Divine Intelligence, represents the heavenly fountain or super-mundane source, whence the soul originally draws her being, and as such is concerned directly, not with her exile and wanderings in material conditions, but with her final recovery from generation and return to the celestial abodes. Consistently with this idea, Isis is represented sometimes as the spouse, sometimes as the mother of Osiris, the Saviour of men. For Osiris is the microcosmic sun, the counterpart in the human system of the macrocosmic Dionysos or Son of God. So that those authors who confound Isis with Demeter equally and quite comprehensibly confound Osiris with Dionysos, and regard the former as the

---

[1] In a letter, dated " Christmas 1885," in the *Theosophist* of March 1886 (p. 410), Anna Kingsford—replying to a critic—says: " Isis never represented the Soul or sixth Principle (third) of the universe, but the eighth sphere; not properly a Principle but an influence. . . . If, as is certain, Isis was identified with the Moon, and wore as an ensign the double horns of Selene, it is placed beyond doubt that she symbolised the Occult Power of Increase and Decrease, Good and Evil, and cannot possibly, therefore, be identified with the Soul whom she rejoices or afflicts according to an inflexible law. . . . Her counterpartal analogy in the microcosm, or individual, is found in the Genius,—the Guardian Angel of Christian theosophy. This Genius is good or bad, helpful or hindering, bright or dark, favourable or hostile, according to the state of grace (Karma) which the Soul has acquired. The Genius sheds upon the Soul the light derived from her own celestial Sun."

In a further letter, dated 2nd April 1886, in the same Paper (p. 607), Anna Kingsford—replying to a further criticism by the same writer —says: " Where I say that Isis is ' not properly a Principle,' I mean, of course, as I thought would be clearly understood, not one of the seven Principles which make up the microcosm (Man) or the macrocosm (World) if from the term ' World ' the satellite of the earth be excluded."—S. H. H.

central figure of the Bacchic Mysteries. The Hermetic books admit three expressions of Deity: first, the supreme, abstract, and infinite God, eternally self-subsistent and unmanifest; secondly, the only-Begotten, the manifestation of Deity in the universe; thirdly, God in man, the Redeemer, or Osiris. On one of the walls of the Temple of the Sun at Philæ, and on the gate of that at Medinet-Abou, are inscribed these words: "He has made all that is, and without Him nothing that is hath been made," words which, fourteen centuries or more afterwards, were applied by the writer of St John's Gospel to the Word of God. The microcosmic Sun, or Osiris, was the image and correspondence of this macrocosmic Sun; the regenerating principle within the man, begotten by means of the soul's experience in Time and Generation. And hence the intimate association between this regenerating principle by which the redemption of the individual was effected and the divine power in Nature, personified by Isis, whose function it was to minister to that redemption by the ordination of events and conditions appropriate to the soul's development. Isis is thus the secret motive-power of Evolution; Osiris is the ultimate ideal Humanity towards the realisation of which that Evolution moves.[1]

[1] Besides the translation of the Hermetic Fragment, Koré Kosmou, in *The Virgin of the World*, to which reference has been made (p. 127, *ante*), but which has long been out of print, there is a translation of it by G. R. S. Mead in his *Thrice Greatest Hermes* (vol. iii. p. 93), with an interesting commentary thereon.—S. H. H.

THE METHOD OF THE MYSTICS[1]

THE solution of the religious problem offered by the method of the mystics appears to be that which is destined to triumph in the present age. This is no new method, but one that has been in the world, obscurely and secretly, from the very dawn of religious thought, having its representatives and exponents in the ancient systems of both East and West, Buddhist, Alexandrian, and Christian. Their method consists in regarding the exterior and phenomenal presentation of religion as but the scaffolding necessary to the construction of the edifice—its mythologic scenery, to use Professor Tyndall's expression—and not the religion itself. The true faith is interior and spiritual, and has for ages been in the course of elaboration within and by means of these exterior appliances. Representing an eternal verity, and based in the spiritual consciousness, it is independent of letter and form, tradition and authority, and superior, therefore, to all assaults of intellectual criticism. What this age is witnessing is the removal of the now superfluous scaffolding, and the disclosure, in all its finished perfection, of the true Catholic Church of the future.

The difference between exoteric or popular religion and mystic or *acroatic* religion may be thus defined. In the former, sacred personages and occurrences are understood in the physical and obvious sense, as phenomenal and relative, and related to particular times and places, and dependent for verification upon individual testimony. In the system of the mystic, on the contrary, sacred personages and events denote principles and operations which affect the spiritual Ego, and are to this what physical transactions are to the material personality. As these principles and operations belong necessarily to universal experience, they are unrelated to times, places, and persons, and are to be sought, not on the historical plane, but on that of the mind and spirit; not, as the Buddhist would say, in the "worlds of form," but in the "formless worlds."

---

[1] Abstract, by Edward Maitland, of the Lecture given by Anna Kingsford, on the 13th May 1885, to the Hermetic Society, and published in *Light*, 23rd May 1885, p. 251.

THE METHOD OF THE MYSTICS

Images and symbols of religious verities have their true and legitimate use in leading the soul to the apprehension of that which they imply. But when regarded—as the popular religionist regards them—as themselves essentials and coefficients in spiritual processes, they become instruments of delusion. The essential is related to the essential, the corporeal to the corporeal. The things of God are similars to themselves; the things of Cæsar are similars to themselves. To God belong the things of God; to Cæsar the things of Cæsar. The redemption of the soul cannot be effected by means of coin on which is stamped the image and superscription of the physical. No events occurring in time, no acts of an historical personage, can "save" our souls. These events and acts must be translated into spiritual verities, and realised individually and experimentally, if they are to have any efficacy for the spiritual selfhood.[1]

The method of the mystics consists, then, in transmutation, or the conversion of the terms of the outer into the inner, of the physical into the spiritual; of the temporal and phenomenal into the eternal and noumenal. In them the key of the Scriptures, and of the functions and sacraments of religion, is found in the alchemic secret of transmutation. All the metals, says the alchemist, are gold in their essence, and by an application of the

---

[1] In a note to "Asclepios on Initiation," in *The Virgin of the World*, Anna Kingsford says: "Mankind necessarily passes through the stage of nature-worship before becoming competent to realise the celestial order and the being of the heavenly Gods. For before the empyrean can be reached by the human intelligence, it must traverse the spheres intermediate between earth and heaven. Thus the *images* of the Gods are worshipped before the Gods themselves are known; nor are these images necessarily of wood or stone. All personalities are eidola (idols) reflecting the true essentials, and having, as it were, a portion of Divinity attached to them and resident in their forms, but none the less are they *images*, and however powerful and adorable they may appear to the multitude who know not divine religion, they are to the Hermetist but types and *personæ* of essentials which are eternally independent of manifestation and unaffected by it. The signs of the truly Divine are three: transcendency of form, transcendency of time, transcendency of personality. Instead of form is Essence; instead of time, Eternity; instead of persons, Principles. Events become Processes; and phenomena, Noumena. So long as the conception of any divine idea remains associated with, or dependent on, any physical or historical circumstance, so long it is certain that the heavenly plane has not been reached. Symbols, when they are recognised as symbols, are no longer either deceptive or dangerous; they are merely veils of light rendering visible the 'Divine Dark,' towards which the true Hermetist aspires. Even the most refined, the subtlest and most metaphysical expression of the supreme Truth, is still symbol and metaphor, for the Truth itself is unutterable, save by God to God. It is Essence, Silence, Darkness" (p. 88).—S. H. H.

Divine art can be made to appear in their essence. But the uninitiate judge superficially and reject as dross that which the adept knows to be gold. Gold is the alchemic formula for spirit; and as the precious metal lies concealed under the semblance of the baser, so the true secret of all sacred Scripture—its spiritual significance—is hidden under the letter in such wise that, though invisible to the vulgar, it is evident to the eye of the illuminated.

Following, therefore, the invariable rule of his order, and applying to the text of sacred tradition the "universal solvent" formed by the two words *now* and *within*, the mystic sees in the exposition of revelation, from Genesis to the Apocalypse, the history, not of past events in the external and sensible world, but of the soul, and of operations in perpetual process in the sphere to which the soul—whether universal or individual—belongs.

KARMA[1]

THE doctrine of Karma is really an occult application of the doctrine of the Conservation of Energy, and means Spiritual Heredity. In one form or another it has always constituted an element in transcendental Theosophy, being—while specially developed in the Buddhist system—present in all others, Hebrew, Greek, and Christian. It is a corollary of the doctrine of physical re-births. That which is re-embodied in virtue of the operation of Karma is the true selfhood, or "character." But so long as re-births continue, this selfhood is not free of matter; but carries with it from birth to birth a clinging remnant of its phantom investment, called Kârma-rûpa, and only when it has finally got rid of the impurity thus contracted are the bonds which attract and bind it to the earth-life dissolved, and it is free to seek a loftier sphere. It is in order that this inner, essential being may grow and expand that re-births are necessary. We come back, as Lessing said, again and again so long as earth has lessons to teach us.

All that has been in its nature eternal and noumenal in any incarnation; all that has contributed to build up the true and interior man, is absolute and permanent, and will survive all ephemeral elements in our past personalities. The true Ego of the individual, on attaining Nirvâna, resumes in itself all that is lasting and noumenal of its past existences, and perceives them as constituting an uninterrupted whole—a continuous chain of cause and effect—and is known by other souls, similarly redeemed, in all its various characters. For only that which in its nature is divine can endure perpetually.

It is the doctrine of Karma and of continuity of existences which alone explains the inequalities and incongruities of life and vindicates the Divine justice. And, seen from this point of view, life has a far vaster scope than is compatible with the idea of a

[1] Abstract, by Edward Maitland, of some remarks made by Anna Kingsford at the close of a Lecture on the doctrine of Karma, given by the late C. C. Massey, on the 27th May 1885, to the Hermetic Society, and published in *Light*, 6th June 1885, p. 275.

single existence, which makes the soul independent of the discipline of earthly experience, inasmuch as it denies such experience altogether to the vast number who die in infancy. That the Christian Scriptures do not explicitly recognise the doctrine is no argument against its being a Christian doctrine. It was already in the world in Buddhism; and Christianity, as the complement and crown of Buddhism, had no need to reiterate it. Besides, the function of Christianity was to recognise a stage in the soul's elaboration at which Karma ceases to be operative. For the man who has "put on Christ" has entered already into Nirvâna, "the peace which passeth understanding." He is saved from the earthly elements and the necessity of further revolving on the wheel of re-births. "Hence," says Trismegistus, "he who knows God has overcome the power of destiny, and the ruling of the stars." Few who bear the Christian name attain to the Christian estate. "For strait is the gate and narrow is the way that leadeth unto life, and few there be that find it." Yet this does not mean that the many are lost; but that they must bear their Karma, and return again and again until they find that only way. To remain only Buddhist, by being regenerate only in the human will, is not to win the salvation which is of Christ. The will of man takes the Kingdom of Heaven by violence, that is, by the intellectual way. But they who are in Christ take it by the way of the soul. Two thieves were crucified with Christ, and a third—Barabbas—was dismissed, and had no part in the Lord's Passion. The thief on the right hand represents the will of man—the human will preached by Buddha, saved and regenerate by means of the Divine Will. The thief on the left is the animal will which must be left behind and abandoned; the rebel will, which mortification and crucifixion only can overcome; and the thief which is released to the multitude is the outermost principle, the mere titanic or structural nature-force, which has nothing in Christ. Thus, although the doctrine of Karma is implied in Christianity, it is not made conspicuous, because Christ "destroys Karma, and him that hath the power of death."[1]

[1] To a clerical correspondent in *Light*, who had stated that the doctrine of the transmigration of souls is one which "may not be repulsive to minds who hold lightly to revelation, but which to believers in a Revealed Word of God is abhorrent," Edward Maitland replied: "I object to this utterance as at once uncharitable, arrogant, and ignorant. It is uncharitable, because it imputes infidelity to all believers in the doctrine in question, numbers of whom hold firmly to 'revelation and the Revealed Word of God,' and yet find the doctrine in no way 'abhorrent'

to it or them. It is arrogant, because it assumes the infallibility of its utterer's own interpretation of the Bible. And it is ignorant, because the only key to the interpretation of the Bible—the Kabalah, or transcendental philosophy of the Hebrews—shews clearly that the main theme of the Bible is no other than the *Gilgal Neschamoth*, or *passing through of souls*, the process being described in numberless passages under the form of narratives, apparently personal and historical, but really relating to eternal verities, in some of which the doctrine is either so clearly implied or so thinly veiled as to make it wonderful that it should have come to be ignored. But however this may be, the doctrine was clearly not ' abhorrent' to Jesus Christ, or He would have returned a very different answer to His disciples when they implied their belief in it by asking of Him, "Did this man sin, or his parents, that he was born blind?'—a belief which, as every Biblical student knows, was prevalent among the Jews excepting, of course, the Sadducees or infidel part of them" (*Light*, 1884, p. 419).—S. H. H.

BIBLE HERMENEUTICS[1]

HERMETIC doctrine affirms that all causes originally rise in the spiritual sphere. In the beginning the material and objective is the ectype of the essential and subjective. Thus, the first chapter of Genesis sets out with the declaration: " In the beginning God created the heaven and the earth." Matter is not viewed by writers of the Kabalistic school as self-subsistent and eternal in nature. In its grossest form, Matter is the last term in a descending category, the first term of which is the Godhead itself. Matter is thus not *created*, in the vulgar sense of the word, but evolved; and, in the process of cosmic flux and reflux, it is destined to be again involved and transmuted into essence. Hence it follows that the higher principles of the microcosm, itself the offspring and resumption of the macrocosm, represent and reproduce the higher principles of its parent, even to the inclusion of Divinity, as the supreme source of the world and ultimate of Man. Emanating as macrocosm from God, the universe culminates as microcosm in God. God is the Alpha and Omega of the whole vast process. Now Holy Writ addresses itself not to the lower, but to the higher nature of man. The word of God is spoken to the intellectual and spiritual nature in man as distinguished from the inferior grades of his complex being. Evidently, then, the subjects of Biblical exposition cannot be the things of sense and of matter, but the things of

---

[1] Lecture given by Anna Kingsford, on the 13th April 1886, to the Hermetic Society, and, shortly afterwards, published as or included in Anna Kingsford's " Prefatory Essay on the True Method of Interpreting Holy Scripture," in her edition (then in course of preparation) of *Astrology Theologised*. (See *Life of A. K.*, vol. ii. pp. 224, 226, and 227; and *Light*, 1886, p. 207.) It is from this source that the present Lecture has been taken, and while I have excluded therefrom all passages which—as referring to *Astrology Theologised*—I thought could not have been included by Anna Kingsford in her Lecture, it is possible that I have included therein some passages which did not form part of her Lecture. The excluded passages deal at considerable length with the Creative " Week " of Genesis, and the application of the Allegory to the evolution of Man considered as the Microcosm; and with Fate, Heredity, and Re-incarnation—as to which latter subjects see pp. 220-224. *post.*—S. H. H.

the intelligible and formative world. The Bible is written for the Soul in man, not for his elemental and creaturely natures which, as we have seen, pertain to his lower perishable states, and are not included in the Covenant. Wherefore, surely, it is absurd and irrational to read the "History of Creation," given in Genesis, as though it treated of the mere outward and objective universe, which, in comparison with the inner and subjective, is phantasmal and unreal. Correspondentially, of course, it does so include the outer and objective, because every plane of Nature reflects and repeats the plane immediately above it. But of these planes there are seven, and each successive medium, counting from above downward, is grosser and less capable of exact reflection than the one preceding it, so that when the lowest plane of matter, as we know it by means of the five bodily senses, is reached, the similitude of the first and highest plane has become blurred and indistinct. Not all media are equally reflective. The first plane or medium may be compared to a crystal for translucence, and the last to turbid water. So that we must not look to the first chapter of Genesis for a perfect and exact picture of the physical creation, seeing that it deals with this creation only in a sense remote in series from its original and direct point of application. First, and primarily, the Bible has a *spiritual* meaning addressed to the spiritual and intellectual natures in man, the Sol and Luna of the Microcosm; secondly, it has a philosophical meaning for the Mercurial nature; thirdly, an astrological meaning for the astral nature; and, lastly, a physical meaning for the material nature to which the higher planes are unattainable. But, it must be borne in mind that the three lower meanings thus ascribed to it are not the word of God, because, as we have said, this word is only addressed to the Soul, and not to stocks and stones and elements. In the third Book of Kings there is a marvellous parable which perfectly sets forth in order every one of these four meanings, each with its proper character, effect, and dignity:—

"Behold the word of the Lord came unto Elias, and said: Go forth and stand upon the mount before the Lord. And behold, the Lord passeth, and a great and strong wind before the Lord, overthrowing the mountains and breaking the rocks in pieces, but the Lord is not in the wind. And after the wind an earthquake, but the Lord is not in the earthquake. And after the earthquake a fire, but the Lord is not in the fire, and after the fire a still small voice. (Sound of gentle stillness, Heb.) And when Elias heard it, he covered his face with his mantle and stood in the entering of the cave."

"The Lord passeth," and His coming is foreshadowed and heralded, indistinctly and confusedly, by the formless inarticulate wind, typical here of the lowest and universal expression of Force and Matter. "But the Lord is not in the wind. And after the wind, an earthquake," the sundering and solution of the mere external and physical or earthly plane by the volcanic and electric forces of the more interior mental nature, with its sciences and hermeneutic subtleties. Now the Lord is drawing nearer, but even yet He " is not in the earthquake." " And after the earthquake, a fire," the ethereal penetrative and burning energy of the third principle in man, the human Soul, with its clear luminance of introspection, and its immortal quickening activity. Now, indeed, the Lord is at hand, but even yet He " is not in the fire." " And after the fire, *a sound of stillness*." Yes; for the Spirit, "the Lord," the Fourth Principle in man is Rest, is Silence, is the " Divine Dark " of St Dionysius and the mystics. The word spoken by God is " a word in the ear": a secret whispered only to the Beloved; heard only by the Saint in the recess of his inmost heart. " And when Elias heard It, he covered his face with his mantle." For the Lord had come at last, and he knew that he stood in the Divine Presence. The real and inmost meaning of holy utterance is not reached until its physical, scientific, and intellectual interpretations have been all exhausted. The wind, indeed, may announce the coming and bear the echo of the sacred Voice, but without articulate expression; the earthquake may open the earth and disclose occult significations beneath the Letter which surprise the mere literalist; the fire may cleave the heaven and rend the darkness with its brilliant and vivid finger, but the formulate and perfect Word is inbreathed only by the Spirit. Truth is unutterable save by God to God. Only the Divine Within can receive and comprehend the Divine Without. The word of God must be a spiritual word, because God is Spirit. Accordingly, we find saints and mystics, Catholic and Protestant alike, accepting Holy Writ, both Old and New, in a sacramental sense. Rejecting the Letter they lay hold of the Spirit, and interpret the whole Bible from end to end after a mystical manner, understanding all its terms as symbols, its concretes as abstracts, its events as processes, its phenomena as noumena. The hermeneutic science of the saint has threefold characteristics—form is no more, time is no more, personality is no more. Instead of Time is Eternity, instead of Form is Essence, instead of Persons are Principles. So long as the dross of any merely intellectual or physical concept remains unconverted into the gold of spiritual meaning, so long the supreme interpretation of the text is unattained.

For the intellectual nature, next highest in order, Biblical hermeneutics are of a philosophical character, which, according to the tendencies and tastes of the interpreter, variously wears a poetic, a masonic, a mathematical, an alchemic, a mythologic, a political, or an occult aspect. To occupy worthily this plane of interpretation much learning and research are needed, often of an extremely abstruse and recondite kind. The philosophical hermeneutics of the Bible are closely connected with the study of hidden and unexplored powers in nature, a study which, in former times, was roughly designated "magic," but on which a younger generation has bestowed new names.

Large acquaintance with etymology, paleontology, geology, and the secrets of ancient systems of doctrine and belief is necessary to Biblical exegesis conducted on intellectual lines. Therefore it is, of all modes of exposition, the most difficult and the most perilous, many rival exegetes claiming to have discovered its key and clamorously disputing all interpretations other than their own. Thus the philosophical method is fruitful of schools and polemists, few among the latter becoming really eminent in their science, because of the enormous labour and erudition involved in it, and the brevity of human life.

Thirdly, we have the astronomical and astrological plane, which may briefly be summed up as the interpretation of Biblical writings on the basis of the Solar Myth. This is the method by which the intelligence of the astral mind is best satisfied; it involves no acceptance of doctrine, theological or religious, and no belief in the soul or in spiritual processes and eternal life. The solar theory is that, therefore, which is formally accepted by most modern exponents and reviewers; it is easily understood by men of average scholarship and perspicacity; it lends itself with readiness to all the dogmas and most of the language of both Testaments, and, with equal facility, explains the formulas of the Creed and the Church Liturgy.

Last and lowest comes the meaning which the crowd imputes to the Bible, and in which no real attempt at interpretation is implied. On this plane of acceptance, the literal sense alone of the words is understood throughout, obvious allegory is taken for history, poetical hyperbole for prosaic fact, mystic periods for definite measurements of time, corporeal sacrifice for spiritual at-one-ment, ceremonial for sacrament, and physical acts in time for interior and perpetual processes. This is the plane which produces fanatics, persecutors, and inquisitors, which fills our streets with the cries and tumult of salvationists, and our pulpits with noisy "evangelists," which sends forth missionaries to "convert" the "heathen" Buddhist, Brahman, or Jew, and wastes tears and lives and treasure untold in frantic and futile endeavours to "christianise" the world. The formula of this class of exponents is "justification by faith," and, apparently, the more monstrous the blasphemy against divine goodness, and the more extravagant the outrage against science involved in any article of belief, the greater the "justification" attained by its acceptance. The word of God, therefore, originally and primarily addressed to the secret ear of the soul, becomes, when conducted through all these various and increasingly grosser media, at length an inarticulate and confused sound, just as an image, conveyed through various and increasingly turbid strata of fluids, becomes at last distorted, blurred, and untrue to its original. Some similitude in form and colour of course remains, and from this we may divine the aspect of the object whose shadow it is, but the features of the shadow may be indistinct and grotesque, while those of the original are flawless and resplendent. Such a shadow is popular religion compared with Divine Truth, and the Letter of Holy Writ compared with its spiritual meaning. Do we then argue that the spiritual meaning is the only meaning intended, and the image afforded of it by all lower planes wholly false and fanciful? No; for we admit alike the philosophical, the astronomical, and the historical element in the Bible; we desire only to point out with emphasis the fact that all these, in their degree, transmit an ever-increasingly vague and inaccurate likeness of primal Revelation, and are, in their order, less and less proximately true and absolute. No man can be "saved" by the historical, the astronomical, or the philosophical, be his faith never so firm and childlike. He can be "saved" only by the spiritual, for the spiritual alone is cognate to that in him which *can* be saved, to wit, his spiritual part. Revelation is illumination imparted by God to the God-like principle in man, and its object is the concerns of this principle. Revelation may, indeed, be couched in solar or astronomical terms, but these are its vehicle only, not its substance and secret. Or, again, it may be conveyed in terms ostensibly descriptive of natural phenomena, of architecture, of national and political vicissitudes. None of these, however, are really the primal subject-matter of Holy Writ, for all of them relate to things belonging to sense and to time, which cannot be brought into effectual affinity with the soul, whose proper relation is with the noumenal and eternal. Such things pertain to the province of the sciences—physics, biology, history, paleontology, and so forth—and can be appropriately and intelligently dealt with by these only. They are not subjects for revelation; they in no wise interest the soul, nor can they affect the salvation of man. Moreover, as all knowledges accessible on planes other than the spiritual must of necessity be partial and relative only, mere approximations to facts, and not facsimilia of facts, there can be no sure and infallible record of them possible to man. History, for instance, belongs entirely to the past and irrecoverable, and depends on the observation of and impressions produced by certain events at periods more or less remote; the recorders of the events in question being endued with the spirit and views of their time, and judging according to the light which these afforded. The same events in our age, appealing to minds of wholly different habits of thought and experience, would present an aspect and bear an intepretation wholly different. We need but to attend an assize or police court to learn how variously the same fact or episode presents itself to various witnesses. And when to the element of uncertainty created by natural defects and differences in the faculties of observation and memory possessed by different individuals is added the impossibility of reviewing events of a long-distant past from the modern standpoint, and the consequent necessity of accepting the ancient standpoint or none at all, it becomes obvious that there is, virtually, no such thing as history in the sense usually ascribed to that word, that is, as a record of actual occurrences as they actually occurred. Even contemporary history is only approximately true; the history of a generation past lends large ground to controversy, and that of the long past insensibly slips into legend, and thence into myth. Mankind has no art by which to photograph events. Character leaves its mark for a time on the world's records, and great sayings survive indefinite periods, but acts and events soon become contestable, and the authorship of our finest systems of philosophy and of our most precious axioms and rules of conduct loses itself in the haze of antiquity. The Lord's Prayer, the Beatitudes, and the Golden Rule remain facts, but what scholar knows who first gave them utterance? The Pythagorean, Buddhist, and Chinese philosophies, as also the Parsee and Jewish religions, are facts, but were there ever such men as the traditional Pythagoras, Buddha, Kung-foo-tsze, Mithras, Zoroaster, or Moses? No one to-day can with certainty affirm or deny even so much as their existence, to say nothing of their deeds, their miracles, their adventures, and the manner of their birth and death. And to speak of later times, what do we know, undoubtedly and indisputably, of such prominent personages in English and French chronicles as Roland and Oliver, Bayard, Cœur de Lion, Fair Rosamond, Joan of Arc, Anne Boleyn, Mary Stuart, and a thousand other heroes and heroines whose actions and adventures form the theme of so many speculations and assumptions? They have left on the historic page an impression of character, but little more. Concerning their real deeds, and the actual part they played in the events of their time, we can affirm nothing with assurance. And as the footfall of time, and the gradual decay and destruction of record, literary and geographical, slowly stamps out the burning embers of the past, darkness, more or less complete, falls over the remoter ages and blots them from our view. Decade after decade it becomes increasingly difficult to pluck any certain and solid crumb of fact from the grip of the Biblical exegetes, the etymologists, the biologists, the paleontologists, and all the scientific kith and kin. Every assertion is contested, every date, circumstance, and hero must fight for place and life. Assuredly there will come a day when the figure of Jesus of Nazareth, which for eighteen centuries has filled the canvas of the world, and already begins to pale, will become as obscure and faded as is now that of Osiris, of Fo-hi, or of Quetzalcoatl. Not that the Gospel can ever die, or that spiritual processes can become effete; but that the historical framework in which, for the present age, the saving truth is set, will dissociate itself from its essentials, fall, and drift away on the waves of Time. Spiritual hermeneutics will endure because they are independent of Time. Spiritual processes are actualities, daily and eternally realised in the experience of the microcosm, " as they were in the beginning, are now, and ever shall be." No man can know, philosophically, anything that occurs externally and objectively to himself; he can know only that which occurs internally and subjectively. Concerning the first, he can have an opinion only; concerning the second, he has experience. Nor, again, can any man believe any fact on the testimony of another, but only upon his own witness, for the impression received through the senses of one man, no matter how profound, is incommunicable to the organism of another, and can produce no conviction save to the mind of the man receiving the sensory impression. To believe implies assurance, and assurance can be imparted only by experience.

In matters of history and natural phenomena, moreover, none but the ablest observers and best educated critics can indicate, or determine probabilities, and to be even a sound critic or observer great natural endowments and acquired erudition are needed. It is incredible that God should demand of every man exceptional gifts of intellect and a university education as necessary conditions for the comprehension and acceptance of His Word. Yet, if that Word be indeed directly or intimately dependent on processes of natural phenomena or historical occurrences, it is eminently necessary that every person seeking salvation should be versed in the sciences concerned with them, because no assurance of the truth of Biblical data can be gained save by competent examination and test, and if no assurance, then no belief. It will be observed that contention is not here raised against the accuracy on the physical plane of either facts or figures contained in Sacred Writ; it is simply sought to shew that the unlearned cannot possibly have any valid means of judging or affirming their truth, and that, therefore, belief under such circumstances is a mere form of words. Not long ago, when defending the proposition "there is no such thing as history"—conceived, that is, as a record of consecutive and ascertained facts—I was met by a clergyman of the Established Church with the contention that *broad* facts are always ascertainable, and that, in respect to sacred history, belief in such broad facts only was necessary to salvation. We need not, for instance, said he, trouble ourselves over much about the details and dates of the gospel narrative, nor does it greatly matter whether Christ was born at Bethlehem or at Nazareth; or, again, whether He was crucified on the Feast of the Passover or on the day following; the essentials of faith lie in the great events of His birth and crucifixion. But, said I, if the only evidence we possess of these great events depends on the assertions of recorders whose testimony does not agree together in detail, what does the worth of the evidence itself amount to? In the celebrated "Story of Susanna," the wisdom and perspicacity of Daniel are shewn by his refusal to give credence to an alleged "broad fact," precisely because the witnesses did not agree in detail. But had Daniel been of the mind of my objector, he would have discarded the petty difference between the elders concerning the kind of tree under which they caught Susanna with her lover, he would have been content with their agreement as to the "broad fact," and Susanna would have been stoned. The three facts most essential to the belief of the Christian who deems the acceptation of the gospels as literal history necessary to salvation, are precisely those concerning which detail is all-important, and the witness offered the most uncertain and meagre; to wit, the Incarnation, the Resurrection, and the Ascension. The dogma of the Incarnation is supported by the record of two only of the four Evangelists, and, as an historical fact, depends solely on the testimony of one witness, and that one Mary herself, for no other could have related the tale of the Annunciation or certified to the miraculous conception. As for the dogma of the Ascension, the information supplied in regard to this event is contained, not in the gospels at all, but in the Acts of the Apostles, for the only reference made to the Ascension in the gospels consists of a single sentence in the last verse of St Luke's record, a sentence omitted by some ancient authorities, and noted as dubious in the Revised Version of 1880–1. Surely, then, the Incarnation and Ascension at least cannot be classed in the category of "broad facts," and yet, to regard them as unimportant details which might safely be overlooked, would be fatal to Christian faith and doctrine as understood by the Established Church. Stripped of these two dogmas—the Incarnation and the Ascension—there is nothing disputable on scientific grounds in the gospel history as a record of actual occurrences. It is credible that a man should possess unusual magnetic and psychic powers, or should swoon on the cross and recover from a death-like stupor in the course of a few hours when under the care of friends. But that a man should be born of a virgin, rise from the dead, and should bodily ascend into the sky are marvels for which overwhelming and incontrovertible testimony should be forthcoming. Yet these are precisely the three events for which the evidence is most meagre, and on two of which no stress is laid in either the sermons or epistles of the Apostles. Certainly, the dogma of the Incarnation is not once alluded to in their teaching, and it does not appear in any book of the New Testament that the disciples of Jesus or the founders of the Christian Church were acquainted with it. Whether a knowledge of the

Ascension is implied in the epistles or not is a more open question, but at any rate no express reference is made to it as an historical event. Yet, if for such reasons we should reject the spiritual power of the Gospel and deny its dogmas, or the dogmas of the Catholic Church, in their mystical sense, we should demonstrate our own ignorance and fatuity. For every such dogma is certainly and infallibly true, being grounded in the eternal experience of the human soul, and perpetually confirmed thereby. It is not the crucifixion of Jesus of Nazareth on Golgotha eighteen centuries ago that can save us, but the perpetual sacrifice and oblation, celebrated sacramentally in the Mass and actually in our hearts and lives. So also it is the mystical birth, resurrection, and ascension of the Lord, enacted in the spiritual experience of the saint, that are effectual to his salvation, and not their dramatic representation, real or fictitious, in the masque of "history."

For how can such events reach or relate themselves to the soul, save by conversion into spiritual processes? Only as processes can they become cognates to the soul and make themselves intelligible to and assimilable thereby. Throughout the universe the law of assimilation, whether in its inorganic or organic aspect, uniformly compels all entities and elements, from crystals to the most complex animate creature, to absorb and digest only that which is similar to itself in principles and substance. And if by the law of natural things the spiritual are understood, as all apostles of hermetic doctrine tell us, then it is obvious, by the light of analogy as well as by that of reason, that the spiritual part of man can assimilate only that which is spiritual. Hence the Catholic doctrine of transubstantiation, most necessary to right belief, whereby the bread and wine of the mere outward elements are transmuted into the real and saving body and blood of the Lord. Can bread profit to salvation, or can physical events redeem the soul? Nay, but to partake the substance of God's secret, which is the body of Christ, and to receive infusion of Divine grace into the soul, which is the blood of Christ, and by the shedding of which man is regenerate. These processes are essential to redemption from the otherwise certain and mortal effects of original sin.[1] It is not, therefore, part of the design of hermetic teaching to destroy belief in the historical aspect of Christianity any more than to dissuade the faithful from receiving Christ sacramentally, but to point out that it is not the history that saves, but the spiritual truth embodied therein, precisely

[1] As to " original sin," see p. 135, *ante*.

as it is not the bread administered at the altar that profits to salvation, but the Divine body therein concealed.

Life is not long enough to afford time for studying the volumes upon volumes of attack and defence to which the Christian tradition has given birth. It is more profitable to leave these contentions where they are, and to enquire, not whether the details of the story itself are accurate, nor even if the chief facts it relates were really enacted among men on the physical plane, but, rather, what it all signifies when translated into the language of absolutes. For phenomena cannot be absolutes, and we have shewn that only absolutes can have an intelligible meaning for the soul.

"VIOLATIONISM," OR SORCERY IN SCIENCE[1]

BELIEVERS in the conclusions of the exponents of physical science are apt to bring against the students of Spiritual Science the charge of reviving the old tricks and evil-doings of sorcery. Some persons who make this allegation believe that sorcery, whether ancient or modern, never had, nor can have, any other basis than mere imposture and ignorant credulity; others believe or suspect that it represents a real art of an unlawful and abominable character. I propose to shew that sorcery has indeed been revived in modern times to a considerable extent, but that its revival has taken place, not in the domain of Spiritual Science, but in that of physical science itself.

A further object of my address is to suggest to those who, like myself, hold as a fundamental doctrine of all Spiritual knowledge, the Unity of Substance, and who think it incumbent on them to give the knowledge of that doctrine practical expression in universal sympathy with all forms of sentient being, that it is high time for them to enter the lists actively against the worst manifestation of Materialism and Atheism the world has yet seen, and to declare their recognition of the simple and obvious moral issue of faith in a good God, namely, the duty of Love for all incarnations of the Divine Substance, and horror and reprehension of cruelty as such, whatever plea may be advanced for its practice.

It would be difficult to find stronger evidence of the banefulness of the influence exerted by the materialistic spirit of the day than that which is furnished by the apathy and uncertainty of the public generally in regard to the practice known as vivisection. To

[1] Lecture given by Anna Kingsford, on the 23rd January 1882, to the British National Association of Spiritualists, and published in *Light*, 4th February 1882, pp. 55-58 (see p. 8, *ante*). Edward Maitland says that it was one of her "most notable contributions to the anti-vivisection cause," and that it "attracted much attention both at home and abroad, being reproduced in various languages," and that it "represented, besides her own medical knowledge, much research at the British Museum" (*Life of A. K.*, vol. ii. p. 47).

I hope, shortly, to bring out a volume of Anna Kingsford's and Edward Maitland's Addresses and Essays on Vivisection, which will include much material of the greatest value for the anti-vivisection cause.—S. H. H.

the vitalised minority of persons, the spectacle thus afforded is as amazing as it is deplorable. That any human being, claiming to be civilised, should, through indifference or doubt, hesitate to condemn an organised system of torture, on whatever plea instituted, is in itself sufficiently surprising. But when all the aggravating circumstances are taken into the account—especially the innocence and helplessness of the victims—the prevalent attitude of the public mind becomes explicable only as the result of some moral epidemic.

From the ordinary point of view, the utilitarian and the moral, this question has already been amply discussed, and with these it is not now my purpose to deal. There is a third aspect of it, especially interesting to the student of psychological and occult science, and one which, for want of a more precise definition, may be described as the Spiritualistic. Persons to whom the chronicles of the modern vivisector's laboratory and the records of ancient and mediæval sorcery are alike familiar must doubtless have noted the family resemblance between the two, and will need only to be reminded that the practice whose ethics are now so prominently canvassed in medical conclaves, and on popular platforms, represents no new feature in the world's history, but is in every detail a resuscitation of the old and hideous cultus of the Black Art, whose ghost was deemed to be for ever laid.

The science of medicine, placed originally under the direct patronage of the Gods, whether Egyptian, Oriental, Grecian, or Teutonic, and subsequently under that of the Christian Church, was among all nations in the days of faith associated with the priestly office. The relation between soundness of soul and soundness of body was then held to be of the closest, and the health-giving man, the therapeut, was one who cured the body by means of knowledge, Divine alike in its source and in its method. In Egypt, where the order of the Theraputæ seems to have had its origin, healing was from the earliest times connected with religion, and there is good reason to believe that the practice of medicine was the exclusive and regularly exercised profession of the priesthood, the first hospital of which we have any record being within the consecrated precincts of the temple, and the sick being placed under the immediate care of its ministrants.

More than one deity was associated with medical and therapeutic science. According to Diodorus (lib. i.), the Egyptians held themselves indebted for their proficiency in these respects to Isis. Strabo speaks of the methodical treatment of disease in the Temple of Serapis, and Galen makes similar observations with regard to a temple at Memphis, called Hephæstium. As is well known, the name Pæan, the Healer, was one of the most ancient designations of Apollo in his capacity of Sun-god. This title, and the function it implies, are ascribed to him in the Orphic Hymns, in the Odes of Pindar, and in the writings of Hippocrates, Plato, and all the later poets and historians, both Greek and Latin. Ovid attributes to Apollo the declaration: "Medicine is my invention; throughout the world I am honoured as the Healer, and the power of the herbs is subject to me."

Æsculapius, reputed the son of Apollo, gave his name to medical science; and his temples, the principal of which were at Titana in Sicily, at Epidaurus in Peloponnesus, and at Pergamus in Asia Minor, were recognised schools of medicine, to whose hierophants belonged the double function of priest and physician. These medical temples were always built in localities noted for healthiness, and usually in the vicinity of mineral springs, that at Epidaurus, the most celebrated of them all, being situated on an eminence near the sea, its site having been determined doubtless rather by the beauty of the scenery and the purity of the air, than by the tradition that Epidaurus was the birthplace of Æsculapius himself.

The course of treatment adopted comprised hydropathy, shampooing, dieting, magnetism, fumigations, gymnastics, and herbal remedies, internally and externally administered, these remedies being in all cases accompanied with prayers, music, and songs called νόμοι. In the hospitals of Pergamus and Epidaurus the use of wine was forbidden, and fasting was frequently enjoined. It was also held indispensable that the professors of so divine an art as that of medicine should be persons of profound piety and learning, of sound moral and spiritual integrity, and therefore of blameless lives. It was, as Ennemoser observes in his *History of Magic*, deemed necessary that the aspirant after medical honours should be "a priest-physician. Through his own health, especially of the soul, he is truly capable, as soon as he himself is pure and learned, to help the sick. But first he must make whole the inner man, the soul, for without inward health no bodily cure can be radical. It is therefore absolutely necessary for a true physician to be a priest."

This was also the idea of the early Hebrew and Christian Churches, whose physicians always belonged to the sacred order.

Many of the primitive Christian religious communities were schools of medicine; and the visitation of the sick, not only in the priestly, but in the medical capacity was held to be a special function of the clergy. The custom still survives under a modified form in Catholic countries, where "religious" of both sexes are employed in hospitals as nurses and dressers, the higher duties of the calling having been wrested from them by the laity—often too justly designated the "profane."

Such, universally, was the early character of medical science, and such the position of its professors. "Priest" and "Healer" were religious titles, belonging of right only to initiates in Divinity. For the initiate only could practise the true magic, which, originally, was neither more nor less than the science of religion or the Mysteries, that Divine knowledge, won by reverent and loving study of Nature, which made the Magian free of her secrets and gave him his distinctive power.

Side by side with this true magic, sanctioned by the Gods, taught by the Church, hallowed by prayer, there grew up, like the poisonous weed in the cornfield, the unholy art of the black magician or sorcerer, whose endeavour was to rival, by the aid of sub-human or "infernal" means, the results obtained legitimately by the adept in white or celestial magic.

And as, on the one hand, in order to attain the grace and power necessary to perform Divine works or "miracles," the true Magian cultivated purity in act and thought, denying the appetites, and abounding in love and prayer; so, on the other hand, in order to achieve success in witchcraft, it was necessary to adopt all the opposite practices. The sorcerer was distinguished by obscene actions, malevolence, and renunciation of all human sentiments and hopes of Heaven. His only virtues—if virtues they can be called—were hardihood and perseverance. No deed was foul enough, no cruelty atrocious enough, to deter him. As the supremacy of the Magian was obtained at the price of self-sacrifice and unwearying love and labour for others, so the sorcerer, reversing the means to suit the opposite end, sacrificed others to himself, and cultivated a spirit of indiscriminate malignity. For the patient and reverent study by means of which the Magian sought to win the secrets of Nature the sorcerer substituted violence, and endeavoured to wrest from her by force the treasures she gives only to love. In order to attract and bind to his service the powers he invoked, he offered in secluded places living oblations of victims the most innocent he could procure, putting them to deaths of hideous torture in the belief that the results obtained would be favourable to his wishes in proportion to the inhumanity and monstrosity of the means employed. Thus, as Ennemoser observes, " the sorcerers inverted nature itself, abused the innocent animal world with horrible ingenuity, and trod every human feeling under foot. Endeavouring by force to obtain benefits from hell, they had recourse to the most terrible of infernal devices. For, where men know not God, or having known, have turned away from Him to wickedness, they are wont to address themselves in worship to the kingdom of hell, and to the powers of darkness."

Such, precisely, is the part enacted by the vivisector of to-day. He is, in fact, a practitioner of black magic, the characteristic cultus of which has been described by a well-known writer on occult subjects as that of vicarious death. " To sacrifice others to oneself, to kill others in order to get life,—this was the great principle of sorcery " (Eliphas Levi). The witches of Thessaly practised horrible cruelties ; some, like Canidia, of whom Horace speaks, buried infants alive, leaving their heads above ground, so that they died of hunger ; others cut them into pieces and mixed their flesh and blood with the juice of belladonna, black poppies, and herbs, in order to compose ointments deemed to have special properties. The well-known history of Gilles de Laval, Seigneur of Retz and Marshal of Brittany in the fifteenth century, may serve as an illustration of the atrocities perpetrated in secret by professors of sorcery. This man, distinguished for the military services he rendered to Charles VII., and occupying an honoured and brilliant position in the society of the day (as also do most of our modern sorcerers), was yet, like the latter, guilty of the most infamous practices conceivable. More than 200 children of tender years died in torture at the hands of the Marshal and his accomplices, who, on the faith of the doctrines of sorcery, believed that the universal agent of life could, by certain processes conducted under approved conditions, be instantaneously fixed and coagulated in the pellicule of healthy blood. This pellicule, immediately after transfusion, was collected and subjected to the action of diverse fermentations, and mingled with salt, sulphur, mercury, and other elements [1] (Eliphas Levi).

[1] These formulæ, prescribed by the ancient science of alchemy, have reference, of course, to truths of which the terms used are symbols only. But the sorcerer, not being an initiate, understood these terms in their ordinary sense, and acted accordingly.—A. K.

An almost exact parallel to the modern vivisector in motive, in method, and in character is presented by the portrait thus preserved to us of the mediæval devil-conjurer. In it we recognise the delusion, whose enunciation in medical language is so unhappily familiar to us, that by means of vicarious sacrifices, divinations in living bodies, and rites consisting of torture scientifically inflicted and prolonged, the secrets of life and of power over nature are obtainable. But the spiritual malady which rages in the soul of the man who can be guilty of the deeds of the vivisector, is in itself sufficient to render him incapable of acquiring the highest and best knowledge. Like the sorcerer, he finds it easier to propagate and multiply disease than to discover the secret of health. Seeking for the germs of life he invents only new methods of death, and pays with his soul the price of these poor gains. Like the sorcerer, he misunderstands alike the terms and the method of knowledge, and voluntarily sacrifices his humanity in order to acquire the eminence of a fiend. But perhaps the most significant of all points of resemblance between the sorcerer and the vivisector, as contrasted with the Magian, is in the distinctive and exclusive solicitude for the mere body manifested by the former. To secure advantages of a physical and material nature merely, to discover some effectual method of self-preservation in the flesh, to increase its pleasures, to assuage its self-induced diseases, to minister to its sensual comforts, no matter at what cost of vicarious pain and misery to innocent men and animals, these are the objects, *exclusively*, of the mere sorcerer,—of the mere vivisector. His aims are bounded by the earthly and the sensual; he neither cares nor seeks for any knowledge unconnected with these. But the aspiration of the Magian, the adept in true magic, is entirely towards the region of the Divine. He seeks primarily health for the soul, knowing that health for the body will follow; therefore he works through and by means of the soul, and his art is truly sympathetic, magnetic, and radical. He holds that the soul is the true person, that her interests are paramount, and that no knowledge of value to man can be bought by the vicarious tears and pain of any creature soever. He remembers above all things that man is the son of God, and if for a moment the interests of Knowledge and of Love should seem to be at variance, he will say with equal courage and wisdom: "I would rather that I and my beloved should suffer and die in the body, than that to buy relief or life for it our souls should be smitten with disease and death." For the Magian is priest and king as well as physician; but the sorcerer, whose miserable craft, divorced from religion, deals only with the lower nature, that is, with the powers of darkness, clings with passionate despair to the flesh, and, by the very character of his pursuits, makes himself incapable of real science. For, to be an adept in this, it is indispensable to be pure of heart, clear of conscience, and just in action. It is not enough that the aim be noble, it is necessary that the means should be noble likewise. A Divine intention presupposes a Divine method. As it is forbidden to man to enrich himself by theft, or to free himself by murder, so also is it forbidden him to acquire knowledge by unlawful means,—to fight even the battles of humanity with the weapons of hell. It is impossible to serve humanity by the sacrifice of that which alone constitutes humanity —justice and its eternal principles. Whenever the world has followed the axioms of the vivisector, whenever it has put sword and flame and rack to work in the interests of truth or of progress, it has but reaped a harvest of lies, and started an epidemic of madness and delusion. All the triumphs of civilisation have been gained by civilised methods: it is the Divine law that so it should be, and whoever affirms the contrary is either an imbecile or a hypocrite. The vivisector's plea that he sins in the interests of humanity is, therefore, the product of a mind incapable of reason, or wilfully concealing its true object with a lie. That, in the majority of cases, the latter explanation is the correct one is proved beyond doubt by the nature of the operations performed, and by not a few incautious admissions on the part of some of the school itself. To multiply pamphlets, "observations," and "scientific" discussions; to gain notoriety among followers of the cultus, to be distinguished as the inventor of such a "method" or the chronicler of such a series of experiments, and thereby to earn wealth and position, these constitute the ambitions of the average vivisector. And, if he go beyond these, if some vague hope of a "great discovery" delude and blind his moral nature as it did that of the miserable Seigneur de Retz, we must, in such case, relegate him to the category of madmen, who, for the poor gains of the body, are willing to assassinate the soul. Madness such as this was rife in those mediæval times which we are wont to speak of as the "dark ages," and the following examples, selected for the striking resemblance they present to the "scientific" crimes of the nineteenth century, may, with the instances already given, suffice as specimens of the abominations which the delusions of sorcery are able to suggest.

"The Taigheirm was an infernal magical sacrifice of cats, prevalent until the close of the sixteenth century, and of which the origin lies in the remotest times. The rites of the Taigheirm were indispensable to the worship or incantation of the subterranean or diabolic gods. The midnight hour, between Friday and Saturday, was the authentic time for these horrible practices; and the sacrifice was continued four whole days and nights. After the cats had been put into magico-sympathetic (sur-excited) condition by a variety of tortures, one of them was put alive upon a spit, and, amid terrific howlings, roasted before a slow fire. The moment that the howls of one agonised creature ceased in death, another was put on the spit—for a minute of interval must not take place if the operators would control hell—and this sacrifice was continued for four entire days and nights. When the Taigheirm was complete, the operators demanded of the demons the reward of their offering, which reward consisted of various things, such as riches, knowledge, fame, the gift of second sight, etc."—Horst's *Deuteroscopy* and Ennemoser's *History of Magic*.[1]

Let the following extracts from publications circulated among the vivisectors of to-day be compared with the foregoing, and the reader will himself be enabled to judge of the exactness of the parallel between the black art of the past and of the present.

"Dr Legg's experiments on cats at St Bartholomew's Hospital included a great variety of tortures. Among others, their stomachs were opened, while the cats were pinned alive on a table, their livers were pricked with needles, the stomachs were then sewn up, and the cats left in that condition until death ensued from prolapse of the bowels, some of the animals surviving the torture as long as twenty-six days."—*St Bartholomew Hospital Reports*.

"Burns were produced by sponging the chests and bellies of dogs with turpentine five or ten times in quick succession, setting fire to it each time; and scalds, by pouring over the dogs eight ounces of boiling water nine times in quick succession. All the

---

[1] Among the practices of Japanese sorcerers in the present century, the following is cited in Mr Pfoundes' book *Fu-so Mimi Bukuro*: "A dog is buried alive, the head only being left above ground, and food is then put almost within its reach, thus exposing it to the cruel fate of Tantalus. When in the greatest agony and near death, its head is chopped off and put in a box."—A. K.

dogs died, either in a few hours, or at the latest, after five days."
—*Edinburgh Medical Journal*, 1869.

"Delaroche and Berger baked hundreds of animals to death in ovens, the heat being gradually increased until death ensued. Claude Bernard invented a furnace for roasting or baking animals to death, the details and diagram of which apparatus are given in his *Lessons on Animal Heat*. Magendie has also shewn by numerous experiments that dogs perish at the end of about eighteen minutes in a furnace heated to 120° (centigrade), and at the end of twenty-four minutes in one heated to 90°; or in one at 80° at the end of thirty minutes."—Béclard's *Treatise on Physiology*, and Gavarret's *Animal Heat*.

"Professor Mantegazza has recently investigated the effects of pain on the respiratory organs. The best methods for the production of pain he finds to consist in planting nails, sharp and numerous, through the feet of an animal in such a manner as to render the creature almost motionless, because in every movement it would feel its torment more acutely. To produce still more intense pain, it was found useful to employ injuries followed by inflammation. An ingenious machine, constructed expressly for the purpose, enabled the professor to grip any part of an animal with pincers with iron teeth, and to crush or tear or lacerate the victim so as to produce pain in every possible way. One little guinea-pig far advanced in pregnancy endured such frightful tortures that it fell into convulsions, and no observations could be made on it. In a second series of experiments, twenty-eight animals were sacrificed, some of them taken from nursing their young, exposed to torture for an hour or two, then allowed to rest an hour, and then replaced on the machine to be crushed or torn for periods varying from two to six hours. Tables are appended by the professor in which the cases of 'great pain' are distinguished from those of 'excessive pain,' the victims of the last being 'larded with nails in every part of the body.' All these experiments were performed with much patience and delight."
—*Of the Action of Pain, etc.*, by Professor Mantegazza, of Milan, 1880.

The two following experiments are cited from Baron Ernst de Weber's *Torture-chamber of Science*, and also from the *Courrier de Lyon*, 8th June 1880:—

"The body of a pregnant bitch at the point of delivery was cut open to observe whether in her dying and mutilated condition she would not attempt to caress and lick her little ones."

"The forehead of a dog was pierced in two places with a large gimlet, and a red-hot iron introduced through the wounds. He was then thrown into a river, to observe whether in that state he would be able to swim."

Professor Goltz, of Strasburg, writes: "A very lively young dog which had learnt to shake hands with both fore-paws had the left side of the brain extracted through two holes on the 1st December 1875. This operation caused lameness in the right paw. On being asked for the left paw the dog immediately laid it in my hand. I now demand the right, but the creature only looks at me sorrowfully, for he cannot move it. On my continuing to press for it, the dog crosses the left paw over, and offers it to me on the right side, as if to make amends for not being able to give the right. On the 13th January 1876 a second portion of the brain was destroyed; on February 15th, a third; and on March 6th, a fourth, this last operation causing death."

M. Brachet writes: "I inspired a dog with a great aversion for me, tormenting him and inflicting on him some pain or other as often as I saw him. When this feeling was carried to its height, so that the animal became furious every time he saw and heard me, I put out his eyes. I could then appear before him without his manifesting any aversion; but if I spoke, his barkings and furious movements proved the indignation which animated him. I then destroyed the drums of his ears, and disorganised the internal ear as much as I could. When an intense inflammation had rendered him completely deaf, I filled up his ears with wax. He could now no longer hear or see. This series of operations was afterwards performed on another dog."

The prize for physiology was, by the French Institute, awarded to the perpetrator of the above "experiments."

In Cyon's *Methodik*, a "Handbook for Vivisectors," we read the following: "The true vivisector should approach a difficult experiment with joyous eagerness and delight. He who, shrinking from the dissection of a living creature, approaches experimentation as a disagreeable necessity may, indeed, repeat various vivisections, but can never become an *artist* in vivisection. The chief delight of the vivisector is that experienced when from an ugly-looking incision, filled with bloody humours and injured tissues, he draws out the delicate nerve-fibre, and by means of irritants revives its apparently extinct sensation."

"VIOLATIONISM," OR SORCERY IN SCIENCE

Have we in this nineteenth century indeed expunged from among us the foul and hideous practice of sorcery, or rather, if comparison be fairly made between the witchcraft of the "dark ages" and the "science" of the present, does it not appear that the latter, alike for number of professors, ingenuity of cruelty, effrontery and folly, bears away the palm? No need in this "year of grace" to seek in the depths of remote forests, or in the recesses of mountain caves and ruined castles, the midnight haunts of the sorcerer. All day he and his assistants are at their work unmolested in the underground laboratories of all the medical schools throughout the length and breadth of Europe. Underground indeed they needs must work, for the nature of their labours is such that, were they carried on elsewhere, the peace of the surrounding neighbourhood would be endangered. For when from time to time a door swings open below the gloomy stone staircase leading down into the darkness there may be heard a burst of shrieks and moans, such as those which arose from the subterranean vaults of the mediæval sorcerer. There still, as of old, the Wizard is at his work, the votary of "Satan" is pursuing his researches at the price of the torture of the innocent, and of the loss of his own humanity.

But between the positions of sorcery in the past and in the present is one notable and all-important difference. In the past it was held a damnable offence to practise the devil's craft; and once proved guilty, the sorcerer, no matter what his worldly rank or public services, could not hope to escape from death by fire. But now the professors of the Black Art hold their Sabbat in public, and their enunciations and the recitals of their hideous "experiments" are reported in the journals of the day. They are decorated by princes, fêted by great ladies, and honoured with the special protection of State legislation. It is held superstition to believe that in former ages wizards were enabled by the practice of secret abominations and cruelties to wrest knowledge from nature, but now the self-same crimes are openly and universally perpetrated, and men everywhere trust their efficacy.

And in the last invention of this horrible cultus of Death and Suffering the modern sorcerer shews us his "devils casting out devils," and urges us to look to the parasites of contagion—foul germs of disease—as the regenerators of the future. Thus, if the sorcerer be permitted to have his way, the malignant spirits of fever, sickness, and corruption will be let loose and multiplied upon earth, and as in Egypt of old, every living creature, from the cattle in the field to the firstborn son of the king, will be smitten with plague and death. By his evil art he will keep alive from generation to generation the multitudinous broods of foul living, of vice, and uncleanness, none of them being suffered to fail for need of culture, ingrafting them afresh day by day and year by year in the bodies of new victims; paralysing the efforts of the hygienist, and rendering vain the work of the true Magian, the Healer, and the teacher of pure life.

. . . .

The report in *Light* (pp. 57–58) says that an interesting discussion followed this address. "The question of the suffering in the animal creation, both that inflicted by animals upon each other, apparently in part by way of amusement and torture, and also that caused by the 'blind, unreasoning forces of nature,' was referred to by more than one of the speakers, and it was suggested that an argument might be based thereon by vivisectors in partial defence of their position.

"In her replies to the various remarks, Dr Kingsford took the ground that there must be, somewhere or somewhen, compensation or justification for all that we call evil, and for all suffering. In thinking this out, she was brought face to face with a succession of problems which had led her to the belief that evil and suffering are the result of a degradation, of a departure from the Divine; that, in fact, the ferocity and the cunning of a man-eating tiger, for instance, were the ferocity and cunning of a human spirit, who in a previous incarnation had indulged in those passions.[1] The lecturer also ably and eloquently defended

---

[1] In a note in *The Virgin of the World*, Anna Kingsford says: "In the Divine Pymander, it is clearly set forth that if a human soul continue evil 'it shall neither taste of immortality nor be partaker of the good, but being drawn back it returneth into creeping things; and this is the condemnation of an evil soul.' Yet, Trismegistus hastens immediately to explain and qualify this statement by adding that such a calamity cannot befall any truly human soul—that is, a soul possessing the divine mind, however fallen from grace—for so long as the soul retains this living fire it is the soul of a man, and man 'is not to be compared to any brute beast upon the earth, but to them that are above in heaven, that are called Gods.' But there is a condition so low and lost that at length the divine flame is quenched, and the soul is left dark and Godless, a human soul no longer. 'And such a soul, O Son,' says Hermes, 'hath no mind; *wherefore neither must such an one be called Man.*' Therefore, while it is true that 'no other body is capable of a human soul, neither is it lawful for a man's soul to fall into the body of an unreasonable living thing,' so also is it true that a soul, bereft of its Divine Particle which alone made it human, is human no longer, and, following the universal law of affinity, straightway gravitates to its proper level, sinking to its similars, and drawn to its analogues. Nevertheless, when its purgation

her comparison between the 'sorcerer' and the mere 'scientist,' pointing out that the aim and ambition of both was the acquisition of knowledge for the benefit of the external, the material, the sensuous man only. Whereas the knowledge sought for by the true priest, the Magian, the real healer, is that which is for the good of the inner, the Divine man, and such knowledge need not to be obtained through the infliction of pain and suffering on others."

is accomplished, such a soul may 'come to itself and say, I will arise and go unto my Father.'

"There are some Rabbis indeed who have thought such an occult significance to lie hid in the parable of the prodigal; swine being accounted universally a figure of lust and sordid desire. The Hermetic doctrine, thus interpreted, is identical with that of the Kabalah on the same point, and also with the teaching of Apollonius of Tyana" (pp. 12–13; see also *The Perfect Way*, iii. 21, etc.; *Clothed With the Sun*, pt. i. Nos. xii., xxi.).

THE SYSTEMATISATION AND APPLICATION OF PSYCHIC TRUTH[1]

It is proposed in this paper to offer some remarks which may serve as a contribution towards the utilisation of modern spiritualistic experiences, by showing the relation borne by them to the two great needs of human life—a System of Thought and a Rule of Life. It is proposed to indicate in what manner the facts and phenomena with which the last thirty years have made us personally acquainted, and which are usually, but erroneously, regarded as constituting Spiritualism, may be made to serve as a basis for the construction of a Philosophy which shall be at once a Science, a Morality, and a Religion. Now, a Rule of Life is obviously impossible without a System of Thought; and, equally obviously, a System of Thought includes and involves a Rule of Life. For as it is the function of a Rule of Life to enable us by its observance to make of our existence the most and best that we have it in us to be, so it is the function of a System of Thought to supply such explanation of the nature of existence as will make such result possible. Only when we have learnt how and of what we are constituted, can we at all hope to realise the potentialities of our nature. And knowledge, if it be real, involves being and doing.

Of no Knowledge which the world holds are these axioms so predicable as of that which demonstrates the spiritual nature of Life and in particular of Man, its highest manifestation on this planet. For this is a Knowledge, not of accidents, but of essentials; and it bears relation, therefore, to our conduct in all departments of activity. A Spiritualist in this sense of the term—the only true sense—is not merely one who accepts a certain hypothesis, as affording the most probably correct solution of certain special isolated phenomena, and in respect of all other subjects and departments of Knowledge is left free and unaffected by his hypothesis; but he is one who, knowing the

[1] Lecture given by Anna Kingsford, on the 22nd May 1882, to the British National Association of Spiritualists, and published in *Light*, 3rd June 1882, pp. 264-267 (see p. 8, *ante*).—S. H. H.

THE SYSTEMATISATION OF PSYCHIC TRUTH

nature of Self, and consequently of the Kosmos, occupies a comprehensive and unassailable standpoint, from which all human sciences and practices must be judged. Having such conception of the high purpose and use of the knowledge he holds, the true Spiritualist is emphatically a Philosopher, a religious man; being, after the Latin root of the word, of a piece throughout, bound together, a whole, harmonious, consistent personality, at one in himself, and therefore at one with all existence; and like the Sun in the solar system, ranging round himself as centre all that appertains to his own system. And precisely in so far as a man fails thus to systematise knowledge and truth, he fails in being a true Spiritualist. For this noble and dignified name belongs of right only to the man who understands that Spirit is the Real, and Matter the Appearance, and that while the second exists in Time, the first *is* eternally. Just as he is a Materialist who, unable to penetrate beyond the Phenomenal, contents himself with the study of causes and effects which can never be other or more than secondary, and therefore inexplicable in themselves, so he is a Spiritualist whose thought transcending the Material reaches and finds room for God, and relegates all other secondary knowledges dealing with Matter to the domination and direction of spiritual knowledge. But the title of Spiritualist is no fitting designation for the mere habitué of the séance-room, who, having satisfied himself of the genuine character of the various manifestations of which he has been witness for a more or less lengthened period, and added to his collection of acquired facts the certainty that there are such things as ghosts, and that the current hypothesis of modern schoolmen is inadequate to classify the phenomena of talking tables, trance-mediums, and "materialisations," regards such knowledge as technical merely, and differing from other specific knowledges only as geology, for instance, may differ from botany or from physiology. Such, nevertheless, is the meaning which, unhappily, has become attached to the name of "Spiritualist," and with which meaning both scoffers and believers appear, for the moment, content. Hence it is that even the adherents of the movement frequently exhibit an inclination to treat of Spiritualism as of a special branch of study, comparable to any other at present recognised by the world; accidental, or, at best, complementary in its character, and strictly limited in its range and its subject-matter. Thus, Spiritualists are exhorted, not by outsiders, but by those professing to be of their own number, to confine themselves to their ghosts, and to leave all such questions as vivisection, vaccination, vegetarianism, marriage laws, women's rights, and other matters, characterised as "extraneous," to "experts" who can discuss them from a standpoint of knowledge appropriate to each. I wish to say, very strongly and earnestly indeed, that I entirely dissociate myself from any such conception of Spiritualism or of Psychology as is implied by such advice as this, recently set forth in an organ professedly dedicated to the interests of spiritual teaching; and that, for my part, I distinctly refuse to accept such a view of the "whole duty of Spiritualists." Were Spiritualists really no more in their science than the geographer, anatomist, or the astronomer in his, then the gamut of the whole subject would be soon enough learnt and exhausted. The utmost the science could do for a man would be to convince him that in some undefined way, existence is prolonged beyond the period of life in the body,—whether for eternity or for a limited time only, however, no ghost would be able to tell him,—for inaccuracies, opinions, and prejudices abound with the "dead" as with the living,—and that man may become possessed by study and cultivation of certain powers, vulgarly regarded as miraculous. With such a poor and mean view of the scope and destiny of Spiritualism, however, no earnest mind will for a moment rest content. Spiritualism really represents, not a new branch of experimental science, but a *new platform* from which to view and to examine all other sciences. It is quite reasonable to require the geologist to stick to his minerals and not to meddle with the department of the botanist or of the architect, for all these are representatives of physical sciences, and all alike occupied with analysis or synthesis on the material plane. But the Spiritualist is on this plane no longer; he has passed through and above it, and for him the whole face of human history and human motive is changed. As one viewing a landscape from mountain altitudes sees far otherwise and far more widely and comprehensively than one surveying the same tract of country from the level ground, so the Spiritualist from the philosophical standpoint to which he has attained must needs conceive of Life in its entirety a very different idea from that entertained by the mere physicist. It is therefore in the last degree unreasonable to exhort a man whose whole being is "lightened and lifted higher" to refrain from concerning himself with subjects which, if he be a true Spiritualist, he must find it impossible to expunge from the range of his illuminated vision.

Why, indeed, it may be asked, is he a Spiritualist at all, if it be not to obtain the right and the power to judge the comparative values of things, and to discern what is truly worth the labour and the devotion of the human mind ? Why should the traveller give himself the trouble and fatigue of ascending mountain-passes, and of encountering the difficulties and inconveniences of the journey, if not for the vantage-ground he will thus attain, from whence to survey the surrounding valleys and reaches which from lower ground would be beyond his horizon ? Precisely then as we reasonably claim that the psychic man should rule and control the physical man, in other words, that the spirit or mind should direct and legislate for the body, so it is reasonable that we should claim the right of the Spiritualist to direct and order the courses of mere physical research. For, since the knowledge which constitutes the Spiritualist is, as already stated, a knowledge not of accidentals capable of isolation and separate treatment, but of fundamentals and universals, it follows that no subject possessing a practical application can rightly be regarded as outlying the cognition of the Spiritualist, or belonging to a department into which his entrance would be an intrusion. Indeed, the very nature of his science is such that he cannot, if he would, refrain from bringing it to bear upon all the relations and aims of Life. The possession of a universal truth imposes an obligation of a royal nature, and makes its initiate at once an overseer and an arbiter. It is to set forth in succinct terms the nature both of this truth and of the obligations it imposes that this paper has been prepared. In other words, it is desired to supply, as clearly and concisely as may be, a "schema" on which to construct a System of Thought and Rule of Life based on the facts collectively known as Spiritualistic. It will be seen, in the unfoldment of this schema, why the writer regards Spiritualism not merely as a new knowledge, but as a new Criterion of knowledges ; the Rod in the hand of the Angel, wherewith to measure and gauge the value and soundness of all human toils and structures.

Utility is a word which conveys two different meanings to two different classes of men. To the Materialist, the highest conception of utility bears, necessarily, relation only to material objects and to secondary conditions ; the Spiritualist, equally necessarily, connects such idea with spiritual ends and applies it to primary causes. Now it is a fundamental truth, recognised by Spiritualists from prehistoric times, that the apparent interests of the physical or *sense*-man are often in diametrical opposition to those of the psychic or *spirit*-man. Necessarily, therefore, the Spiritualist will apply to the examination of human sciences and customs a test altogether different in kind from any that can be framed by the Materialist. And the nature of the test thus applied is, in itself, a criterion of the standpoint occupied by the critic. It is impossible for the Spiritualist, occupying the loftier platform, to lower his point of view to that of the Materialist, and to compare notes with him upon the respective values to physical humanity of certain practices, the nature of which renders them wholly unlawful and unacceptable to the *spirit*-man. Such practices may indeed have their " experts," just as may robbery, brigandage, fraud, false coining, assassination, seduction, sorcery, poisoning, and the like, but they are, in their primary out-birth, Satanic, and with their secondary utilities the Spiritualist can have no concern. All the evil sciences just named have secondary utilities which bring bread to the hungry, relief and pleasure to the miserable, wealth to the poor, vengeance to the outcast. No Materialist can, by any possibility, be a just judge in such issues. His noblest standard of right is formulated in the words: "*The greatest good of the greatest number.*" And by "greatest good" he always means either physical or intellectual good applicable to temporary ends. Both these belong to the *sense*- and *time*-man, the first kind to the body merely, the second to the mundane mind. But the measure of right formulated by the Spiritualist is expressed in the Italian axiom: " Farvi migliori; questo ha da essere lo scopo della vostra vita." And to do the best, in disregard of, or even in the teeth of, all the interests of secondary utilities will, in the long run, prove the only true and real service. It is bound to prove so, by the very constitution of the Kosmos, and by the Nature Itself of God. "*He*," says Christ, "*who will save his life shall lose it, and he who shall lose his life for my sake, the same shall find it.*" Here we have a succinct statement of the paradox ever confronting Man; the conflict between the apparent interests of the illusory, and the real interests of the permanent. To see only the apparent and illusory is to be in the position of a man following a marsh-light circling hither and thither without goal or definite intent. At one time, one course may appear to him safest and best, at another, conclusions may seem to him to lie in a quite different direction. Yet, all the time, he may be, according to his knowledge, honest and earnest. Of all classes of mankind, the Spiritualist alone is able to systematise knowledge, and to trace for his feet a rule of life. He may be likened rather to the Wise Men in sacred story who, guided not by an earth-light, but by a heavenly Star, followed its steadfast leading to the abode of the Christ.

These prefatory remarks will suffice to suggest what manner of counsel it is I desire to press on my hearers. I would earnestly recommend to them to be constructive and consecutive; not to be content with having acquired, here and there, a few isolated and scattered facts of a more or less occult nature, but, having once assured themselves that these facts are trustworthy, and essential in their nature, and therefore part of the Divine order, to seek out for themselves their sequences, and not to rest until by reason, study, comparison, and thought, they have arrived at a comprehension of the three Unities of the Kosmic Drama—(action, time and place)—and, consequently, at the formulation of a System. The lines upon which such systematisation should be attempted are indicated by the terms of the basic doctrine of Spinozic and Swedenborgian philosophy—borrowed from the old Hermetic teaching,—that everything existing in Time and Space has a subsisting correspondence of eternal and infinite nature. That therefore nothing material and ephemeral is without a substantial Idea, preceding, interpreting, and surviving it, and that no *merely* physical or transient entity is conceivably possible in a *real* Kosmos. Hence, to know the character, value, and place of any object or action, it must be transferred in thought to the spiritual or noumenal plane, and judged, not according to that which it *seems*, but that which it *is*. We have thus to deal with a world within a world; and the study of the Spiritualist should be so to regulate his conduct as to be in immediate relation, not with the outer and phenomenal, but with the inner and true. Forms interpret and reveal Ideas, and only Ideas are related to the Spirit of Man. Therefore, while for the Materialist forms may represent the absolute, and he may model his behaviour to suit the secondary utilities related to these; for the Spiritualist, Ideas alone are absolute, and the course of his action must be related wholly to them; realising thus the Pauline axiom: "Our conversation IS in Heaven."

It is not then permitted to the Spiritualist, as it is to the Materialist, to be without a system. It is not permitted to the Spiritualist to be in any sense a specialist, or to "run with the hare and hold with the hounds." It is not permitted to him, for instance, to believe in the undying quality of the human soul, and in the righteousness of God, and yet to have vague and dubious notions about the definition of Divine Justice, the ordering of the Kosmos, and man's moral duties, differing in nowise from the notions of his materialistic neighbours. It is not permitted him to hold that God is just, as he conceives justice, to himself and to his kind, and unjust, as he conceives injustice, to other creatures not yet man. If he find himself content to let such things rest in doubt, to conceive it possible that some of God's ways may be evil, and that man therefore may be Godlike in pursuing and abetting injustice; that it is right certain knowledges or apparent benefits should be suffered to increase by means which he would not willingly see employed by a divine personage; if he is able to quiet his conscience with the reflection that it is enough for him to have ascertained the immortal nature of himself and of his friends, and to believe that reform, in virtue of that knowledge, is no business of his,—then such a man, whatever else he may be, is certainly no Spiritualist. To be a Spiritualist is to hold, first, the basic Principle of Existence to be pure Being, the "Substance" of Spinoza, the Brahm of the Hindûs. Secondly, it is to hold that this Principle is Good, and that consequently that which is called evil is not essential but accidental, not real but illusory. Thirdly, that as the constant and unvarying aim of the Spiritualist is to struggle back through Matter, through Accident and Illusion into Spirit, this aim compels him to conflict with the opposing wave which meets him in one continual outflow from Spirit to Matter, from Good to Evil. These fundamental knowledges will lead him to catalogue as good all actions and thoughts (which are internal actions) the basic principle of which is pure, and applicable to true essentials and to the human Ego stripped of its externals. Such actions only are calculated to hasten the return to Spirit, and the coming of the "Kingdom of God." On the other hand, he will be led to catalogue as evil all actions and thoughts the basic principle of which is impure, and by its character inapplicable to essential and heavenly states. Such actions are calculated to perpetuate Maya, or Illusion.

Thus judgment is, for him, at once pronounced on such practices as Vivisection, Flesh-eating, Inoculation of Disease, and every class of gross, luxurious, and impure living. Cleanliness and Justice are the two factors of the Godly Life. The direction of the good or Spiritual impulse is towards the *Volatilisation of the Fixed*, that of the evil or Material impulse is towards the *Fixation of the Volatile*. Thus are posited the two hypothetical modes of force—Centripetal and Centrifugal; of which the first has the Sun, or God, for its point of attraction; and the second has the orbit of Saturn. (He that hath ears to hear, let him hear.) Thus, also, is posited an illustration of the two modes of personality belonging respectively to heavenly and to mundane men;—the Divine, and the Satanic. The Divine personality, (a better word is needed, for the signification to be conveyed is that of being, not of seeming,) consists in the perfection of the interior or essential consciousness; the Satanic personality is the strengthening and fixation of the exterior or material consciousness. The first of these personalities is by nature Eternal, the second, Temporary. An action is good in proportion as it leads inwards towards the development and manifestation of the Son of God, or spiritual Ego in man; an action is bad in proportion as it leads outwards towards the development and creation of the devil in man. The good action has therefore a tendency towards a focus, towards permanence and light; the bad action has a tendency towards void, dissipation, and darkness.

As on the physical plane the law of progress has been from the impersonal to the personal, and from unorganised to elaborate, so the order of spiritual evolution is from the void and chaotic to the formulated; from vague good—which we call evil—to distinct and perfected good. Spiritual or heavenly personality becomes stronger with every good thought and action, as it is weakened by every evil action. In proportion as an action is distinctly human, that is, distinctly of the spiritual character, insomuch it tends away from rudiments towards perfection. In ethics, the "survival of the fittest" means the "survival of the best," because the tide of tendency in spiritual evolution is towards Righteousness, and this in invariable, and in the main, consistent inflow, ever centralising and personalising. I say "in the main," because, from point to point, there is a back tide, a retrogressive stream towards Negation and Loss, and this it is which represents Evil. The inflowing stream represents Order and the Obedient Will; the reflux, Disorder and Sin. To flow inwards and upwards is to tend towards Spirit and Essential Being; to flow outwards is to tend towards Matter and Illusive Existence. Thus man, in the first act of sin, depicted in Genesis, is not to be regarded as choosing a positive (evil) in preference to a positive (good), for there cannot be two positives:

—but as preferring Substance under its aspect of Maya (Matter) to Substance under its essential aspect. For, as all is God, evil in the popular sense is an absurdity. Evil is then simply circumferential or remote good, and as such its characteristic is impersonality, or absence of organisation. It is unreasonable, blind, insane; and philosophers in all ages have identified wickedness with madness and disease.

One of the fundamental principles of the spiritual Evolutionist necessarily is that Man is the outcome and therefore the purposeful result of Genesis; and therefore, that *there is in the whole Kosmos nothing but Man*, either in the making or the marring. The making is represented by the in- and up-flowing main-stream; the marring, by the back-flow. This proposition is a self-evident corollary of physical evolution, keeping pace with the latter, and underlying its manifold transmigrations and vicissitudes. Like a distinct silver clue unwinding and revealing itself in ever-increasing strength and brightness, the gradual evolution of Personality leads the soul onward through a labyrinth filled with monstrous and ghastly shapes, chaotic gloom and vistas of bewildering mirage,—onward by means of suffering,—which is but another name for experience,—until she reaches the daylight of Humanity. The recognition of this law of spiritual progress entails upon Man the obligation of considering all creatures as his rudimentary selves, with unblossomed potentialities of humanity lying latent in their inner being. Such knowledge gives him new views of his relations towards them, and of their claims on his regard and brother-love. Moreover, the recognition of the higher spiritual evolution flowing side by side with that of the physical, and being itself the propelling cause of the latter, must influence all considerations of mere physical relations and benefits in a manner impossible to the conception of the Materialist. Such recognition must inevitably tend to lower the value of secondary or physical knowledges relating to the exterior existence, while bringing into prominence spiritual knowledges, and to enhance the value of these last so greatly as to render them all-sufficient to human needs.

And such, assuredly, they will prove in the end, because essentials involve derivatives, and the greater includes the less. All knowledges on whatever plane are attainable by Divine methods. The only condition for such attainment is that the Divine method should first be diligently sought and mastered. The Kingdom must first be established, then shall come the power and the glory of it. As it is written: "*Seek ye first the Kingdom of God and His justice, and all these things shall be added unto you.*"

For Love is the universal Solvent; and Love's method is in all its unfoldings, consistent with its object and intent.

Such as these, faintly and inadequately traced, are the lines of the Royal Way by which the Spiritualist passes from Earth to Heaven. Co-worker with God, he heads the stream rolling ever inward towards the "Sea of crystal mingled with Fire." With this inward-flowing stream, the new tendencies of modern scientific methods constitute in many respects a directly colliding element, a retrograde movement in diametrical violation of the advancing and spiritualising impetus of the Kosmic force. Thus it becomes the immediate business of the Spiritualist, against whose breast this backward wave first breaks, to warn those behind him of the coming danger, and so prevent them from being carried away by it, or, at least, to take care that it does not implicate him, and sweep him out of his steadfast course.

The name of "Spiritualist" should therefore before and above all things signify "Anti-Materialist," if Materialism be understood to imply a method of thinking which, attributing to accident and to fortuitous arrangement of merely phenomenal and automatic atoms the genesis of Life, is necessarily incapable of assigning to the religious sense any real value or meaning. Regarding Man as sprung from and returning to Negation, at once the product and the heir of the Void, the Materialist must necessarily view all moral sentiment as merely utilitarian in character, and therefore he naturally enough expects such sentiment to yield with a good grace to arguments based on temporary expediency. He is a "dead man," in the Apostolic sense of the phrase, because for him all Nature is but a corpse in whose arteries no Divine pulse-beats thrill.

But the Spiritualist is, as I have attempted to shew, essentially a *living* man. Seeing in Matter but the vehicle and manifestation of Spirit, and in the primary Divine Being the source and centre of all the manifold expressions of existence, it is his prerogative —nay, his obligation—to test all beliefs and customs, social and secular, by reference to essential principles, and to translate every action and rule of conduct to the spiritual plane. Hence he becomes a universalist, and everything his immediate and proper concern. It is impossible for him to have "opinions"; he alone of all men has a right to certainty, and is bound by virtue of his system to decide with certainty the issues of all controversies. And the test by which he thus decides is Principle.

Now of Principle in its true and primary sense the Materialist can obviously know nothing. Living in time, and for secondary utilities, his only guide and standard of action must needs be Expediency, and in regard to Expediency there may, of course, be many and widely differing opinions. For Expediency is kaleidoscopic, and every new shake may give a new pattern, but Principle is one and indefeasible. Expediency is of this world, and all its relations are ephemeral; Principle is prophetic and absolute. It is the universal "Thus saith the Lord" of the old Hebrew "man of God." On the lines of such conception of the comprehensive character and application of Spiritualism was based the Theocracy of Moses. No subject was too secular or too remote to be brought within the reach of the "Lord's" immediate instruction. The "Lord," of course, stands for the Divine in Man; and though such records as we possess of the ancient Hebrew legislation do not, obviously, represent the original Mosaic system, yet the formula still remains as evidence of the universal and all-including application of the Divine Word. But the Material tendencies of the day in which we now live have changed all this. We are told not to mix up secular science and mundane interests with things sacred and spiritual; and to keep distinct places in our minds for week-day opinions on one hand, and for Sunday certainties on the other. Thus it naturally comes about that with the old universalism we have lost the old unanimity. Spiritual knowledges have ceased to interpret for us intellectual problems, and we allow men occupying a totally different plane from ours to be our umpires and autocrats in matters which ought to be decided by the Divine Oracle.

Now of Principles,—which though spoken of in the plural number are, it must be remembered, as integrally one as the spectrum rays are one light,—the first and foremost, and that which constitutes the stability of the Universe, is JUSTICE. And forasmuch as of Justice the root is Wisdom,—for none can be just unless he first understand,—Wisdom is one with Love, and God is Love. So is Justice one with God, and is God. And man is God-like, precisely according to the degree in which he loves and practises Justice. Therefore, whether in the domain of science, morals, politics or sociology, the nearer we get to Principles the nearer we get to Essentials, and, consequently, to the Divine. And, on the contrary, the more we incline to Expediency the lower the ground we take, and the less likely it is to prove firm under our feet. Building upon Principle, we build upon the Rock, and neither storm nor flood shall prevail against our house. But Expediency is as the shifting sand, which the ever-varying tides of Time and Custom suck and undermine, and drive hither and thither, and on which no wise man sets his habitation. Principles alone are real and eternal, and a man may know his grade in respect of Divine things by the degree of his preference for Principles above persons, things, and circumstantial accidents. These essential truths, faithfully followed even in narrow ways and dark places, will at length bring a man safe to the footstep of the Throne. Whereas he may gain a whole world of expediencies, and yet lose his own soul.

To become a Spiritualist simply in order to converse with ghosts implies a very poor kind of advantage. But to be a changed man, to take new and illuminated views of Life, to look with the "larger other eyes" of the Gods on Life's problems, duties, and ordeals, to hear a Voice behind us saying—"This is the way, walk ye in it ; and go not aside to the right hand nor to the left,"—to have exchanged doubt for knowledge, hesitation for decision, strife for peace, expediency for principle ;—this is to have systematised and applied Psychic Knowledge, and to have become a true Spiritualist.

And because the percipience and experience necessary to make such theoretical and practical application of his system come to the Spiritualist only by means of thought, study, and heart-searching, it is, I submit, of the strongest urgency that those burning questions with which the lay and scientific worlds are now ablaze should be examined and argued by Spiritualists from the platform which is peculiarly and exclusively theirs. Of what use to be "the salt of the earth" unless we give forth our savour ? Of what good to be the candle of the world if we submit to be put under a bushel instead of giving light to all that are in the house ? And of what avail will Spiritualism prove to ourselves or to the age unless it make the world purer, sweeter, more just and more Godly ?

Wherefore I at least, as one Spiritualist among many, will be instant in season and out of season, with voice, pen, and desire, to hasten the advent of the Kingdom of God, and the age of the " new heavens and new earth in which Justice dwelleth."

. . . .

In the following number of *Light* (p. 270) the Editor, " M.A.

(Oxon.),'' referring to this magnificent appeal by Anna Kingsford to Spiritualists to take their stand against vivisection and other inhuman practices, said: " I hope it is not a sign of unregenerate cruelty of heart, or something worse, that I cannot without a strong sense of the extreme inappropriateness of such language hear ' practices ' that it is not difficult to identify with experiments which, at least in a vast majority of cases, have a beneficent and useful end in view, compared to ' robbery, brigandage, fraud, false coining, assassination, seduction,'—there is more, but this will, perhaps, do. I do not know how high that platform may be whence this higher criticism finds its way to us ; but the vituperative language, when it does get down to us, is ' of the earth earthly,' with a very human tendency to mere scolding, etc.''

To this Anna Kingsford replied as follows : [1]—

" To the Editor of ' Light.'

" Sir,—Permit me to tell ' M.A. (Oxon.) ' that he mistakes in supposing *Light* to be the journal alluded to in my paper recently read before the B.N.A.S.

" He mistakes also in imputing to me vituperative language. If he will read my paper he will find that the comparison made between vivisection and the crimes he cites is made only to confute the plea that vivisection is useful, by demonstrating that the worst malpractices have likewise their utilities, ' beneficent ' to those who engage in them. As for this charge of ' scolding,' it is, alas, a word which has been applied in various shapes to all earnest reformers. That which to the man who agrees with the reformer is noble and uncompromising indignation, becomes to his opponent vituperation and abuse. So was it with our Lord, whose anger against the false teachers of His day led Him to heap on them such epithets as ' children of the devil,' ' liars,' ' vipers,' ' hypocrites,' and the like ; and, not satisfied with words, to proceed even to the use of physical force, driving out of the Temple with scourges the purveyors of sacrifice dues, and violently upsetting their seats and their goods. Noble vituperation was this !—the violence of a great heart ; the rage of a true revolutionist. All real reformers have done the like, for without enthusiasm no cause is won. Therefore, if such be ' scolding,' I too will ' scold ' with Jesus, with Paul, and with all who in the

[1] *Light*, 1882, p. 289.

earlier ages withstood evil in high places and carried their protest unabashed into the presence of princes and magistrates. Or, coming to later times, I too will 'scold' with such men as Joseph Garibaldi and William Lloyd Garrison in the service of a cause which is equally that of freedom and humanity, and than which I know of none more righteous.—I am, Sir, yours,

"ANNA KINGSFORD, M.D.

" 11 CHAPEL STREET, PARK LANE, W.,
    " 10th June 1882."

ESSAYS AND LETTERS

THE CONSTITUTION OF MAN[1]

THERE is, generally, so much misapprehension as to the *modus operandi* of the soul's progress, and, consequently, so much warm contention between two sections of Spiritualists on the question, that I am moved, contrary to my custom, to write for public reading a brief recapitulation of the ancient and true doctrine on this important subject. This doctrine I first received, not from any extraneous or obsessing "spirit" or "control," but from the divine and interior Spirit,[2] concerning whom something will be said in this paper. Subsequently, I discovered that the revelation thus made to me was not new, but was contained and formulated in the Hebrew Kabalah, in Hindû philosophy, and not less clearly in the mysteries of Egypt and of Greece. Man is a twofold being, comprising in himself a celestial and terrestrial personality. The inner person—the celestial—is dual, and this duality is composed of Soul and Spirit. The outer personality is also dual, and is terrestrial and evanescent. Its component parts are Body and astral Shade. In the Kabalah the three first of these constituent elements of man are named, from within outwards—Jechidah (or Chokhmah), Neschamah, and Ruach—the *anima bruta*—of which last, the outer portion, or shade, is termed Nephesch.

The four constituent elements of human nature reappear under many symbols throughout all sacred scriptures. In Genesis, they are first allegorised as Four Rivers, whose names, to an initiate, are sufficiently significative, and in Ezekiel and the Apocalypse they are figured as the Four Faces of the Living

---

[1] Article written by Anna Kingsford, and published in *Light*, 1882, p. 127. It was the outcome of a debate on Re-Incarnation, which had been got up by the Spiritualists, and in which she and Edward Maitland had taken part. (See *Light*, 1882, pp. 103-105 and 111-113; and *Life of A. K.*, vol. ii. pp. 49-50.)—S. H. H.

[2] See Preface, pp. 3 and 7, *ante*.

Creature ; of which faces that of the eagle represents the Spirit (Jechidah) ; that of the angel or woman, the soul (Neschamah) ; that of the lion, the astral or mundane spirit (Ruach and Nephesch) ; and that of the ox, the body.

In the Egyptian and Greek Mysteries, these four characters were the Personæ or Masks of the Sacred Drama represented in the cavern temples where the rites of initiation were performed. This sacred drama, it need hardly be said, formed the pattern and prototype of the mystery play of early Christian times, which, so late as the seventeenth century, was still continued in Catholic countries. These sacred plays, whether "pagan" or Christian, were represented in pantomime, that is, by gesture only, and they took place at the festival of the Sun's Birth, whether as Mithras, Bacchus, or Christ. They are still continued in our day, vulgarised as Christmas pantomime, but preserving, nevertheless, with marvellous exactness, every detail and every accessory of their sacred original.

Their four characters are familiar to us as Harlequin (the Spirit) ; Columbine (the soul)—these two representing the celestial duality ; Clown (the mundane spirit) ; and Pantaloon (the body)—these two last representing the outer or terrestrial dualism.

Harlequin, like his ancient prototype, is always masked, and supposed therefore to be invisible and nameless. He wears a glittering dress of many hues, typical of the Heavenly Bow, or seven Divine Spirits and their several Tinctures. He carries a *bâton* or rod, the well-known Rod of sacred Mythos, the symbol of Divine will and power. With this rod he accomplishes any transformation he desires. By striking objects with it he converts their appearances, and removes or displaces them. The wills of persons with whom he comes in contact are amenable to its control, and at the desire of its owner they acquire new perceptions or lose their senses. Harlequin's spouse, Columba—the dove or human soul—is his inseparable companion. She is beautiful, aerial, and obedient to all his directions, but, unless with the rod of her spouse, she can herself work no wonders. He is the shining One, the all-pervading, the all-powerful ; she is his faithful and lovely counterpart, Divine only in being his.

The astral or mundane spirit is represented by the Clown, whose characteristics are, unlike those of the celestial pair, of a wholly material order. He is adroit, cunning, worldly-wise, and humorous. There is nothing spiritual or Divine about him ; he has no power of transmutation, and all his machinations are adapted to low or gross objects. In short, he is the faithful presentation of the earthly mind. His proper colour is red, as is that of the lion, whose part he fills. This personage controls and directs his inseparable companion, the Pantaloon or body, who is always appropriately represented as a decrepit, foolish, weak creature, with no power or foresight of any kind. The body is, in fact, a mere slave, the sport of the earthly mind, or intellect, and an object of contempt to the two celestial characters. The body, under the mask of Pantaloon, is shewn to be but a feeble entity, supported by a stick, infirm, despicable, and continually buffeted. He is the fool of the play, as the Clown, or mundane spirit, is its jester or trickster.

The pantomime, of which these four characters are the personæ, opens with some mystic prologue or allegory, of which Harlequin and Columbine, the Divine Spirit and soul, are hero and heroine. Usually, they are presented as prince and princess, whose faithful and mutual love excites the rage and jealousy of the infernal deities, or "bad fairies." Their ordeals—which are none other than the Trials of the Mysteries—form the action of the drama, and their final union and eternal happiness, which are consummated in the "transformation scene," set forth the supreme object of all religious discipline and doctrine, the Marriage of the Spirit and the Bride, which constitutes the final act of the mystery-play known as the Apocalypse of the Diviner.

Of course the whole action of the pantomime is, from beginning to end, astronomical, and depicts the course of the sun through the twelve zodiacal houses. Hence it was, and still is, represented only at Christmas-tide, when the solar course begins. Twelve is the solar or male number, as thirteen is that of the lunar or female cycle. In the "Tarot" of Egyptian origin the sacred number was the latter, as being that of Isis, the goddess of the Egyptian Mysteries. This "Tarot" survives among us in the familiar game of playing-cards, as M. Vaillant and Eliphas Levi have clearly demonstrated.[1] The "Tarot" is composed of four suits, two of which are red and two black. The red represents the Celestial dualism, the two black the Terrestrial. Of these the Diamond, or stone of the Apocalypse, is the Spirit,

[1] The original "Tarot," according to some authorities, was composed of fifty-six leaves or "cards," the additional four being the cavaliers or horsemen. These horsemen represent the Nephesch, intermediate between the "King" and the "Knave," which element is usually included in the sign of the "King."—A. K.

or Holy Ghost, of the human Microcosm, the essentially pure and shining One. The heart is the soul, the seat of aspiration, love, and desire, the feminine element of the human kingdom. The sword (or spade-head) is the earthly mind, incisive and relentless, like its Kabalistic symbol, the lion. Hard as iron and sharp as a blade, the human intellect analyses, delves, penetrates, and attacks. Lastly, the Club is the body, a figure which, like that of the ox, conveys an idea of physical attributes related to the earth only.

Of these four suits there are three "Court" cards, which, in their proper order, are Queen, King, and Knave. Modern usage has inverted the sequence of the first two. The Queen is Columba, the soul; the King is the Astral Lion, or mind; the Knave is the body. But of all these, the chief, at once Alpha and Omega of the whole series, is the Ace or Unit, the primordial Spirit. This Unit takes all "tricks," and controls alike Queen, King, and Knave. He is the First of numbers and the Last, whose will is paramount and whose supremacy is absolute.

The series of each suit is twelve, corresponding to the Twelve Zodiacal Signs and the Labours of Hercules, the solar hero. In mystic language these twelve numbers represent the Twelve Degrees of Regeneration, of which the crown and completion is the Thirteenth Act of the Soul, that is, the Marriage of the Son of God. Hence thirteen, represented by the Ace, is the perfect number, and the marriage supper is therefore celebrated by thirteen personages, viz. Christ and the Twelve Apostles.

The Unit or Ace is, in Greek, spoken of as the Nous. This word, as Bryant demonstrates, is identical in meaning with the name Noe or Noah, the architect of the Ark or Microcosm. Noe's three sons, Sem, Japheth, and Cham, are the representatives respectively of soul, mind, and body. Of these three the most blessed and the worthiest is Sem, the soul, the lord of the East and the progenitor of the chosen race. Japheth, as the mind, is appropriately the father of the European nations, pre-eminent in intellectual civilisation and inventive art; while to Cham, or the body, is assigned the parentage of the lowest races of humanity. "Cursed is Chanaan," says the oracle, "a servant of servants shall he be." Here we have a repetition of the anathema pronounced on the old Adam, whom, in fact, Cham symbolises. The body, mere perishable dust and earth, is the servant alike of Spirit, soul, and mind. His father and his brothers dominate, control, and subjugate him. The story of the crime by which Cham, or the body, brought this curse upon himself is another rendering of the Edenic allegory, and refers to the materialisation of the holy mysteries, or, in other words, to the sin of idolatry. The secrets of the Divine Spirit, Noah or Nous, are profaned by a materialising and earthly-minded priesthood, and thereby rendered gross and ridiculous,—subjects of criticism and mockery. Spiritual truths are wrested to physical meanings, and that which belongs only to the celestial is idolatrously represented as pertaining to the body and to things phenomenal and terrestrial. To this Cham or Chanaan, the Club, or emblem of earthly generation, was in Egyptian symbolism appropriated.

Now, of the two dualisms of the human kingdom, one is transmigratory, the other is not. The body and astral element of man are renewed at every successive birth, and at every death they pass away, the body into dust, the astral mind, according to its deserts, to the "Summer Land," or to the shades of gloomy Tartarus. The "Summer Land" is known to mystics as the Lower Eden. There after death abides the Ruach, or mundane spirit of the good man, retaining all the memories and affections of his one life. Thence he comes to the circle of his still incarnate friends, gives evidence of his identity, embraces and caresses his dear ones, and relates to them the beauties and blessedness of the astral light in which his home is made, and out of which he has created gardens, palaces, flowing streams, and moving forms. This mundane spirit is a personal entity, and, in fact, is the external Ego of the man, the "I" and "Me" of the character whose family name he still bears.

But the essential germ of the Microcosm, the Divine dual particle of soul and Spirit, very rarely returns to earth in such fashion. It is only on solemn occasions and for special purposes, so rare as to be events, that such return is permitted. This celestial pair constitute the transmigratory fire, whose light composes the Hindû "Karma." This celestial duad it is that represents the Spiritual personality of the man, a state or being as opposed to an entity, the sum-total of what the man is, as opposed to what he seems. This essence, immortal and progressive in its nature, because at once Divine and human, passes on and reanimates new forms. The name of this interior Ego is not that of the Ruach, who responds to the "Christian" or family appellatives of earth; its name is known only to God. It passes on from form to form, and from avatar to avatar, until it attains Nirvâna. The circumstances and conditions of a re-birth represent, therefore, as the *Bhagavad-Gita* tells us, the Karma of the preceding existence.

Nirvâna is the annihilation of the exterior personality, and the apotheosis of the interior personality. Thus it is true that existence is an evil, nay, it is the supreme evil to escape from which is the continual aim and aspiration of the saint, and the extinction of which is found only and finally in the bosom of God.

When, therefore, a man says, as the non-Re-Incarnationists are fond of saying, " I do not like the idea of a succession of births," or " I do not wish to return," or " I will not return voluntarily," it is the external self that speaks, the Ego of the Ruach. Let him be content, he will *not* return. He will go to the " Summer Land," to the Elysian Fields—the Lower Eden.[1]

But his interior, his Divine particle, if ever it is to attain beatitude, will obey the Divine Will, and continue the course of its existences, whether few or many, until the final Marriage of Spirit and Soul. This act consummated, it becomes thereby purified from existence, and enters upon the condition of absolute being.

In this brief exposition, I have purposely avoided all direct references to holy writings, whether Hebrew, Hindû, or other, in order not to encumber my statement with citations.

ANNA KINGSFORD, M.D.

P.S.—Since the above exposition was read by me in my private circle, a friend has sent me a copy of the *Theosophist* for October

---

[1] Edward Maitland, replying to one who denounced the doctrine of Re-Incarnation as " repulsive," says : " The first question to be decided is whether it is *true* ; and that, if true, it can seem repulsive only through being misunderstood, since, as a part of the Divine order, it must of necessity partake of the perfection of that order. As understood by me, it is both beautiful and true in the highest degree, and necessary to account for the facts both of existence in general and of my own experience in particular. And though Swedenborg failed to attain to the knowledge of it during his earth-life, it is really involved in his favourite doctrine of Correspondence. For it is according to the law of Correspondence that the soul, like the body, should use up many exterior coverings in the course of its pilgrimage, ' putting off bodies like raiment, and as a vesture folding them up, itself remaining while they perish.' And it is but reasonable to suppose that it would continue to do so until sufficiently perfected through experiences of the body to be capable of looking beyond the body and appreciating higher conditions of being " (*Light*, 1882, p. 155).—S. H. H.

1881, which I had not previously seen. It contains, under the heading "Fragments of Occult Truth," the substance of the teaching of which I am myself the recipient from a wholly independent and interior source. In the spelling of the Biblical names, I follow the Catholic version of the Scriptures.

A. K.

CONCERNING RE-INCARNATION[1]

CONVINCED as I am that the right understanding of the doctrine variously known as Transmigration, Metempsychosis, Re-Birth, and Re-Incarnation is the very basis and ground-work of all spiritual philosophy, I beg to supplement, as briefly as is consistent with the subject, the short paper I have already contributed to *Light*.[2]

Dr Wyld seems to find something absurd in the idea that man is a complex being. Yet this belief—I ought rather to say, this knowledge—is as ancient as the Mysteries themselves. Not to cite Eastern philosophy, which is full of illustrations and apologues to the point, let me refer him to the Homer of his schooldays, where, in the Odyssey XI., he will find this passage, part of the recital given by Odysseus of his descent into Hades, or the under-world, and of his discourse with the ghosts of the dead: "There also I descried the mighty Heracles — *his phantom*, I say, *for as for himself* (namely, his true soul), he is enjoying himself at the table of the Immortal Gods. . . . And presently he—the phantom—recognised me, and on beholding me, spoke lamenting." [3]

Let it be observed that in this passage the true soul of the Hero is represented as not being in the land of shadows at all. The "phantom" with which Odysseus converses, and whose discourse is reported in the lines immediately following, is but the outer Ego or exterior personality of Heracles. These phantoms, the poem tells us, love the earth, and are fain to return to it, and to manifest themselves to their living friends, the method by which they seek to materialise being precisely that recounted by Lady Hester Stanhope in her *Travels*, by Madame Blavatsky (*Isis Unveiled*), by Eliphas Levi, and, in short, familiar to all students of magic and the occult.

---

[1] Letter written by Anna Kingsford, and published in *Light*, 1882, p. 168. (See *Life of A. K.*, vol. ii. pp. 57-58).—S. H. H.

[2] The reference is to her Article on "The Constitution of Man." (See p. 184, *ante*.)

[3] See letter written by "A. K. and E. M." in *Light*, 1883, p. 475.

It is surely strange that, at this time of day, a Theosophist of Dr Wyld's understanding should need to be reminded of the witness of Paul and of all Christian writers who have had spiritual experiences, to the strife which continually rages in every human kingdom between the outer and the inner will,—between the old and the new Adam,—between the interior and the exterior self. The fleshly or earthly self is that Ruach, or Mind, which constitutes the mundane individual; the heavenly or spiritual self is that essential soul "whose name is known only to God." It is in order that this essential and inner man may grow, expand, and finally become all in all, that progress and re-births are necessary. In its initiatory stages a tiny spark—to speak in metaphorical language—it grows and gathers strength by successive purifications, and at length returns to the bosom of God, a glorious and "consuming fire."[1]

The conflict between the two selves is a matter of personal experience; therefore of this doctrine, which is the very fundamental doctrine of all religion, whether Oriental or "Christian," the witness is, chiefly, in oneself. Speaking personally, I am profoundly sensible of this conflict, and am daily reminded that I am a compound personality.

With regard to the dissolution of this compound personality at death, it appears to me no more surprising or difficult of belief than the phenomenon of skin or shell-casting common among certain animals; which phenomenon, being by the ancients regarded as a type of Re-Incarnation, caused these creatures to be venerated as religious symbols.

All that has been in its nature eternal and noumenal in any transient incarnation, all that has contributed to build up the true and interior spirit of the man, is absolute and permanent, and will survive all ephemeral constituents of past personalities. To appropriate a phrase from Mr Noel's work on Immortality: The conception of true personality consists in the "absolute unity and self-identity of the spirit in its innermost self, wherein all its phenomenal lives are known, understood, resumed, felt to be indeed one." Thus the spirit, the true Ego of the man, on entering Nirvâna, resumes in itself all that is lasting and noumenal of its past manifold existences. For only that which by nature is Divine can survive eternally. Thus there are two kinds of

[1] This word "consuming" is used to denote the property of this immortal spirit, which is to convert impurity into purity, and to lick up and appropriate, as does a flame, the fuel supplied to it, transmuting into spirit that which was matter.—A. K.

memory, or consciousness;—that of the exterior, and that of the interior, Ego. The work of the saint is to centralise his consciousness, and to prevent it from becoming dissipated. As says the *Bhagavad-Gita*: "The Yogee who, labouring with all his might, is purified of his offences, and after many births made perfect, at length goeth to the supreme abode."

It is no concern of mine to defend such holy personages as Krishna, Buddha, Pythagoras, or Apollonius of Tyana against Dr Wyld's criticisms. The reputation of these men and the wisdom of their many great disciples need no championship. But I will add a word in respect to Swedenborg, whom Dr Wyld is accustomed to cite as an authority on his side.

In Swedenborg's voluminous writings we have unfolded a series of pictures reaching from Hell to Heaven. At times the seer was carried aloft to the highest; at others, he groped amid the manifold illusions of the astral and magnetic. Hence many incongruities, obscurities, and contradictions are apparent in his works, and are admitted even by his warmest admirers. Vistas of wondrous and far-reaching spiritual interpretation are opened before the reader's mind, to be suddenly crossed and obliterated by grotesque images which alike bewilder and repel. Swedenborg's exterior manner of life was not, in effect, such as to assure the constant level of his interior perspicacity. Although abstemious and temperate, he did not, on principle, or invariably, refrain from the eating of flesh, and thus exposed himself to dangers of which no one who has not had similar experience can gauge either the nature or the extent. For many reasons I exercise considerable caution when studying his writings, as I do also when studying those of a modern seer who somewhat resembles him, Thomas Lake Harris. I doubt much whether, if Swedenborg were now living among us and were one of our circle, Dr Wyld would be inclined to attach more importance to his experiences than he does to those of certain of his friends with whom he frequently converses. "But no man is a prophet in his own country, or in his father's house." There is one at least, whom I do not name, for it would be unbecoming to do so, who is no stranger to heavenly visions and voices, and who, to my knowledge, has freely communicated her experiences to Dr Wyld. In these visions there has never been anything either incongruous or inconsistent, and the life of the recipient is such as to preclude danger of the kind to which Swedenborg was exposed.[1] And in all

[1] Anna Kingsford was a vegetarian.—S. H. H.

these visions the doctrine to which Dr Wyld so emphatically objects is ever strenuously and forcibly insisted upon as the very basis of human philosophy, and of a right understanding of Divine justice, and of the progress and evolution of the soul. The person of whom I speak could not, without renouncing religion itself, and turning traitor alike to her whole past experience and to the Divine light whose guidance she follows, and from whose interior illumination all her knowledge is derived, reject as illusory teaching so attested and so conveyed; teaching, moreover, which alone is capable of interpreting satisfactorily to human reason and intelligence a natural system of apparent incongruities and injustices, utterly inexplicable on any other hypothesis.

Will Dr Wyld, or any other champion of the "one-life" theory, explain, for instance, the problem of brute suffering and misery? Will he tell us why a good and wise God should have, by the exercise of His arbitrary power and will, produced such creatures as the snake, the wolf, or the tiger? Will he account on the theory of the "one life," which in the case of the lower animals involves no eternal evolution in the "spheres," for the heart-rending suffering of the dumb, intelligent, and loving dogs, horses, and other domestic creatures whom man has adopted as his friends and servants, and whose moral qualities often furnish him with an example or a rebuke? I will tell him frankly, that rather than adore a God who could deliberately have made these poor souls and endowed them with feeling and intelligence for no other end than to become the victims of the sportsman, the vivisector, or the cobra, or to wear out their lives in suffering and toil, with no prospect of the education and progress which toil and suffering bring to human spirits,—rather, I say, than adore or reverence such a Being as this, I would turn Agnostic or Atheist to-morrow, and cry "forward" to the disciples of a Monteil or of a Bradlaugh.

There is evidence in Dr Wyld's present article, and in a former paper published by him in these pages, that he has never rightly comprehended the doctrine he impugns, else he could not possibly maintain it to be "entirely antagonistic to the central doctrine of Christian Theosophy—*i.e.* that the Logos is in every man, and that there is no salvation save by it," with more to the same purpose.

If I were to ask Dr Wyld whether he considers, for instance, that this mystic Logos is as developed and as potent in the breast of a Billingsgate costermonger or of a Dahomey savage as in that of a St Theresa or of a Swedenborg, he would answer: "No, but it will be developed after death, in other spheres, and under spiritual conditions more favourable to its growth." I should then ask him how a soul which needs objective and material conditions for its evolution and training is to obtain them in a state from which they are excluded; and why a soul which, admittedly, has *not* detached itself from matter and from material attractions should be enabled miraculously to defy the universal law of Affinity, and gravitate, after physical dissolution, to ethereal and spiritual spheres, rather than return, as we should naturally expect it to do, to renew its progress and education in God's great preparatory school, the material world?

In my view, and in that of those who think with me, life has a much vaster and lengthier scope than is afforded by the span of one human existence; and not until the soul has rid herself of all affinity for matter, and of all mundane affectional cares and desires, will she, by the operation of a natural and immutable law, be free to mount to the "higher spheres" and to enter on a course of evolution unconnected with material limitations. Until that time arrives, however, the same causes which have hitherto operated to detain the soul within the earth's atmosphere will, undoubtedly, continue to operate. In such a view, at once scientific, reasonable, and just, I can see nothing either "repulsive" or "ludicrous." But I am fain to confess that both these attributes appear to me to be exemplified by the description I have heard given by Dr Wyld of the spiritual sphere upon which he supposes all souls to definitely enter after their one earth-life. He said that there, the man whose supremest earthly joy had been in his pot of ale at the tavern, would still continue the same delights in a spiritual existence; as doubtless also would the sportsman, the prize-fighter, or, shall I add, the vivisector? It did not appear to him a necessary truth that as the "spiritual sphere" represents rather a *state* than a *place*, no soul whose condition is incongruous and dissimilar with it can enter upon it. For Dr Wyld's idea of "Brahma's bosom" is not that of a state of rest between one incarnation and another, but of a new progressive world into which the infant of a day old enters on definitely and with as perfect certainty of having done with earthly limitations as the veteran of a hundred years of struggle and experience.

Clearly, then, in the view of the "one-life" school, the education of objective Incarnation, and the lessons of the body, are not necessary to the soul, since myriads of souls, undergoing physical dissolution at the very moment of birth, pass into the world of spiritual conditions and escape them.

Blessed, thrice blessed indeed, then, are still-born babes, and cruel and accursed is the hand of the physician who seeks to retain the departing soul within its earthly tenement! "How far better for my infant," ought to be the cry of the mother, "that he should escape the bitter pains and experiences of earth and be brought up and trained by the angels!" For, according to "Tien-Sien-Tie"—one of the recently declared champions of non-Re-Incarnation [1]—this earth is the platform only for the acquirement of *identity*; and this object is as amply attained by an existence of a day or of a week as by one of a century.

As a last word, I would record my belief, expressed with all possible love and sympathy for those whose views differ from my own, that too much of the personal *likes* and *aversions* of the exterior Ego have been brought to bear on this question. On every side one hears the cry, "I can't bear the idea of coming back to earth!" "This world is a beggarly place!" "The very notion of a re-birth is repulsive to me!" "I have had enough of the world!" Alas, all these cries are but signs of impatience and self-will, the voice of the unregenerate soul. It would be better to hear it said humbly and in self-abnegation: "Thy will, my God, be done! Though the way be long, and the path such as I would not, let it but bring me at last to Thee, and I am more than content. For I know that Thine order is more beautiful, and that Thy method is love; therefore, I pray that not my will, but Thine may be all in all!"

ANNA KINGSFORD, M.D.

[1] See *Light*, 1882, pp. 103–105.

THE DOCTRINE OF "SHELLS"[1]

To the Editor of "Light."

"Sir,—As this is a question of extreme importance, practically no less than philosophically, and we have been largely referred to in the discussion of it in your columns, and our teaching impugned, we shall be much obliged if you will allow us to supplement "C. C. M.'s" able exposition of the Theosophical doctrine concerning it by some remarks tending to elucidate it yet more fully.

For the attainment of a sound conclusion upon any subject it is indispensable that there be, first, sound premisses, and, secondly, sound reasoning from these premisses. For, however excellent in itself may be the superstructure constituted by the latter, it can have no stability unless the former also be secure. It is the second only of these conditions which has been fulfilled by the Hon. Roden Noel. He has reasoned correctly from his premisses, but those premisses are in themselves defective. Hence, notwithstanding the knowledge and skill displayed in his superstructure, it lacks that first condition of stability, a firm foundation.

The consequences of this characteristic of Mr Noel's treatment of the subject are, even to his own position, disastrous in the extreme. Not only does he deprive of their only possible explanation some of the principal and most incontestable facts of spiritual cognition, but, even while seeking to uphold the current orthodox presentments of the doctrines of the Trinity, the Logos, and Creation, he, in denying the possibility of differentiation of the Ego, and ignoring the differentiation of Substance, makes the Trinity, the Logos, and the Universe one and all alike impossible!

This assumption—so fatal—of the indivisibility of the Ego has its rise in a misconception of the nature of the Substance and the constitution of the entity concerned. Mr Noel not only treats as simple that which is complex, but, in likening the

[1] Letter written by Anna Kingsford and Edward Maitland, and published in *Light*, 1883, p. 63. (See *Life of A. K.*, vol. ii. pp. 107-109).—S. H. H.

astral envelope, or "Shell," to a material fabric, such as a coat, and arguing that the former is, when separated from its central Ego, as devoid of consciousness as the latter, he compares things which differ so essentially as to have between them no point of similitude, and which are, therefore, incapable of comparison, namely, living, conscient Substance with lifeless, manufactured stuff.

The following account of the nature and constitution of the individual system will render the Theosophical position clearly intelligible. Taking it for granted that those of your readers who are sufficiently interested in the question to follow this discussion have already made themselves familiar with *The Perfect Way*, we shall refrain from repeating what we have there said respecting the fourfoldness of the constitution of Existence, and come at once to the question of the nature and mode of distribution of Consciousness.

Remembering that Spirit *is* Consciousness, and that, therefore, all differentiations of Spirit—the material, the astral, and the psychic—are modes of Consciousness, originally proceeding from and indefeasibly permeated by Spirit, it becomes obvious that the consciousness of the Ego of any individual system consists in the sum-total of the consciousnesses of all its individual particles, and, though single, is the resultant of the innumerable minute individual personalities which, bound harmoniously together, compose the system.

The consciousness of the Ego thus resulting depends, necessarily, both in quantity and quality, upon the character and condition of the constituent elements of its system. Consciousness, therefore, is not so much a Thing as a Condition, as the following illustration will shew. Let us imagine an incandescent globe, consisting of several concentric spheres or zones, each zone of course containing all those which are nearer to the centre than itself. Of this fiery ball the radiant point, or heart, occupies and constitutes the innermost and central zone, and each successive zone constitutes a circumferential *halo* more or less intense according to its proximity to, or remoteness from, the radiant point. But each such zone is secondary and derived only, and is not in itself a source of luminous radiation.

This illustration applies alike to Macrocosm and to Microcosm. In the human kingdom the interior zone, which immediately contains the radiant point, the Divine Spirit, and is Nucleus to its Nucleolus, is the Soul, Psyche. And by this one indivisible effulgence the successive zones are illuminated in unbroken continuity, but the source of this effulgence is not in them. As his radiant point is the Divine spark, or spiritual Ego, so this effulgence is Consciousness. And inasmuch as Spirit is Consciousness, and Consciousness is manifold, and all things are modes and manifestations of it, the Ego, though One, comprehends in its Unity many personalities. Were it not so, there could be no Universe, no Man, but only one point of Light, spreading no rays—a thing against reason and altogether impossible, since it is the very nature of light to be radiant, that is, to emit itself.

Similarly, in the human system Consciousness emits Consciousness, and transmits it first to the astral, and last to the material man; first, that is, to the *Anima bruta*, which, after death, constitutes the *Phantom, Ruach*, or "Shell"; and, last, to the physical body. But the more concentrated the Consciousness, the brighter and more effulgent the central spark. And every part of man is conscious in its own mode and degree, and capable of independent expression. Thus in the phenomenal manifestations of *Somnambulism*, either the *Anima bruta* and the physical body exhibit consciousness, while that of the soul is suspended; or the soul exhibits consciousness, while that of the spheres exterior to it is suspended. And the part which remains conscious (a thing dependent on the characters and desires of the person or persons concerned in the manifestation) is capable of reflection, of thought, of memory, even of intelligent invention, according to its kind and its endowments. For in being diffusive, Consciousness is also divisible.

Now, if from our supposed incandescent globe we take away the central radiant spark, the whole globe does not immediately become dark, but the effulgence lingers in each zone according to its position in regard to the centre, the outermost first becoming dark. So is it at the dissolution of the man. From his outermost and lowest sphere, the physical body, the consciousness speedily departs. In the shade, Nephesch, which is an emanation from the dead body, as the "Astral" is from the living,—Mr Noel seems to confound the shade with the Ruach—consciousness lingers a brief while. In the *Ruach* (*Anima bruta*, astral soul, or *Shell*) consciousness lasts long, it may be for many centuries, according to the strength of the lower will of the individual, manifesting the distinctive characteristics of his outer personality. In the soul, the immediate receptacle of the Divine Spirit, the consciousness is everlasting as the soul herself. And while the *Ruach* remains below in the astral sphere, the soul, *Psyche*, obeying the same universal law of gravitation, detaches herself and mounts to the higher atmosphere suited to her, there to undergo purification prior to her further evolution; unless, indeed, she be wholly gross and devoid of aspiration, in which case she remains " bound " in her astral envelope as in a prison.

For being an agglomeration of all the essences of the myriad consciousnesses which compose the human system, the soul is as the apex of a flame—its upper, purer, and intenser part—having for fuel the body, and for the lower part the astral sphere. And from these it is separable as is a flame from its fuel, or as one part of a flame from another part, yet leaving an energetic flame behind it, and it is capable of transference to other affinities as a flame is transferable from one mass of combustible material to another.

Meanwhile the *Ruach*, or astral Shell, on its detachment from the soul, continues to operate in the same manner as before such separation, just as does Mr Noel's hypothetical old coat after he has ceased to wear it. For to everything belongs its proper behaviour. The coat holds its parts and its warp and woof together; and maintains its colour, shape, consistency, and all other of its characteristics, after he has parted with it. It was a coat when he wore it. It is a coat still.

And so with a man's astral Ego. In his lifetime its proper function was to reason and think *electrically* (as distinguished from psychically). It is not a coat; it is Substance having life. And when the soul puts it off, it continues to be what it was; for it is of thought-nature, and it keeps its nature as does the coat. And just as it would be a miracle were the coat, on being discarded, to change its nature and become something else than a coat—say, non-material; so it would be a miracle were the astral phantom, when the soul separates from it, suddenly to change its nature and become something else—say, non-substantial, and devoid of the characteristics it hitherto possessed. Matter remains matter, and psychic substance remains psychic substance. Mr Noel would make differentiation in the substantial world impossible, a procedure of which the consequences have already been indicated.

This, as we have remarked, is not only a philosophical but a practical question, and we now come to the latter aspect of it. The phantoms of the dead resemble mirrors having double surfaces. On one side they reflect the earth-sphere and its picture of the past; on the other they receive influxes from those higher spheres which have received their higher Egos—these consisting, as already described, of the most sublimated essences of the lower. The interval, however, between the two is better described as of condition than of place or time; for these belong to the physical and mundane, and have no existence for the freed soul. This is because there is no Far or Near in the Divine.

The *Ruach*, however, has hopes which are not without justification. It does not all die. The soul, on attaining Nirvâna, gathers up all that it has left within the astral of holy memories and worthy experiences. To this end the *Ruach* rises in the astral sphere by the gradual decay and loss of its more material affinities, until these have so disintegrated and perished that its substance is thereby lightened and purified. But continued commerce and intercourse with earth add, as it were, fresh fuel to its earthly affinities, keeping these alive, and so hinders its recall to its spiritual Ego. And thus, therefore, the spiritual Ego itself is detained from perfect absorption into the Divine.

The *Ruach* survives only insomuch as it is worthy of such recall. The astral sphere which it inhabits is also its place of purgation. And "Saturn," who, as Time, is the "devourer of his own children," even those who being born only of Time have in them no Divine, enduring element, devours the dross, and suffers only that which is ethereal to escape.

This "death" of the *Ruach* is gradual and natural. It is a process of disintegration and elimination extending over periods greater or less according to the character of the individual. Those which have belonged to evil persons, having strong wills and disposed earthwards, persist longest and manifest most frequently and vividly, because they rise not, but being destined to extinction are not withdrawn from immediate contact with the earth. These are all dross; there is in them no redeemable or redemptive element. The *Ruach* of the righteous, on the other hand, complains if his evolution be disturbed. "Why callest thou me?" he may be represented as saying. "Disturb me not. The memories of my earth-life are chains about my neck. The desire of the past detains me. Suffer me to rise towards my rest, and hinder me not with evocations. But let thy love go after me and encompass me. Rise thou with me through sphere after sphere."

Thus even though, as often happens, the *Ruach* of a righteous man remains near one who, being also righteous, has loved him, it is still after the true soul of his dead that the love of the living friend goes, and not after his lower personality represented in the *Ruach*. And it is the strength and divinity of *this* love which helps the purgation of the astral soul, being to it an indication of the way it ought to go, "a light shining upon the upward path" which leads from the astral to the celestial and everlasting.

A knowledge of the physical is an indispensable aid to the comprehension of the metaphysical. The chemist is well aware that a great number of substances which to ordinary observation appear indubitably simple, both in their nature and in their operation, are in reality complex and divisible. Thus water, once universally regarded as an element, is now known by all to be a complex substance composed of two elements united in invariable proportion, and easily divisible into its factors. The same occurs with a number of chemical bodies which, though behaving as simple in many combinations, yet are divisible by analysis into several elementary substances. To all ordinary perception these bodies appear simple entities, since they exhibit affinities as such, but when the right test is applied, they dissolve and separate into their distinct constituents.

Similarly with the human body. The material of the brain is constituted of countless cells and connecting fibres, and each cell has its own consciousness according to its kind and degree. Nevertheless the resultant of all these concordant functions is one Perception and one Consciousness. There is also a Consciousness of the nerves, another of the blood, and another of the tissues. There is a consciousness of the eye, another of the ear, and another of the touch. And so with every bodily organ. And all these work continuously in the body, each according to its kind and its order, yet the intellect of the man knows nothing of it. And if one of these living organs be interrogated, it answers after its own kind.

If, then, man comprises in his own physical body so many diverse parts which he can neither direct nor discern, why should it appear strange that his ethereal Self should be similarly multiple? The *Anima bruta* is as an organ of the Spiritual Man, and though it be a part of him, its acts, its functions, and its consciousness are not identical with those of the *Anima Divina*. Consciousness *is* divisible, and diffusible, in man as in God, in the planet as in the universe. And One Law is throughout all, for "He who worketh is One."

THE WRITERS OF "THE PERFECT WAY."

January 1883.

EXTRANEOUS SPIRITS AND OBSESSION[1]

PRAY allow me to vindicate the position ascribed by you to the Theosophists—but which has also been that of all genuine seekers after *Divine* communication since the beginning until now—from the reproach of selfishness in declining the control of extraneous spirits. The motive is neither a selfish one, nor is it the fear of affording access to low or bad spirits, but the positive knowledge that it is not only dangerous and injurious to oneself to weaken the bond between oneself and one's own animating, indwelling spirit by suffering another spirit, whether high or low, to enter in and take possession, but it is injurious to the obsessing spirit itself. To use the faculty of holding converse with visitors, whether from the world of men or the world of spirits, is one thing; but to abdicate the ownership of one's house, and suffer another to occupy it, the owner being meanwhile altogether unconscious of that other's character and proceedings, is another thing, and one that is as unwise and perilous in the case of a spiritual as of a material visitor. It is not by seeking outwards that a man can attain the interior unfoldment which alone can advance him spiritually, or qualify him to help others. Only by climbing the ladder within oneself can one reach the kingdom within, which alone is divine. And to seek to climb by the ladder of others is both to fail oneself, and to keep those others back by strengthening the bonds which bind them to earth. No doubt some of those who speak in trance are really uttering that which they know of their own spirit, even though they may suppose it to be an extraneous one. But in this case the speaker is conscious, and understands that which is imparted. The true spirit of a man never controls his client, nor, if it can help it, steps aside to allow another to enter. It is a common mistake to suppose that all sudden and vivid suggestions of ideas or other intimations come from without. A spirit does not cease to be a spirit by becoming incarnate, and it is at least more respectful

[1] Letter of E. M. in *Light*, 8th December 1883, p. 531.

to one's own spirit to give it the credit for what it tells us, than to set it aside in favour of some wandering stranger. No doubt such visitants may, and do, gain by association with persons of pure and high intent, but it is enough for this end that they frequent the atmosphere of such persons. . . .   E. M.

THE HISTORIC "JESUS"

I.[1]

To the Editor of "Light."

SIR,—

. . . .

One of the most vital of all religious questions is the question whether the Gospels are historical or allegorical—whether, that is, they are intended as a relation of the physical history of some one actual but exceptional man, or as a dramatic presentation of the spiritual history of every man regenerate, the question whether the portraiture is wholly ideal, or drawn, more or less exactly, from some actual person or persons, being left open as comparatively unimportant. . . . Everything turns on the questions (1) as to the sense in which they spoke of Jesus Christ, and (2) as to the correctness of the belief which regarded Him as an historical person rather than as a spiritual ideal. The controversy turns upon the method and intention of Scripture, and how far religion is addressed to the senses or to the soul. It requires, therefore, for its determination a combination of much learning with profound spiritual insight, and is not to be settled off-hand on the strength of any individual testimony, conviction, or preference, however strong. E. M.

II.[2]

To the Editor of "Light."

SIR,—I do not think Mr. Roden Noel and the "leaders" of the Hermetic Society are so much in disagreement as Dr Wyld seems to think.

The "leaders" of the Hermetic Society have never denied, nor wished to deny, the historic Jesus. They have but pointed

---

[1] Letter written by Edward Maitland, and published in *Light*, 1884, p. 454.
[2] Letter written by Anna Kingsford, and published in *Light*, 1885, p. 331. It is also reprinted in *The Life of Anna Kingsford*, vol. ii. pp. 228–229.

out that not the historic but the spiritual Christ is the real essential of Christianity, and subject of the Gospels.[1]

I have—speaking for myself—distinctly stated at recent meetings of our Society, that I should be grateful to anyone who could reconcile for me the difficulties and discrepancies abounding in the way of belief in the historical Jesus. I should be glad to receive any really logical and scholarly rectification and explanation of the many serious and important misstatements and inconsistencies undoubtedly existing in the Gospels. These difficulties do not concern mere details, but the chief facts of the life itself.[2] I do not doubt the achievements of Napoleon, but then it is a matter of no moment to the souls of the world to-day whether Napoleon achieved anything or not. So neither I, nor any other person interested in eternal things, cares to verify his history or his acts. As for the miracles, they are no sort of difficulty to me. I am not in the position of the non-Spiritualist. But does not Dr Wyld see that he proves too much in proving the modern phenomena of Spiritualism to be identical with the "mighty works" of Jesus? What, then, was Jesus no more and no greater than the medium of to-day, but merely a better medium!

I have said that I should be glad to be able to think the Gospel stories true, because so to think would bring me into closer union and harmony with many friends whose sympathy is dear to me. But, for myself, such a belief would add nothing to my faith in Christ. For I am quite sure that there is, virtually, no such thing as history. The things that are truly done, are not done on the historical plane; nor has any fact in the history of the world ever been truly chronicled. For no man can know

---

[1] Many of Anna Kingsford's Illuminations refer to Jesus as an historical character, some of them refer to Him as one whom she remembered in a past life. For instance, in an Illumination "Concerning Christian Pantheism," it is stated, "The crucifixion of Jesus was an actual fact, but it had also a spiritual signification; and it is to the spiritual meaning, and not to the physical fact, that the whole of the mystical writings of the Christians refer" (*C. W. S.*, pt. i. No. xxvii.). See also her Illumination "Concerning the Actual Jesus" (*ibid.*, No. xxxiii.), giving some most interesting details connected with the crucifixion as from an eye-witness; and declaring that His birth—that is, the birth of the physical man—"was most certainly an ordinary birth"; and distinguishing between certain incidents in the life of Jesus that are "allegories of which the signification is spiritual" and incidents that are "real facts." In another Illumination, "Concerning the Previous Lives of Jesus," Anna Kingsford relates an incident which she was assured "actually occurred," and that she had borne part in it, though no record of it survives (*ibid.*, No. xxxiv.).—S. H. H.

[2] See her Lecture on "Bible Hermeneutics," p. 146, *ante*.

any fact, and cannot, therefore, set it down. The knowledge one man has of any given fact is not the knowledge of another; man is incompetent to know facts, for he has no possible means of knowing them. Only Omniscience can know facts.

But man can, and does, know his own spiritual experience, and this is, indeed, the only needful knowledge. Jesus Christ comes in the flesh when He is incarnate in man; and this is the way in which He comes to all mystics, in which only He can come.

It does not matter to me, therefore, whether the Gospels are true or not on the merely outer plane. They are true, essentially, and, for my soul, my true self, the historical and the physical *are not*. Nothing done on that outer plane can save my soul; it must all be transmuted into spiritual terms and spiritual application before it can have any true saving value and grace.

As for the doctrine of re-births, I do not want to enter into that question again, because already in these columns, in reply to Dr Wyld, I once undertook a disquisition of some length about it.[1] There are no re-births any more for the soul that has found Christ Jesus, and is one with God. Unto which grace may we all be brought.[2]   ANNA KINGSFORD, M.D.

3rd July.

[1] See her letter "Concerning Re-Incarnation," p. 191, *ante*.
[2] Shortly after the publication of this letter, Anna Kingsford, writing to Mrs Atwood—to whom reference has been made—said: "If you follow, as you doubtless do, the career of the Hermetic Society in the pages of *Light*, I trust you have taken note of Dr Wyld's aspersions and criticisms on our position in regard to the 'Historic Jesus.' As I rejoice to know that you share in our view in regard to this matter, you would oblige me, infinitely, if you would send to *Light* a comment of your own on Dr Wyld's letter, and add the undisputed weight of your scholarly knowledge and research to the Hermetic view, which, at present, it seems, we are almost alone in supporting. Of course, I know full well that the common understanding of men—even so-called 'Spiritualists'—is wholly incapable of grasping theosophic methods and processes in the manner necessary to comprehend the spirit of scripture written by and for initiates: but still, much may be done by testimony such as that you could furnish:—enough, I conceive, to demonstrate, at least, the fact that one so versed as yourself in the study of mysticism, recognises and endorses the view of 'Christ' which we are seeking to maintain. The more I observe the course of the world from day to day, the more convinced I become that true history is really not to be looked for on the phenomenal plane at all. Nothing really happens on that plane:— nothing, that is, that is a true thing; essentials do not belong to that plane, and only a foolish and uninstructed person would seek them there. . . . How right you are when you say that ' myths are truer than all history ' ! They are, of course, *the only history* of which the soul can have cognisance; for she *can* know only the hyper-physical, and the sacred myths are its records and archives. But those who write and think like Dr Wyld, appear to me to imagine that flesh and blood, not soul and spirit, are to inherit the Kingdom of Heaven."—S. H. H.

III.[3]

To the Editor of "Light."

Sir,—Dr Wyld's letter of the 4th inst. reads so much more like the product of a desire to "bring a railing accusation" against those who presume to differ from him, than of a desire to elucidate truth, that were I to follow my own impulse I should leave it unnoticed. As, however, there may be among your readers some who imagine that, because a charge is unanswered, it is therefore unanswerable, I will indicate, as briefly as possible, its chief fallacies.

In the first place, there are in the Hermetic Society no persons whom Dr Wyld is entitled to call its "leaders," for the simple reason that the term "leaders" implies *followers*; and the members of the Hermetic Society are wholly unpledged and independent, and are not, therefore, followers of any persons whatever, but purely and simply of truth.

In the next place, Dr Wyld has misrepresented the position of those whom he assails. We have neither "denied the historic Christ," nor that "Jesus Christ has come in the flesh," though we may differ from Dr Wyld as to the sense to be ascribed to the latter expression.

Respecting this sense, it is necessary to remember that the fact that there was a difference of opinion in the Primitive Church —not whether Christ had come at all—but whether the manner of His coming had been such as to constitute the anticipated coming "in the flesh,"—shews that the phrase bore a meaning so subtle and occult as to be readily susceptible of misconception.

Had Christ indeed "come in the flesh" in the sense insisted on by Dr Wyld, and been an altogether exceptional personage, miraculously engendered, a performer in public of numerous stupendous physical marvels, and so different in kind from other men as to be superhuman rather than a merely superior human, the fact would—we may well believe—have been so palpable and flagrant that no question could have arisen about it; and certainly it would not have been so depreciated by Paul. But so far from this being the case, there was a numerous party which held that Jesus was but an angelic or phantasmal appearance, unrelated to humanity, and that consequently no manifestation

[1] Letter written by Edward Maitland, and published in *Light*, 1885, pp. 341–342.

of Christ in and through humanity or the "flesh"—meaning thereby human beings—had occurred.

Dr Wyld, however, not only assumes the right to be positive *now* about a matter concerning which there was doubt *then*, but takes a view which, as it seems to us, neither the Apostles nor their opponents held; and hastens to invoke anathema upon those whose respect for religious truth prompts them carefully to search the Scripture for its real meaning and intention, instead of foisting upon it their own preferences and foregone conclusions. It is evidently but an ungracious reception that the promised "Spirit of Truth," when He comes, will receive at the hands of the Dr Wylds of the period, in case He ventures to differ from them. As it is, it may well be that in refusing to accept the mode of coming I have suggested as a "coming in the flesh," Dr Wyld incurs for himself the condemnation he seeks to pass upon us.

Even if we had made the denial ascribed to us by Dr Wyld, the fault—if a fault at all—would, by his own shewing, be a venial one, since he holds that "the historic Jesus, as a *bare fact*, may have very little influence on the souls of men," and that notwithstanding His "full possession and transmutation by the Divine Word," Jesus so slightly transcended the medium of the period that a "replica of almost every miracle attributed to Him may be found in modern Spiritualistic phenomena"! And, further, even if we had denied the "historic Jesus," we should not therein necessarily have affirmed that such Divine possession and transmutation had never occurred to any human being on this planet, seeing that similar experiences are ascribed in the Bible to two other persons, Enoch and Elijah; so that Dr Wyld, when he cites the transmutation of Jesus as an unique event, shews himself to be as slenderly acquainted with the Old Testament as he obviously is with the New.

The very paper on which Dr Wyld mainly bases his strictures admits the probability of there having been some special figure which served as chief model for the character delineated in the Gospels. We have denied only the proposition that there is in the Gospels anything that can, without an abuse of language, be called a history of such a person, or that is not true as mystically interpreted of every regenerate man.

As if despairing of proving his case by reasoning, Dr Wyld betakes himself to assertion, and this in the most dogmatic fashion. "I assert," he says, "that there is not one discrepancy of importance in the four Gospels," but only "a few verbal discrepancies," and these such as to afford confirmation of their genuineness by shewing that they were not fabrications. The hardihood of this utterance, extreme as it is, is not its only objectionable feature. As a direct unqualified contradiction of us it is also discourteous. There are plenty of ways of expressing dissent from an opponent without plainly implying that one considers him so unworthy of heed as to be best met by a flat contradiction. The presumption of it, too, is amusing, or, at least, would be so but for the melancholy proof it affords of the utter failure of its utterer to have followed the developments of modern research in these grave matters. Dr Wyld evidently supposes that he will have settled the question to his satisfaction when he has succeeded in discrediting us; whereas he has, on the contrary, to deal with the vast array of competent and candid scholars who in the last half century have devoted themselves to the inquiry, with the result of demonstrating absolutely the hopeless disaccordance of the Gospels, both with each other and with contemporary history, and the large extent to which they are reproductions of legends, and compilations from literatures long pre-existent; and, consequently, their non-historical character. These are results irrefragably established for all who have carefully and candidly examined the grounds on which they rest. And yet they are to be disposed of by the simple *ipse dixit* of one who is so much of a tyro in the subject that little over three years ago, in a discussion upon it, he expressed surprise at learning, among other discrepancies—all of which have sorely exercised the orthodox—that the Gospels disagree as to the day of the Crucifixion! As he had taken their agreement in this and other respects for granted then, so now. For his letter shows that he has not improved the interval by acquiring further knowledge of the subject.

To cite but a few of the contradictions to which a belief in the Gospels as historical and concordant commits its holder. He must believe both that Jesus was miraculously born of a virgin mother and the Holy Ghost, and was not derived from the house of David; and also that He was born naturally of Joseph and Mary, since only through Joseph could He have been " of the seed of David according to the flesh." He must believe both that Jesus did go down into Egypt, His parents having fled thither on the night following the visit of the Magi, in order to escape the massacre ordered by Herod; and also that He did not go into Egypt, but remained where He was born to be circumcised after eight days, and, after forty days, to accompany His parents to Jerusalem for His mother's purification, a visit which was repeated every successive year for twelve years, and consequently that there was no persecution or massacre by Herod. He must believe both that the mother of Jesus was so fully aware of His Divine nature and mission as to treasure in her heart every incident concerning Him; and also that she failed wholly to comprehend His allusions to His peculiar nature and destiny, and joined His brethren in an attempt to withdraw Him from a public career on the ground of madness. He must believe that Jesus was crucified both on the day of the Passover, and again on the day after the Passover; that the resurrection occurred under four different and incompatible sets of circumstances, a different set being detailed and positively stated in each Gospel; that the ascension occurred both, as described in the Gospel of Luke, on the same day as the resurrection, and also as stated in the Acts, which purports also to be Luke's, forty days after the resurrection; and that Judas both returned the money paid for his treachery and hanged himself, and also did not return the money but bought a field with it, and died therein of an accident. It is, of course, open to Dr Wyld to plead that the parentage, birth, crucifixion, and ascension are not matters of importance, and I am quite willing to allow him this loophole for escape. But he cannot avail himself of this plea and still retain his belief in the historical character of the documents which thus differ respecting them, seeing that they, not to mention the system founded on them, treat them as of the utmost importance, and that, if not historical on these points, they are not entitled to be regarded as historical at all; but, if of serious import, must be regarded, as we regard them, namely, as mystical.

As for the pretended doubts about Napoleon, Dr Wyld forgets that there remains a very substantial residue of indubitable fact in his case, while in that of Jesus there remains nothing after the doubtful parts are eliminated.

Had Dr. Wyld really desired to promote knowledge he would not have omitted to notice the striking demonstration given by me of the fact that so far from Jesus being represented as claiming for Himself an exceptional physical birth, He is represented as disclaiming anything of the kind, inasmuch as He is made to declare it necessary to every man that he be born again precisely as He Himself is described as having been born, namely, spiritually;—" Water and the Spirit," and " Virgin

Mary and the Holy Ghost," being but symbolical formulas for the soul and spirit of which man when regenerate is "born again." But Dr Wyld passes over this conclusive proof that the subject of the Gospels is really not a particular human personality, but the interior and spiritual personality of every regenerate man; and, as if under the impression that an assertion needs only to be repeated often enough to convert it into a fact, he proceeds to reiterate his disbelief in the doctrine of physical re-births or "re-incarnation."

His remarks here are no less open to objection for their superficiality, their flippancy, and even their insincerity. The negative experience of a majority, however large, proves—as Dr Wyld well knows—nothing as against the positive experience of a minority, however small. Nevertheless, he cites the non-experience of the majority as an argument against the doctrine. The reminiscence of past existences belongs, not to the *spiritualistic*, but to the *spiritual*, consciousness, and to an interior region of this; and it is therefore not comprisable in the order of experiences of which alone, as I am forced to conclude, Dr Wyld has cognisance. Of the profound philosophy of the doctrine, and of the sanctity of the experiences on which it rests, he is obviously unaware, or he would not make contemptuous reference to the latter as by ascribing them to a process of "self-biologising." The reply of Jesus to His disciples concerning this doctrine, though it evaded the question, neither was scornful nor denied it.

Limited to a single earth-life, the experiences requisite to enable a "Captain of Salvation" to be "made perfect through suffering" would indeed be few!

Equally fallacious is his demand for "scientific proof" of the facts of the spiritual consciousness. As if the reality of a remote memory of any kind was capable of sensible demonstration! While his denial of there being any historic confirmation of the doctrine seems to imply that Plato, Pythagoras, and Buddha are names as strange to him as those of Enoch and Elijah appear to be. As a student of such subjects he ought to know that the whole of the ancient religions comprised the doctrine of transmigration, and consequently of re-incarnation. But there are students and students, and Dr Wyld's letter makes it difficult to class him with those who merit to be called serious.

One remark on what Dr Wyld so warmly eulogises as the "testimony" of Mr Roden Noel. The argument from the alleged necessity of a realised ideal of perfection in another as an aid to the pursuit of it in oneself, if valid at all, must be valid in cases other than that where the perfection in question is spiritual. Is it the fact that the belief in the existence of some transcendentally physically-beautiful specimen of humanity is necessary to enable us either to aspire after physical beauty in ourselves or to form a conception of perfect beauty for ourselves? Assuredly not. We none the less recognise and desire beauty because we know of no one perfectly beautiful. And the artist is none the less able to devise a perfect type because he cannot find a perfect model. For all that is necessary for him is to have suitable subjects from which to compile the manifold excellences he desires to combine into a single image. Greek art was a new revelation of the beauty of the human form. Yet it needed not that any one individual be transcendentally beautiful; or even that there be more beauty than usual in the world; but only that there be an enhanced perception of beauty. Why may it not have been so with the inspired artists to whom the world owes the portraits of its Christs? It is none the less a "coming of Christ in the flesh" that His lineaments be distributed among many. But Dr Wyld sides with those who say, "Lo, here is Christ, or lo, there!"

Regretting the length at which I have been compelled to write, and trusting that any reply that may be made will in some degree tend to edification,—I am, etc.,

EDWARD MAITLAND.

IV.[1]

To the Editor of "Light."

SIR,—Historical records differ wholly both in nature and in terms from mathematical or arithmetical formulæ. These represent the only exact science; while there is nothing in the world so inexact as "history."

The fact that two and two make four is a fact essential and abstract; it posits an idea, and is only conceivable and recognisable as an idea. Wherefore it is an eternal verity; because two and two not only made four in the past, but make four now, and will continue to make four so long as the world shall last.

It is not necessary that any inspired writer of antiquity should

[1] Letter written by Anna Kingsford, and published in *Light*, 1885, p. 354.

inform us of such a fact as this, for its evidence does not rest on authority, but inheres in the terms of the fact itself, and on the immediate recognition of the human intelligence.

Dr Wyld is, therefore, comparing things that are not similars.

The same may be said of his statement that fire warms, that food satisfies hunger, and the like. These facts are not historical; I verify them in my own experience every day, and need not that any should testify to me about them.

Mr. Maitland's letter has answered the other objections made to our position by Dr Wyld, and I need not, therefore, notice them.

If, when all the legendary framework, obviously unhistorical and allegorical, is removed from about the central figure of the great Christian Mythos, Dr Wyld still thinks that what is left constitutes of that figure "the most important historic person this planet has ever known," I shall be curious to hear how he will substantiate his opinion. Of the thirty-three years which Jesus is said to have lived, the Gospels affect to give only the events of the last three. Concerning nearly all the rest, they are dumb. Consequently, they give us in no sense whatever "a life" of Jesus; and what they do give is obviously mostly mythical.

What, under such conditions, can we know or divine of the "historical Jesus" as He really was?

We know far more of Gautama Buddha; of Pythagoras; of Apollonius; of Plato; of Socrates.

As for my own personality, I doubt much whether it will be an historical "fact" eighteen centuries hence that I lived at all, much less that I was "President of the Hermetic Society." If ever I pass into "history," no doubt just as many foolish and untrue things will be said of me as are now said of Rosamond Clifford, of Joan of Arc, of Mary Stuart, and of every other personage of the past.

Already, I am aware that many supposed "facts" which are wholly baseless have been told and believed concerning me, and I have observed a similar state of things in respect of several of my contemporaries. ANNA KINGSFORD, M.D.

V.[1]

To the Editor of "Light."

SIR,—Though sympathising with your desire to close the discussion on this subject, I must nevertheless ask to be allowed to make a brief reply to some of the statements contained in this week's *Light*.

To take first the letter of Dr Wyld. The epithets to which he objects applied not to himself, but to his style and argument. If flat contradiction in a matter such as that under treatment is not "discourteous," then, and then only, was I not justified in using the term. I believe, however, that I was justified in using it. Thus much as to the style.

With regard to the argument—to which I applied the other terms complained of—if to use an argument to another which does not satisfy oneself—as, for instance, Dr Wyld's argument from majorities, which he certainly does not regard as sound in regard to things spiritual—is not to be "flippant, superficial, and insincere," then, and then only, was I wrong in using those terms. As it is, I hold that I am justified by the facts of the case. Dr Wyld replied to me by an argument which, he well knows, has no weight with himself.

Dr Wyld's veneration for the "beloved disciple" cannot exceed mine. But the question between us is, not what that disciple wrote, but what was his meaning. Dr Wyld in his present letter simply reiterates the expression before employed in order to stigmatise us as "false prophets," without taking the smallest notice of my suggested explanation of the meaning of the phrase "Come in the flesh"—thereby aggravating his original fault. We maintain no less strenuously than Dr Wyld himself that "Jesus Christ has come in the flesh," and by that coming inaugurated the Christian dispensation. But we differ from Dr Wyld as to the *modus* of the coming, and believe that our view is the true one, and that which the "beloved disciple" himself intended.

Dr Wyld's persistent substitution of the word "mythical" for "mystical"—which I used—is, I hope, due to accident rather than design, for the perversion involves a serious misrepresentation. It is, however, clear from his remarks on the

---

[1] Letter written by Edward Maitland, and published in *Light*, 1885, pp. 363-364; see also p. 379.

Miraculous Conception that his own view of what is implied in that event is neither mythical nor mystical, but materialistic; and that as, for him, "Christ Jesus" denotes, not Man regenerate and purely spiritual, but a physical and historical personality; so "Virgin Mary" denotes, not the human soul become pure and fit to be the "mother" of such "Man regenerate," but a physical and historical personality. But perhaps Dr Wyld is of those for whom Adam and Eve and the serpent are "historical" personages. If so, it is no wonder that he falls foul of us who hold that the Bible teaches by means of parables which, referring to things spiritual and in perpetual course of enactment, are not "historical," but true for all time. It is precisely the insistence of the materialistic, because historical, view that has wrought havoc with Christianity and even with religion itself.

I cannot but regard Dr Wyld's allusion to what he considers the exposure of "Koot Hoomi" as unfortunate for his case. If only by shewing how easily a fictitious personage may come to be accepted as a real one, the history in question is suggestive in a direction the very opposite to that which Dr Wyld would approve. Concerning the case itself I pronounce no opinion. But concerning the spirit in which Dr Wyld has dealt with it I have a decided opinion, and find it not difficult to believe that had he lived—as perhaps he did—some eighteen centuries ago, the "pretensions" of a certain other personage, also intimately associated with "a tree," would have found in him an equally scornful repudiation.

If I have indeed "somewhat overstepped bounds" in alluding to Dr Wyld's admissions in past years, I am sorry for it. But I alluded only to what he has said repeatedly and before others, and was in no sense private, but has since been borne out by his own published letters. If Dr Wyld can say the same of the remarkable utterance he ascribes to me, I shall be content to incur the reproach due. This, however, I know that he cannot do; for, whatever may have been the remarks on which he bases his statement, they were certainly not as he represents them; first, because, however high I may believe to be the authority for the doctrine of re-births, it is contrary to my practice to rest any doctrine on authority, and still less to advance pretentious personal claims; and next, because the expression, "forsaken of the Gods," would imply my belief in a previous enjoyment by him of Divine communion; and happy as I should be to credit Dr Wyld with so high a privilege, he has yet to furnish the grounds which would justify me in doing so. But it may be after all that the solution of our difference here is to be found in the proverbial difficulty which persons of Dr Wyld's nationality are said to have in apprehending a joke.

I do not care to contemplate a harsher explanation of Dr Wyld's mistake in this matter, but am content to ascribe it to some defect either of apprehension or of recollection, and would therefore remind him that, however positive he may feel about his accuracy, all that he can possibly be sure of is his own belief as to what passed on the occasion or occasions to which he refers.

One word of thanks to Madame de Steiger for her excellent letter. She is indeed right, it seems to me, in her reprobation of those who, in their determination to have their human God, have caused Christianity to be discredited, and seriously endangered the whole fabric of religion.

It is impossible for me to deal here otherwise than very cursorily with Miss Campbell's elaborate disquisition. I will therefore content myself with indicating a few of its salient points, as a means to a judgment of the whole.

1. Miss Campbell has sadly mistaken both the scope and spirit of my remarks. For those who, being sincere in their beliefs, defend them by sincere arguments, and even if mistaken have taken pains to learn, I have nothing but respect, no matter what their beliefs are, and to such as these my strictures bore no reference. It was to a particular line of argument, employed by a particular person, that I applied the terms she resents, and her application of them to the whole body of those who share the same views is at once unjust and unjustifiable.

2. So far from my interpretation of Mark iii. being "astounding," it is the obvious and only one possible. The word (v. 21) translated "friends" means undoubtedly, says the learned Dean Alford in his scholarly work on the Greek Testament, "relations," "for the sense is resumed (v. 31) by the word" οὖν,—therefore. Moreover, his note is headed "Charges against Jesus of madness by His relations"; and the text expressly specifies His mother as one of those concerned.

3. After saying she "has never read the works of scholars either on one side or the other," but will "simply let the Gospels speak for themselves," Miss Campbell proceeds to set forth, not at all what the Gospels say,—namely, that Mary, as cousin to Elizabeth, who was of the house of Aaron, must have belonged to the tribe of Levi, and was not therefore of the house of David,

—but what "Roman Catholics are taught in their earliest lessons" by their priests, and is rested by them, not on the Gospels, but on a tradition in apparent discordance with the Gospels!"

Does not my fair, and doubtless amiable, though somewhat impetuous, opponent see that even if her letter does not call for the particular epithets by which I characterised that of Dr Wyld there are yet others which might be used of a scarcely less favourable nature? The most fervent faith and zeal cannot afford to dispense with accuracy of statement and logical coherence. She seems to regard her acknowledged want of study, which means want of knowledge, as a positive qualification for the task of defending her religious convictions. But how if such rule were applied to the discussion of other subjects as, for instance, chemistry or astronomy? Would she not consider as guilty of something not very unlike "presumption" the novice who, "having never read the works of scholars on one side or the other," should undertake to contradict off-hand those who had devoted years to earnest investigation?

If, as I suspect, Miss Campbell thinks the presumption is ours for declining to accept the sacerdotal presentation of these matters, I would refer her again to her Bible, where, as she will find, it is always the priests who, alike in Old Testament and New, incur the Divine reprobation for precisely the degradation of doctrine from which we are endeavouring to rescue Christianity. If she can shew that the *prophets* are against us we shall indeed be answered. But we know and respect the Bible far too well to take our interpretation of things spiritual from any body of priests. Does she suppose that the sacerdotal character has changed since the days of Caiaphas?

Miss Campbell's closing remark that "it is quite open to doubt the mystic sense of the Gospel," shews that she has yet much to learn of her own religion before she is qualified to take part in this controversy. If the Jesus of the Gospels was indeed an historical character, then must His mother have been one likewise. Is it, then, such a character that the Church contemplates when, in its offices of the B. V. M., it puts into her mouth the words, "I dwell in the highest: and my throne is on the pillar of the clouds. I made an unfailing light to arise in heaven: and, as a mist, I overspread the whole earth"? Or when it says of her, "The Lord Himself created her in the Holy Ghost: and poured her out among all His works"? And declares, further, that "the Virgin Mary was taken up to the Heavenly chamber, where the King of kings sits on His starry throne"? To us who accept her as a symbol of the soul, universal or individual, and at once Divine and human, these utterances are intelligible and true. But they represent the mystic sense of the Gospel, and therefore, for your correspondent, though a Catholic, are "quite open to doubt," and the only sense that is imperative is that which, by applying them to an historical personality, makes them something worse than nonsense.

In reference to the "correspondent" whom you answer at such length, I would add to your answer these two remarks: (1) That a careful examination of the subject would shew him that so far from "attacking Christianity" we are doing the one thing that can rescue and save Christianity—namely, restoring to it its spiritual sense; and (2) that the course he proposes to you in the conduct of your paper would be not only "idiotic," but unjust and illogical. *Light* is described on its title-page as a "Journal of Psychical, Occult, and Mystical Research." So that in demanding—as I understand—that it should deal exclusively with things spiritualistic, he demands that it should omit the whole of the subjects it professes to treat saving only a particular department of one of them—Spiritualism being defined as a department of Occultism. It is only recently that you deprecated the establishment of a rival magazine, on the ground that *Light* suffices to meet existing requirements. I feel tolerably confident that were you to do as your correspondent suggests, and exclude the classes of subjects to which he objects, it would very speedily be found that another paper of the kind would really be indispensable.—Yours, etc., EDWARD MAITLAND.

FATE, HEREDITY, AND RE-INCARNATION[1]

THE Ego of the regenerate man must dwell entirely in the seventh (or spiritual) sphere, and, as the mystics of the school of St Dionysius say, become wholly absorbed and merged in the Divine Abyss. The selfhood of the man must be lost in the selfhood of God, and become one with It. Not until this final act of saintship is accomplished is the man free of Fate and astral domination, an ascended man, having passed up " beyond all heavens " or starry planes and powers, and " taken captive their captivity." For, indeed, these powers hold us in thrall until they themselves can be bound by us. The ascended man is the type of the elect who have so perfectly taken up their lower nature into the divine, that Matter and Fate, or Karma, as the Oriental theosophists term it, are wholly overcome, and can no more have dominion over them. There is left in them no dross of the sensual and physical planes to weight them down again into material conditions; they are " born again " into the heavenly estate, and have severed the umbilical cord which once bound them to their mother, the earthy estate. Do men become thus regenerate and redeemed in the course of a single planetary existence? Assuredly not. Astrology, chiromancy, phrenology, and other occult sciences, all inform us that every man is born with a certain definite and determinate Fate, which declares itself in his horoscope, on the palm of his hand, in the formation of his head, in the set of his face, features, limbs, and aspect. Speaking broadly, all these determinations are included and intended under the physiological term Heredity, and they belong to the accidents of evolution. But what *is* heredity, and how can it be explained in the light of Eternal Justice ? The Macrocosm could not stand a moment were it not founded on a perfect equity and governed by an unalterable law of compensation and of the conservation of energy. Every effect is equal to its cause, and one term presupposes the other. And as the Macrocosm is but the prototype in large of the Microcosm, this also is founded on and

[1] From Anna Kingsford's " Prefatory Essay " to her edition of *Astrology Theologised*, pp. 21-26, 42.—S. H. H.

governed by laws in harmony with those which control the solar system whose offspring it is. So that heredity is no arbitrary or capricious effect appearing without adequate cause, but is the result and expression of foregone impetus, developing affinities and sympathies which infallibly compel the entity on which they act into a certain determinate course and direction so long as the energy of that impetus lasts. Expressed in terms of common physics, this is the law of gravitation and of polarisation. But without this explanation all appears as haphazard and confusion. No hermetist denies the doctrine of heredity as held and expounded by ordinary scientific materialists. But he recognises the sense intended by its inventors as comprising only the last term in a complex series of compelling causes and effects. The immediate cause of a low and afflicted birth is obviously the condition, physical and mental, of the parents responsible, on this plane, for the birth. But beyond this preliminary stage in the enquiry the ordinary scientific materialist does not go. He is unacquainted with the hermetic theorem that all physical effects and results are *ultimates*, which must, of necessity, have their first term in a formative sphere. The corporeal world is incapable of engendering causes, it can but transmit them; hence the beginning of things can never be discovered within the limits of material agencies. Therefore, regarding heredity as the ultimation in physical conditions of causes at work behind and beyond it, the hermetist is irresistibly forced to the conclusion that although a man may be born deaf, dumb, epileptic, idiotic, or otherwise afflicted, because his father or mother have been drunken, immoral, or "unfortunate," these latter causes are immediate only, not mediate, and are themselves in their turn effects of previous causes not belonging to the physical sphere, but to one next above and behind it, that is, to the astral, and that this also in its turn has been influenced by the spiritual energies of the Ego whose "nativity" is involved. And he comes to these conclusions because they are consonant with all that he otherwise knows and has observed of the working of the universe. Many persons find it difficult to reconcile belief in the "ruling of the stars," with belief in free-will. It appears at first sight arbitrary and unjust that certain lines of life—even vicious and base ones— should be indicated by the rulers of nativities as the only lines in which the "native" will prosper; and they ask incredulously whether it can be rationally supposed that the accident of the day and hour of birth is, by Divine wisdom and justice, permitted to control and confine the whole career of an intelligent and responsible being. But the difficulties of astrological science, if viewed in the light of " Karma "—as Predestination—not only disappear, but give place to the unfoldment of a most lucid and admirable system of responsible causation. There is but one hypothesis capable of solving the enigma of Fate, and that hypothesis is common to all the great schools of thought—Vedic, Buddhist, Kabalistic, Hermetic, Platonic—the hypothesis, to wit, of multiple existences. Destiny, in the view of these philosophies, is not arbitrary but acquired. Every man makes his own fate, and nothing is truer than the saying that " Character is Destiny." We must think, then, that it is by their own hands that the lines of some are cast in pleasant places, of some in vicious, and of some in virtuous conditions. For in what manner soever a soul conduct itself in one existence, by that conduct, by that order of thought and habit it builds for itself its destiny in a future existence. And the soul is enchained by these pre-natal influences, and by them irresistibly forced into a new nativity at the time of such conjunction of planets and signs as oblige it into certain courses, or incline it strongly thereunto. And if these courses be evil, and the ruling such as to favour only base propensities, the afflicted soul, even though undoubtedly reaping the just effect of its own demerit, is not left without a remedy. For it may oppose its will[1] to the stellar ruling, and heroically adopt a course contrary to the direction of the natal influences. Thereby it will, indeed, bring itself under a curse and much suffering for such period as those influences have power, but it will, at the same time, change or reverse its planetary affinities and give a new " set " to its predestination, that is, to the current of its " Karma." So that the ruling signs of its next nativity will be propitious to virtuous endeavour. " From

[1] The power of the human will is the instrument by which Destiny may be controlled. In a note to an " Hermetic Fragment," published in *The Virgin of the World*, Anna Kingsford says : " By continued and ardent striving towards the purely spiritual and intelligent, the Soul frees herself from the power of Destiny (Karma), and at length passes into beatitude. She transcends natural order, and enters into the divine. This is Saintship. Inversely, by attaching herself to sensible things, and by suffering herself to be borne away by passion and desire towards illusory existence, she becomes caught on the ever-rolling wheel of Destiny, and made subject to the order of Nature, which is that of Metamorphosis. Whereas her true duty and happiness are to aspire continually upwards, addressing herself by means of purified passion and desire towards the One, and away from the Manifold " (*The Virgin of the World*, p. 150). —S. H. H.

a great heart," says Emerson, " secret magnetisms flow incessantly to draw great events."

The reason why the doctrine of Metempsychosis is not put forward as an article of faith in the Christian dispensation appears to me to be because there is no more death or birth for the man who is united with God in Christ. The Christian religion was addressed to this end, and he who enters the Kingdom of Heaven is saved for ever from that of earth. But very few realise this blessed state, therefore says the Lord, "Few there be that find it." Not, assuredly, that all the majority are lost, but that they return to the necessary conditions again and again until they find it. When once the life of Union is achieved, the wheel of existence ceases to revolve. Now the Church takes it for granted that every Christian desires in this existence to attain to union, such union with Christ being, in fact, the sole subject and object of Christian faith and doctrine. Therefore, of course, she does not preach the Metempsychosis. But, as a matter of fact, very few so-called Christians do attain union; therefore they return until the capacity for union is developed. Such development must be reached in mundane conditions; the cleansing fires of an afterworld are incapable of more than purification; they do not supply the necessary conditions for evolution found only and granted only in this life. Now the dispensation of Christ is the highest there is, because regeneration begins for the Christian in the interior principle, and works outwardly. In other dispensations it begins outwardly and works towards the interior. Buddha, in whose system the Metempsychosis is most conspicuous, is in the Mind, Christ is in the Soul. . . . The religion of Buddha is of the will of Man, . . . for it is by violence that the Buddhist takes the Kingdom of heaven, that is, by the Intellectual way. But they who follow Christ take it by the way of sight, that is, by the Soul. For the Soul is feminine, and does not fight. . . . But the Human will is sanctified, being saved by Christ—the spiritual or seventh principle—and taken into Paradise. It is the Thief crucified on the Right Hand of the Lord, who is taken by Him into Paradise, though not into Heaven. The Thief on the Left Hand is the Creaturely will [—the will of the flesh, inherent in the Creaturely nature—] which must be left behind because it reviles the Lord, even though partaking His Passion. But the Thief who is released unto the mob is the robber Barabbas [—representing the mere Organic or Titanic principle—], who cannot be partaker in the death of the Lord. For the Titanic hath nothing in Christ. So that under Buddha we are born again and die again, but under Christ there are no re-births, for Christ saves us out of the world when we are united to God through His merits and sacrifice. . . .

. . . .

It will be understood, in the light of what has already been said concerning Heredity, that, from the point of view I occupy, original sin should not be taken to imply a burden of corruption arbitrarily imputed to new-born babes as the consequence merely of transgression in a remote ancestry, but as that voluntarily acquired and self-imposed " Karma," which every soul accretes in the course of its manifold experiences, and loaded with which it enters upon each nativity. This weight of original sin may be heavy or light; it may grow or decrease with each successive birth, according to the evolution of the soul concerned, and the progress it makes towards release and light. " If," says Mr W. S. Lilly, " a man submits to the law of moral development by choosing to act aright, he will finally be delivered from all evil. But if he rebels, and will not submit to the elevating redeeming influences, he thereby falls under those which degrade, stupefy, and materialise. And as he would cease to be man had he no free-will, and as moral good implies moral choice, it seems inevitable that he should remain the slave of the lower life as long as he will not choose to break away from it " (*Ancient Religion and Modern Thought*). The spirit of this passage is that of the teaching of Yama—or Death—in the *Katha Upanishad*: " They who are ignorant, but fancy themselves wise, go round and round with erring step as blind led by the blind. He who believes that this world is, and not the other, is again and again subject to the sway of Death."

THE MYSTIC MAGI, OR KINGS OF THE EAST[1]

"Cum ergo natus esset Jesus in Bethlehem Juda in diebus Herodis regis; ecci, Magi ab Oriente venerunt Jerosolyman, dicentes: Ubi est, qui natus est rex Judæorum? Vidimus enim stellam ejus in Oriente, et venimus adorare eum."—Matt. Cap. II. i. 2.

I PROPOSE to set before the readers of *L'Aurore*, as briefly and succinctly as I can, that system and method of applied theology which, under various names and disguises, whether as Neoplatonism, as Gnosticism, as Alchemy, or as the Hermetic art, has constituted the wealth of Mystics of all ages; identical always

[1] This Article on "The Mystic Magi, or Kings of the East," and the following one on "Christian Mysticism," were written by Anna Kingsford, in 1886, for publication in the then new French monthy *L'Aurore*, which was under the editorship of Lady Caithness (Duchess of Pomar). They were written in English, and translated into French for publication, but by whom they were translated I know not—it was not by Anna Kingsford. I have in my possession the original MS. of "The Mystic Magi, or Kings of the East," and it is from this that the present Article has been copied. After considerable trouble, I obtained copies of the two Articles in *L'Aurore*. That on "The Mystic Magi, or Kings of the East," appeared in *L'Aurore* (No. i. p. 30) in December 1886, under the title *Les Rois Mages Mystiques*; and that on "Christian Mysticism" in *L'Aurore* (No. iv. pp. 204-211) in March 1887, under the title *La Sainte Vierge Mystique*. (See *Light*, 1887, p. 212.)

The above-mentioned copies of the Articles in *L'Aurore* have been translated into English by my friend Mrs D. S. Hehner, who says: "These articles seem to have been originally written in English, which no doubt was Anna Kingsford's own clear and terse English, and then translated—very inadequately—into French. The typing of the copies of the French Articles in *L'Aurore*, too, is so defective, that it is in places difficult to make out the *sense*. In some cases, words have been omitted; in others, changed altogether. Several sentences read anything but clear in spite of my efforts to render them as well as possible. . . . I have added between brackets words which I thought helpful in order to render the idea. . . . As to the rest, and generally speaking, you can rely on accuracy. I should have liked to be *free* at times, but have not yielded to the temptation. You will find much to alter in order to make the whole perfectly lucid."

The Article on "Christian Mysticism" has—with the exception of a few verbal alterations—been copied from Mrs Hehner's translation from the French, which, it is seen, cannot be a correct rendering of Anna Kingsford's original Article from which the French translation was made, but as it is the nearest idea that I can give of the original, I have thought it better to give it as it stands, coupled with the above explanation.
—S. H. H.

although presented under so many differing modes, but finding its fullest and most perfect formation by the mouth and in the dogmas of the Catholic Church.

Mysticism may, perhaps, be helpfully defined as *experiential* Theosophy. While theosophy, in its broader signification, represents and includes the entire range of Transcendentalism, the science of the Mystic is strictly and finely *spiritual*. It is the science of the Saint rather than of the Adept, and occupies itself immediately and concentratively with the interests of the Soul and the aspirations of the Heart. It takes scant account of occult physics and dynamics, or of the intellectual ceremonials of *la Haute Magie*. In intent and scope it is interpretative rather than exegetic or constructive, and occupies itself with the conversion of the exoteric, material, and general formulæ of faith and doctrine into esoteric, spiritual, and particular meanings, enfranchising the concerns and interests of the Soul from the bondage of the Letter and the Form, and lifting the plane of belief from the level of Tradition to that of Revelation. Thus the religion of the Mystic is essentially spiritual, and all its articles relate to interior conditions, principles, and processes. It is based upon experimental knowledge, and its central figures are attributes, qualities, and sacraments ; not personages nor events, no matter how great or remarkable. These latter, with all the material accessories and accidents they imply, are by the Mystic regarded as constituting the *Vehicle*, not the essential element of religion, since they are not, and cannot be, noumena or absolutes.

I have used the term " applied theology " to express the personal and inward application to the life and in the heart of man of the great dogmas which form the outward and visible fabric of Religion. It is not by any means my purpose to criticise or meddle with these dogmas in their historical sense. I take them as the Church enunciates them, and intend to shew their secret and particular sense as illustrated and developed in the interior world of devout human experience. And in this work I shall endeavour at the outset to distinguish between false and true Mysticism, giving a few simple rules by observing which it will not be difficult to avoid the one and appropriate the other.

First, then, the science of true Mysticism has three salient characteristics : *form* is no more, *time* is no more, *personality* is no more. Instead of Time is Eternity, instead of the Formal is the

Essential, instead of Persons are Principles. So long as the dross of any merely intellectual or physical concept remains unconverted into the gold of spiritual meaning, so long, for the true Mystic, the most inward and secret application of religious dogma is unattained. In all our essays, therefore, at the transmutation of historical into hermetic theology, we must take care that we do not stop halfway at pseudo-psychologic interpretations, and mistake the physiological or the merely recondite for the spiritual. We must get rid of personæ, of places, of events occurring exteriorly to ourselves, or ideas compelling association with material conditions. Suggestive and attractive though some such half-and-half mysticisms may be, they are full of danger, and terribly liable to mislead into spurious theosophy, bewildering hallucination, and even madness. This the old initiates knew right well when they imagined the hermetic allegory which has, for ages, in many lands and under various guises, done duty as a fairy-tale none the less poetic because of its divineness;—how the true Knight, armed with a sword and a silver thread bestowed on him by his fairy godmother, goes in search of the sleeping Beauty in the wood, and by means of that magic clue winds his way safely through labyrinths and tangled mazes in which many other less fortunate knights had become lost, until at last he penetrates into the very heart of the enchanted bower and finds and awakens her who is his destined bride. That silver thread is the secret of the Mystic; it is the test of Spirituality, by holding fast and following which continually, he passes by with safety all the distractions of divergent interpretations and sideways of thought which is not ultimate and absolute in its application, and so emerges finally into the very core and essential of his being where the Divine Beauty sleeps, awaiting his kiss of recognition.

Secondly, and lastly, true Mysticism is strictly orderly, obedient, and reverent of congruities. It is systematised and coherent; it is disciplined and sane. Having found and determined the spiritual value and correspondence of any dogma, personification, or symbol, it abides by it, and does not perpetually shift and break correspondences and meanings, catching at new ones and letting go the old, as fancy may suggest. Recognising many planes of Truth, it is, nevertheless, careful to categorise these planes in orderly sequence, and to relate them appropriately; never transgressing the disciplines of scientific restraint, nor violating the natural and proper harmonies of far and near, real and illusory, ideal and actual. It is thus homogeneous, methodic, law-abiding. It creates no new dogmas or fancy beliefs at hazard, but follows scrupulously and obediently the teaching of the Church Catholic, whose exponent and minister it is.

Obviously, to be a Mystic after such a manner is by no means an easy thing. Much knowledge, much discretion, much experience are needed for the guidance of the aspirant. What, then, is the criterium, what the guarantee of a successful issue in the enterprise? These are found in the exercise of three supreme functions, each a sovereign principle in man: Right Perception, Right Aspiration, Right Judgment. They are, spiritually, the Kings of the East, and their apparition announces the Epiphany of the Divine Life. Theirs it is to cognise, to interpret, to illumine the interior nature, and to demonstrate the perfect reasonableness of the divine science. They are, so to speak, the sponsors for Christ, the Godfathers of the heavenly Babe. They affirm and declare Him; their presence at His cradle and their united act of adoration are the supreme ratification of His supernal origin. Their respective offerings of gold, frankincense, and myrrh symbolise the recognition of the Inward Light in Man by the prophetic, priestly, and kingly attributes of his nature. These three wise principles, whose testimony to the Deific Source of that Light is necessary to our acceptance of It as "God with us,"—Emmanuel—arise themselves in the East or place of the *Aurore*, and are the accredited ambassadors of the Most High.

So lowly, so humble, so insignificant seem the beginnings of the Divine Life when first the holy Soul brings It forth in the seclusion and darkness of her retreat from the world, that she can scarce believe in Its ineffable and miraculous nature. In her deep humility she lays this precious Offspring in a modest cradle concealed from the general gaze, and awaits events in reverent silence. Then come the "Magians," unerring in their witness to the Truth, proclaiming by their act of adoration that this is indeed the Son of God who is born among men, that the reign of Herod—or the lower nature—is at an end, and that henceforward the kingship of the Christ is established and attested. Not that the new king will escape opposition and persecution, for Herod is not to be deposed without a struggle. "The flesh lusteth against the Spirit," the law of Death wars against the law of Life eternal. "Futurum est enim ut Herodes quærat puerum ad perdendum eum."

The advent of the kings signifies, therefore, the time of interpretation, of unveiling, of making known; and the office which they come to fulfil is that of Illumination. The manifestation of the holy Child is the Epiphany in Man, collectively and individually, of the Divine Life, but this can only be discerned and proclaimed for what It is by the consensus of our highest mental, psychic, and spiritual faculties, right perception, right aspiration, right judgment. By the combined verdict of this royal council God certifies to us the truth. And it is thus that Mystics have always apprehended the birth of the Lord within their own hearts, and have unmistakably recognised and joyfully saluted Him. And now, it seems that the day of the Kings of the East is coming in its fulness; not for a few individual Mystics merely, but for the Catholic Church in her entirety; that the hour of making known is at hand, and that, from the rising of the sun, the messengers of God are approaching us with good tidings.

It is my object to unfold the mission of the *Rois Mages*, for this is none other than the evangel of Mysticism itself; the evangel of Manifestation and of Interpretation; the Life of Christ declared and exposed after its spiritual and individual meaning. "Et si cognovimus secundum carnem Christum: sed nunc jam non novimus" (2 Cor. v. 16).

CHRISTIAN MYSTICISM

THE HOLY VIRGIN OF MYSTICISM[1]

"Ecce, concipies in utero, et paries filium, et vocabis nomen ejus JESUM. Hic erit magnus, et Filius Altissimi vocabitur; et dabit illi Dominus Deus sedem David patri ejus; et regnabit in domo Jacob in æternum; et regni ejus non erit finis."—Luke, Cap. I. 31, 32, 33.

IN Christian dogma, esoteric as well as exoteric, the personality of the Holy Virgin is the highest and most important next to that of her Son.

Just as the life and Passion of Christ constitute a representation of and correspond to the interior progress and trials of the mystic, so also the acts and grace of the Holy Virgin find their corresponding expression in a similar way.

If Christ sets humanity free from the curse of Adam, so that the Apostle calls him the second Adam in whom all men are made alive, Mary sets us free from the curse of Eve by expiating through perfect obedience the disobedience of the latter. Thus the promise made to Eve is transferred to Mary, who, as second Eve, crushes the head of the serpent and becomes the Mother of God. Both arcanum and symbol remain identical, so that Eve and Mary stand for one and the same principle in man. This principle is the *Soul,—anima divina*—the interior and spiritual Self which all mystical writers consider as feminine, and which, through union with the descending Influx of the Holy Ghost, conceives in him (man) the divine life and brings forth Emmanuel, the God-in-us.[2]

---

[1] See note on p. 225, *ante*.

[2] In an Illumination "Concerning the Christian Mysteries," received by Anna Kingsford, occurs the following passage: "It is said that the Blessed Virgin Mary is the daughter, spouse, and mother of God. But, inasmuch as spiritual energy has two conditions, one of passivity and one of activity,—which latter is styled the Holy Spirit,—it is said that Mary's spouse is not the Father, but the Holy Ghost, these terms implying respectively the static and the dynamic modes of Deity. For the Father denotes the motionless, the force passive and potential, in whom all things *are*—subjectively. But the Holy Ghost represents will in action,—creative energy, motion, and generative function. Of this union of the Divine Will in action—the Holy Ghost—with the human soul, the product is Christ, the God-man and *Our* Lord. And through Christ, the Divine Spirit, by whom He is begotten, flows and operates" (*Clothed With the Sun*, pt. i. No. xlviii.).—S. H. H.

Esoterically and mystically, the subject of sacred history is the Soul.

In the Old Testament, the soul is depicted, in the first place, as Eve, emerging radiant in beauty and purity from the hands of the Creator. Tempted by the adversary, she yields to his cunning devices. Rejected from Paradise, she is subjected to the bonds of enslavement and suffering. Yet in the very hour of her condemnation she is upheld by the promise of redemption and divine motherhood. In the second place, in the New Testament, she reappears under the figure of Mary, of illustrious lineage, "highly favoured." Greeted with the reversed name of Eve (Ave); overshadowed by the virtue of the Most-High; bearing in her own virgin bosom the Son of the Almighty; taking part in His sufferings, His sacrifice, and His victory; witness of His ascension; recipient of the gift of the Paraclete; assumed into Heaven; and crowned with the twelve stars as the twelve fruits of the spirit.[1]

There is not a single feature of the story of Eve and of that of Mary, which is its sequel, that is not truly applicable to the soul of man; and were it not for this fact, there would be in these stories nothing to relate them to man's spiritual welfare. "Truly unfortunate," says the *Zohar*, "is he who sees in sacred history nothing further than a simple narrative." Each word of the law has a divine meaning, and veils a mystery entirely sublime. History is only the garment of the law. The sages and servants of the Supreme King—they who dwell upon the heights of Sinai—take account only of the soul, which is the foundation of all the rest.

Every sinner can witness in his own interior experience a representation of the grievous drama of the fall. Every saint re-enacts in his regenerate life the mystery of the Holy Virgin's Rosary. Within him, the soul travels through every stage in turn of the joys, of the sorrows, and of the glories of Mary. Even as without Mary there can be no Christ, so without the soul there can be no divine life. Therefore the part which is assigned to Mary in the gospel of the Christian religion is that which is enacted by the soul in the interior of the mystic. That which seduces the soul in the first place and lures her into the evil path, is the attraction of the illusory world, symbolised under the figure

---

[1] The *twelve* fruits of the Holy Ghost are: Charity, Joy, Peace, Patience, Longanimity, Goodness, Benignity, Mildness, Fidelity, Modesty, Continency, and Chastity.—A. K.

of the serpent with its glittering coils and the fascinating power of its eyes.

It is by yielding to this attraction that the soul leaves heavenly realities for the shadows of the terrestrial world, and drags down in her fall the intellect of man (Adam). Intellect and soul fall together, and lose the twofold faculty of desiring and apprehending divine things. No longer in harmony with the latter, they are placed outside divine conditions, and are henceforth conscious of their material surroundings only. That which constitutes sin and the fall, is the substitution of the illusory for the real. That which is the gain of regeneration, is the restitution of the power to love and apprehend again the real. The original sin of which Mary was free, is precisely this state of blindness which prevents cognition of heavenly things and closes to the soul's perception the world of truth and of the Absolute. It is not possible that divine life be generated in a soul afflicted with such blindness. Christ can be conceived only in the Virgin-Immaculate. The converted soul passes from the state of fall into the state of regeneration, and through that very fact becomes virgin, that is to say, no longer entangles herself in material and illusory conditions. She is delivered from earthly attachments; she has rejected the yoke of her companion Adam, compelled to till the earth, in order to be espoused to the Holy Spirit. And as Eve has accepted the annunciation of the serpent, so does Mary accept the annunciation of the Angel. In other words, just as the soul in her frailty has, by preferring the material to the spiritual, yielded to the temptation of illusion, so also the soul in her virtue obeys the voice of angelical nature, and prefers virginity or the spiritual life to dealings with matter.

Western mystics and Hermetists distinguish four separate elements in man—body, mind, soul, and spirit. The alchemists say that the human kingdom is divided into four parts or hypostatic relations called "elements." In *The Golden Treatise of Hermes*, it is stated that the third part of this kingdom is coagulated, but that the rest is fluidic. "Our stone, writes the author, is the resultant of many things, its colours (tinctures) are varied and compounded of four elements. . . . Thou must know that the hen's egg is that which will best help thee to an understanding of the nearness and relatedness of substance to nature. For therein is found a spirituality and a conjunction of the elements and an earth the colour of which is gold." And in fact, if the egg is examined from its external to its internal texture, it is seen to be composed of a shell which corresponds to the body of man, of a fluidic, plastic mass which represents his mental or astral part, of the golden yolk which is the figure of his soul or spiritual individuality, and within this yolk is found the white germ which corresponds to the divine vitality of the Spirit.

It would seem that Christ stated this fourfold division when He compared the Kingdom of God to a little leaven which the woman—the Divine Wisdom—took and hid in *three* measures of meal,—the body, the mind, and the soul,—until the mass had risen, that is, until the whole being had been penetrated by and transformed through the working of the Spirit. This image is entirely alchemical, and sums up the arcanum of transmutation, which is the central doctrine of alchemy. The divine life or leaven operates in the soul as a ferment which gradually, and through her, acts first upon the mind, and then upon the physical man, until the whole individuality is " highly favoured " (*gratia plena*, lit. full of grace), and passes from corruption into incorruptibility. Now it is ever in the soul that this heavenly influence is first felt; it cannot be born in the mind or astral man, still less in the bodily sense; and, as we have already seen, the soul must be in a special state of grace or favour, that is to say, polarised towards divine conditions, before the Divine Child can be conceived within her. The third element—or the soul—being in this state of grace, is, therefore, the kingdom of man,—the human kingdom,—the counterpart of the Holy Virgin. Her Son is the fourth element, or the express Image of the person of the Eternal (One), the Divine Life formed and incarnate as concrete expression of the Deity. It is thus that we read in another part of the Scriptures, " the form of the fourth is like the Son of God" (Dan. iii. 25).

We have said that the acts and the glory of Mary find their corresponding expression in the regenerate life of the saint. What then are these acts and this glory? The Gospels tell us very few of Mary's acts, apart from those of her Son. And it is so, because the special characteristic of the holy and regenerate soul is humility, the suppression of the personal I (I-hood) to the profit of the Divine Self (I AM); the absorption of the human into the heavenly, the surrender of the created for the uncreate.

All the acts of the Son are the acts of Mary; but none belongs to her, as her own. She has part in the birth of her Son, in His manifestation, in His passion, in His resurrection, in His ascension, in His Pentecost, and He is her gift to the world. But it is always

He who operates, while she merely entreats, consents, and responds. It is through the mediation of Mary that her Son overflows into the mind and body of man. St Augustine says: " Totum nos habere volicit per Mariam " (All graces come by the hands of Mary). The regenerate soul is the mediatrix as well as the genitrix of the Divine Presence. This is why the Church tells us of the Ascension of Christ and of the Assumption of Mary.

The Christ being of divine nature and heavenly origin, by His own power causes her to ascend. She is nothing of herself. He is her all in all. Where He dwells, there she must also be lifted by the force of the divine union which makes her one with Him. Thus bound to Him and penetrated by His Spirit, she no longer can remain among earthly conditions, in the realms of illusion. She is dead to material things, she lives only in the spiritual things. She leaves the atmosphere of the earth, carried upwards by the angelical nature wherewith she is clothed; she rises into Heaven, attracted by God. Henceforth she enjoys this divine estate which alone can develop her affinities; she dwells in the Real, and has for ever done with illusion. In the mystery of the Incarnation, which makes Mary the Mother of God, there is a conjunction of human force with divine force. Mary receives her Child by an act of heavenly energy (on her part) which brings about the conception of the Holy of Holies. . . . The divine life incarnate (or Emmanuel) does not spring up spontaneously or of necessity. It is the result of the conjunction of two forces, the union of the divine and the human.[1] The soul is as transparent glass exposed to the rays of the sun (or spirit). It polarises these rays and draws fire from them. The spiritual state corresponding to her condition, and the intimate communion with God which is the result of it, belong to her in the spiritual world.

Then is lit within her *this holy flaming Light* which illumines

---

[1] In a note to " Asclepios on Initiation," in *The Virgin of the World*, Anna Kingsford says: " Hermetic doctrine regards man as having a twofold nature. For he is in one sense a child of the earth, developed by progressive evolution from below upwards; a true animal, and therefore bound by strict ties of kinship with the lower races, and of allegiance to Nature. In the other sense, man descends from above, and is of celestial origin; because when a certain point in his development from below is reached, the human soul focuses and fixes the Divine Spirit, which is peculiarly the attribute of man, and the possession of which constitutes his sovereignty over all other creatures. And until this vivification of the soul occurs, man is not truly Man in the Hermetic sense " (p. 53).—S. H. H.

the world. In Latin, the language of the Church, the name of Mary is identified with that of the Sea, and in the litany of the "Holy Name of Mary" she is addressed as "Mary, ocean of bitterness." . . . From the beginning, water has been regarded as a symbol of the soul, and this term is used throughout the Holy Scriptures and by Our Lord Himself in the same acceptation: "Except a man be born of water and of the Holy Spirit, he cannot enter the Kingdom of Heaven."

Every Christian must, therefore, even as Jesus, be engendered psychically in the virgin soul by the divine Spirit. He must be born again in the Heavenly world and to spiritual things. It is only as a child of soul and spirit that he can apprehend that which is transcendental . . . (1 Cor. xv. 48). Again, "That which is born of spirit is spirit." It is to the soul, needless to say, that Hermes alludes in his *Golden Treatise*, when he mentions the "alchemical water wherein fire resides." . . . This water is Mary, "the Great Deep," over which the Spirit of God broods and moves in the beginning of the work of regeneration, and the fire that dwells in her is the heavenly Light, called "the glory of the only-begotten Son."

The Son of Mary, states the evangelical annunciation, shall sit upon the throne of David, and shall reign for ever in the house of Jacob. The throne of David is the throne of the Beloved, of the King. It is the place of royalty and supremacy, and therefore is given to him who has been anointed with the Christ-principle. The house of Jacob is the image of this system, for Jacob was made the prince, and the representative of God upon earth, and his name is always used in Holy Scripture as denoting a governor of the microcosmic kingdom. This reign in the house of Jacob is, therefore, the expression and exercise of royal supremacy in the human system; the establishment in the midst of it of the glorious law of Spirit; its transformation into the Temple of the Holy Ghost, through the power of the Christ which has been given to us from God, and is made unto us wisdom, justice, sanctification, and redemption (1 Cor. i. 30.)

ANIMALS AND THEIR SOULS[1]

I.

To the Editor of "Light."

SIR,—I shall be glad to have space for some animadversions, not on the recent interesting letters which bore the heading, "Have Animals Souls?" but on that heading itself. For, defining soul, as I believe it ought to be defined, to be that principle in virtue of which organic life subsists, it follows necessarily that, as organised beings, animals have souls, and could not subsist without them. In this view the question to be asked is, not whether animals have souls, but whether they have souls capable of surviving their bodies. For if, as stated in the Hermetic books (*e.g. Asclepios*, Part I.), souls are not all of the same quality, but differ in mode and duration, it may well be that there are some kinds which are capable, and some which are incapable, of continuance after death. In which case the question about the animals would be, as just said, not whether they have souls, but what kind of souls they have. Ancient belief—which was founded not on the preferences or prejudices of the uninstructed majority, but on the knowledges of the initiated few—was unanimous on this subject. Animals not only had souls, but had souls capable of continuance after death. As with men, it was not the death of the body that put an end to them, for they passed through many bodies. But neither were they immortal in themselves, nor were they immortal *as animals*, but passed on into higher forms according to the mode and degree of their unfoldment—form being the expression of qualities—until the human was reached.

This question, or rather a question which involves it, was raised coincidently in the *Theosophist*, for February, p. 274, by a Hindû contributor, who asked for references, other than those of *The Perfect Way*, in support of retrogressive incarnation (*i.e.* from the human back to the animal), and an answer in affirmation of the doctrine was given in the same number, consisting in a citation from Plato's *Phædo*, and some references to the earlier

[1] *Light*, 1887, p. 117.

Greek philosophy; according to which there is an interchange of souls, by transmigration, between men and animals, according to the developments and deserts of the individual. Among the further references which might have been adduced, and of which your readers may like to be informed, are the almost identical statements in the *Divine Pymander*, Book IV., and the *Bhagavad-Gita*, c. xvi.; the rituals and symbols of ancient Egypt, and notably the Sphinx, which unites all extremes of life in one form; the life of Apollonius of Tyana, who is said to have recognised the soul of King Amasis doing penance in the body of a lion; the Biblical parable of Jacob's ladder, on which the souls were seen ascending and descending; and the teaching of the Kabalah. For the Kingdoms of Edom, said in Genesis to pass away and perish, while only the Kingdom of Israel endured, are explained in the Kabalah as denoting the various elementary stages in the elaboration of man which precede and lead up to the perfected humanity, and which, being provisional only, are necessarily incapable of permanence. Meanwhile, until the establishment of the Kingdom of Israel, or advent of the man perfect, the soul concerned ascends and descends this ladder of evolution, gathering according to its needs the experiences requisite for its full edification in the Divine image, when, and when only, "the gift of God, even life eternal," is attained.

According to this doctrine—formerly universal, and it is to be hoped again to become so, being eminently logical and just—there is one soul of men and animals, having many modes and degrees, and passing from form to form in accomplishment of its pilgrimage, a pilgrimage of which the starting-point is the dust of the ground, and the goal the throne of the Most High.

So far, however, is this doctrine of an universal soul common to all creatures from obtaining recognition as yet even among professed initiates in spiritual mysteries, and so slender sometimes is the amount of intelligence brought to the study of those mysteries, that we find volume after volume purporting to be written by proficients in Occultism, in which the animals are confounded with "the animal," and condemned accordingly as inherently and wholly evil, and even pronounced to be therefore lawful subjects of any cruelty which man, in his selfishness, may choose to inflict upon them. As if man were not, by the very indulgence of such selfishness, degraded below the level not only of the human but of the animal, down to that of the infernal, from which there is no redemption.

It is not, however, because animals have souls and continue after death that we are bound to be just and merciful to them, but because we ourselves have souls of which the principles of justice and mercy are the very life-blood, and which we degrade and destroy by being unjust and unmerciful. Suffer as the animals may through our ill-treatment of them, we ourselves suffer yet more thereby. So that the notion, so prevalent, that humanity—meaning men and women—can be benefited by methods involving the ill-treatment of animals is utterly absurd and false. Humanity cannot be benefited by aught that is, by its very nature, subversive of humanity. May the opening in your pages of the question of the souls of animals be the means of bringing all Spiritualists to a sense of the obligation in regard to animals imposed on them by their faith!   E. M.

II.[1]

To the Editor of "Light."

Sir,—I have been long ill and am still too great an invalid to enter into any controversy; but I should like, *apropos* of the subject of Mrs Penny's interesting letter of March 19th on animals and their after-life, to relate a pathetic little story which I heard from a well-known Spiritualist in Paris. At a certain séance held in that city, a clairvoyante saw and described spirits whom she beheld present. Among the sitters was a stranger, an English gentleman, unknown to anyone in the room. Looking towards him the clairvoyante suddenly exclaimed: "How strange! Behind that gentleman I see the form of a large Setter dog, resting one paw affectionately on his shoulder, and looking in his face with earnest devotion." The gentleman was moved, and pressed for a close description of the dog, which the clairvoyante gave. After a short silence he said, with tears, "It is the spirit of a dear dog which, when I was a boy, was my constant friend and attendant. I lost my parents early, and this dog was my only companion. While I played at cricket he always lay down watching me, and when I went to school he walked to the door with me. He constituted himself my protector as long as he lived, and when he died of old age I cried bitterly." The clairvoyante said: "This dog is now your

---

[1] *Light*, 1887, pp. 161–162.

spirit guardian. He will never leave you; he loves you with entire devotion."

Is not that a beautiful story?

I don't think, however, that I should have been moved to give it here but that, while I was at Nice a few days ago, someone sent Lady Caithness a new journal just issued by an "occult" society, or lodge, in which there was a passage which deeply grieved both of us. It was a protest against belief in the survival of the souls of animals. Such a passage occurring in any paper put forth by persons claiming to have the *least* knowledge of things occult is shocking, and makes one cry, "How long, O Lord, how long?" The great need of the popular form of the Christian religion is precisely a belief in the solidarity of all living things. It is in this that Buddha surpassed Jesus—in this divine recognition of the universal right to charity. Who can doubt it who visits Rome—the city of the Pontiff—where now I am, and witnesses the black-hearted cruelty of these "Christians" to the animals which toil and slave for them? Ill as I am, I was forced, the day after my arrival, to get out of the carriage in which I was driving to chastise a wicked child who was torturing a poor little dog tied by a string to a pillar—kicking it and stamping on it. No one save myself interfered. To-day I saw a great, thick-shod peasant kick his mule in the mouth out of pure wantonness. Argue with these ruffians, or with their priests, and they will tell you "Christians have no duties to the beasts that perish." Their Pope has told them so. So that everywhere in Catholic Christendom the poor, patient, dumb creatures endure every species of torment without a single word being uttered on their behalf by the teachers of religion. It is horrible—damnable. And the true reason of it all is because the beasts are popularly believed to be soulless. I say, paraphrasing a *mot* of Voltaire's, "If it were true that they had no souls, it would be necessary to invent souls for them." Earth has become a hell for want of this doctrine. Witness vivisection, and the Church's toleration of it. Oh, if any living beings on earth have a claim to Heaven, surely the animals have the greatest claim of all! Whose sufferings so bitter as theirs, whose wrongs so deep, whose need of compensation so appalling? As a mystic and an occultist, I *know* they are not destroyed by death; but if I *could* doubt it—solemnly I say it—I should doubt also the justice of God. How could I tell He would be just to man if so bitterly unjust to the dear animals? ANNA KINGSFORD.

ROME, 28*th March.*

III.[1]

To the Editor of "Light."

SIR,—No doubt the *Spiritual Reformer* is the paper to which I alluded. I did not know its title when I wrote my last letter to *Light*, because I never had the publication in question in my own hands. The passage which called forth my comments was read to me by Lady Caithness.

In reply to Mr Read,[2] I will briefly state what my belief on the subject is, a belief spontaneously and logically arrived at by my own interior mental processes, aided by the "inner light," of which our good friends the "Quakers" make so much, and rightly; and also emphatically taught amd maintained by the schools of Brahman, Buddhist, Platonic, and Hermetic initiates, whose humble disciple I am. I understand that the Theosophists also hold the same doctrine; indeed I know of no "Occultist" really worthy of the name who repudiates it. The teaching of Hermetic science is in accordance with the tenets of evolution. It maintains that the "soul" is elaborated, individualised, and made permanent by means of successive and progressive incarnations. Beginning in the realm of the elemental and inorganic, it gradually makes its way upward and onward, perpetually enduring and striving, through the organic world—plant-life and animal-life—into the human. At every "death" an astral relict of *persona* is shed, and this is, progressively, less and less evanescent as the selfhood ascends in the scale. Thus the ghosts of horses, dogs, and domesticated, intelligent animals have almost as much "personality" as those of average human beings. But the real "Soul," or Ego, is not resident in the ghost. It may remain connected with it under certain conditions for a

---

[1] *Light*, 1887, p. 219.
[2] In a subsequent letter (*Light*, 1887, p. 255) Anna Kingsford says: "Mr Read has kindly sent me a copy of the *Spiritual Reformer*, which arrived here this morning. I lose no time in recognising Mr Read's explanation and my own misconception. I see that the person with whom I am really at issue is not Mr Read at all, but another writer, from whose suggestions Mr Read distinctly dissents. While I hope he will forgive me for my mistake, perhaps I may be allowed to add that as it is evident from the article in question that *some* Spiritualists do not draw the hard-and-fast line I wrongly attributed to him between the ultimate destinies of men and other animals, it may not be altogether regrettable that I was led to write as I did on the subject in these columns. I am extremely glad to have the *Spiritual Reformer* thus brought to my notice, and to find it a journal of a quality much needed in the present day."—S. H. H.

longer or shorter period—as, no doubt, it was enchained by affection to the ghost of the good dog whose history I recounted in *Light*. This association of Soul and Astral may be the result of meritorious affection, or it may be, on the contrary, the enforced penalty of materiality. Other conditions, such as premature or violent death, may cause it, or special circumstances, peculiar to individual souls. But, sooner or later, the soul disentangles itself from this intermediary state, and passes on to other births, shedding its lower personality, and going on to animate other and higher natures. Thus all animals are *potential* men,—men in the making—and must inevitably, in process of evolution, develop human conditions. No animals are immortal or " glorified " *as* animals ; but, also, no animal perishes,—no, not even the lowest. It is embarrassing, however, that Mr Read should have chosen " flies " to illustrate his remark, because flies and a whole class of creatures psychically connected with them belong to the kingdom of " Beelzebub," " god of flies," in order to explain whose position and function I should be compelled to enter into a long dissertation, chiefly Kabalistic. Suffice it to say here, that these creatures are by Hermetists regarded as " *débris*," and that they are included in the " kingdoms of Edom," which represent the backwater stream of disintegrating " Soul." Occultism is not a simple thing, but it is a perfect thing, and leaves no riddles unexplained. So that it comes to this : All creatures included in the " Kingdom of Israel," or kingdom of the " Divine Intention," are perpetually progressing and passing by the natural process of evolutionary development into higher forms. They are our younger brethren, and will some day put on humanity. As *human beings* they may obtain the " gift of God, which is eternal life through Christ our Lord." *For God is just.* If Mr Read's views were correct, belief in a just and Divine origin and control of the universe would be impossible, for justice involves compensation, and animals have almost a monopoly of martyrdom. If it be a good thing to be immortal, no creature of God can be shut out from attaining to it. The contrary doctrine strikes a fatal blow at the solidarity of the universe, and makes of man a separate creation, unconnected with the rest of living beings. If animals are soulless then man is soulless, for he is flesh of their flesh physiologically and essentially. Hence I say that the very core and root-doctrine of the new dispensation must be and will be the recognition of the Buddhistic precept concerning the brotherhood of all living things, based on the truth that the universe is One, and that One Life (*Atman*) pervades and maintains it. Because *all* are eternal, *we* are eternal, and not otherwise. All things press towards the human, all evolution hastens to develop into MAN.—Faithfully yours, ANNA KINGSFORD.

ROME, 8*th May.*

SIR,—In denying continuity to the souls of animals, Mr Read destroys the lower rounds of the ladder of evolution by which man himself ascends, thus rendering man impossible, since we cannot have the upper without the lower part of the ladder. Can it be that in Mr Read we have an Occultist who holds that man becomes man by some mode other than that of development from lower forms ? It would be interesting in such case to know whence Mr Read derives his doctrine. I, at least, know of no authority for it. E. M.

THE TRINITY

To the Editor of " Light."

SIR,—Your contributor, " 1st M.B. Lond.," who writes under the above heading in your issue of the 25th ult., must penetrate very much deeper into the Christian mysteries before he can be accepted as a competent interpreter thereof. His remarks at the outset on the Athanasian Creed and its framers shew that the subject is wholly new to him; and his explanations of the Trinity, the Christ, and the method of inspiration, while excellent as regards tone and intention, shew that as a student of Divine things he has as yet not mastered their alphabet. Had he studied the mere history of the Athanasian Creed, he would have found that so far from the framers of that famous symbol being persons devoid of culture and logic, easily satisfied, and intellectually the inferiors of the present generation, it was the very profundity of their metaphysical science which has caused them and their ideas to be misunderstood and unappreciated by the present materialistic and superficial age.

I do not propose to inflict upon you a lengthy disquisition on the Trinity or any of the other subjects which, equally with it, your contributor treats at once so inadequately and so confidently. I wish but to shew that the dogmas concerned, when subjected to examination by minds trained to the exercise of abstract thought and acquainted with the terminology and method of ancient mysticism, are neither incomprehensible nor illogical, but constitute symbolical expressions for truths which are necessary, self-evident, and incapable of being conceived of as otherwise, concerning the nature, and mode of operation under manifestation of Original Being, and this, whether as subsisting in the "Heavens" or world of pure unmanifested Spirit, or in the macrocosm of the universe and the microcosm man.

A single and familiar instance will suffice to justify this allegation so far as concerns the doctrine ordinarily regarded as the climax of absurdity—the doctrine of the Trinity. For the

[1] *Light*, 16th July 1887, pp. 324–325.

instance will shew that it is impossible to conceive of anything whatever as having being which does not constitute in some mode a trinity consisting of elements which correspond respectively to the Three Persons of theological dogma.

These elements, in the world merely physical, are Force, Substance, and Phenomenon, the sensible resultant of these. Thus, for example, a stone consists, first, of force; next, of substance—wherein its force resides and operates; and, thirdly, of their joint product, the material object palpable to the senses. Each of these is stone, and yet they are not three stones but one stone. And as the last is that by which the two first are manifested, it constitutes their expression or "word." And as force is the masculine and substance the feminine principle of things, the former, or first person, may be fitly called the father; and the latter, or second person, the mother; and their joint issue, or third person, the son.

This is not, however, the Trinity of the Churches, though it involves that conception. For in the ecclesiastical Trinity the substance, or "mother," in the Godhead, is combined with and merged in the "father," the two making one person; the offspring—expression or "word"—of this dual unity, the "son," being the second person; while the potency which proceeds from the former through the latter (the son being the manifestor of the father-mother, and more properly called the son-daughter), and denotes deity in its dynamic or active, as distinguished from its static or passive mode, is termed the Holy Ghost or Spirit, and made the third person.

Such is the key to the mystery of the Trinity.   E. M.

INDEX

ACHERON, 102.
Actæon, 136.
Acts and graces of Mary, *see* Virgin Mary.
Adam as man external, 97, 110, 112, 113, 132, 187, 230, 232.
    and Eve, 104, 107, 109, 113, 114, 216, *see* Eve.
    "in Paradise," 3, *see* Paradise.
Adam Kadmon, 107, 110.
Adonai, 100–102.
    habitation of, 105.
    the Lord, 98, 100, 105.
    rod of, 106.
    the Only Begotten Wisdom, 101.
    the Word, 98.
Adrasté, 75.
Agnosticism, 36, 75.
Ain-Soph, 105, 107.
Alchemy, the higher, 50, 141, 142, 161, 232, 233, 235.
Amen, 30, 41, *see* Nirvâna.
Anael, 42, *see* Aphrodite.
Angel, guardian, 84, 85, 138.
Angels, 122.
Anima bruta, 199, 202, *see* Ruach.
    divina, 202, 230, *see* Neschamah, Soul.
Animal, the, 237.
Animals, Church and, 239.
    descent to, 168, 169, *see* Re-incarnation, Evolution (and Devolution).
    eating flesh of, *see* Food.
    immortality of, 51, 236–242, *see* Life.
    as potential men, 80, 178, 236, 240, 241, *see* Man.
    some evil, 168.
    souls of, 236, 237, 239.
        transmigrate, 236, 237, *see* Reincarnation.
    sufferings of, 168, 194, 239.
    symbolical, *see* Symbols.
    torture of, *see* Vivisection.
    treatment of, 37, 157, 237–239.
Annunciation to B. V. M., *see* Virgin Mary.

Aphrodite as Counsel, 41, 42.
Apollonius, 169, 193, 214, 237.
Archangels (or Elohim), *see* Anael, Michael, Orifiel, Raphael, Salamiel, Uriel, Zacchariel, Gods, Spirits of God.
Ares as Knowledge, 41, 42.
Argus, 73, 134.
Ark, *see* Noah, Symbols.
Artemis, 134–136, 138, *see* Diana, Isis.
Ascension, 220, *see* Christ Jesus.
Asclepios, 78, 79.
Aspiration, 1.
Assumption of B. V. M., *see* Virgin Mary.
Astral body, *see* Body.
    fluid, 112.
    powers, sevenfold, 134.
    sphere, 200.
Astrology, 221, 222, *see* Stars.
Atheism, *see* Materialism.
Athena, *see* Pallas Athena.
Atman, 82, 129, *see* Spirit.
Atonement, 91, *see* Salvation.
Atwood, Mrs, 46, 47, 207.
Authority, 12, 17, 18, 134, 216, *see* Experience, Understanding.
Avernus, 102.

BACCHUS, 108, 111, *see* Iacchos.
Baptism, *see* Christ Jesus.
Barabbas, 144, 223.
Beauty, *see* Nature.
Beelzebub, 241.
Being, 124, *see* Consciousness, Existence.
    original, *see* En-Soph.
Belief, 30, 31, 32, 121, 153, *see* Faith, Knowledge.
Bible, 88.
    Genesis, a Forgotten View of, 147.
    Gospels, discrepancies, 153–155, 206, 209–211, 217, 218.
    not historical, 86–90, 96, 97, 153, 154, 205, 206, 209–211, 214.
    intention and method of, 87–89, 205, 215.

245

Bible—*continued*
   Gospels are mystical, 88, 206, 207, 209, 211, 214, 219.
     origin of, 86–91, 210.
     truth of, 152, 207.
   hermeneutics, 34, 146–156.
   interpretation of, astrological, 147–150.
     key for, 91, 141, 142, 145, 231.
     literal, 140, 147–150, 153.
     philosophical, 147–150.
     spiritual, 141, 142, 147, 148.
   is mystical, 9, 34, 35, 43, 88, 92, 145–151, 231.
   New Testament, 88, 89.
   Old Testament, symbology of, 44.
   and Re-incarnation, 77, 87, 111, 145, *see* Christianity, Re-incarnation.
   translation of, 6.
   unsealing of, 5.
Binah, 105, 107, 109.
Black Art, *see* Magic.
Blavatsky, Madame H. P., 3, 7, 10, 11, 19, 20, 22, 23, 28, 43, 55.
Blood, veil of, *see* Food, Veils, Vivisection.
Boaz, 105, 107.
Body, astral, 77, 81, 84, 188, 199, 200.
   physical, 81.
   resurrection of, *see* Resurrection.
British National Association of Spiritualists, *see* Spiritualists.
British Theosophical Society, *see* Theosophical Society.
Buddha, 7, 21, 50, 87, 123, 193, 212, 214.
Buddhism, 143, 144, 240.
   and Christianity, *see* Christianity.
   Esoteric, 20, 23, 140.
   and the One Life, 241, 242.
Burial of Jesus Christ, *see* Christ Jesus.

CÆSAR, 100.
Cain, 97, 98.
Cards, *see* Tarot.
Catholic Church, 94–96, 109, 228, *see* Church.
   three divisions of, 121.
   dogmas of, 95, 115, 155, *see* Creed.
     interpretation of, 91.
     are mystical, 10, 15, 18, 34, 49, 155, 218, 219, 226, 227, *see* Christianity.
   the future, 140, 229.
   is Hermetic, 225, 226.

Catholic Church, ignorance of, 34.
   the Mass, 49, 155.
   sacraments of, 95, 126, 141.
   and Transubstantiation, 50, 155.
   and treatment of animals, 239.
   the true and holy, 41, 104, 140.
   has the truth, 16, 49, *see* Truth.
Causes are spiritual, 146, 221.
Cerberus, 103.
Ceres, 130, 131.
Cham, 187, 188.
Chaos, 103.
Cherubim, 122.
Chokhmah, 105, 107, 184.
Christ, recognition of, 16.
Christ Jesus, acts of, 101, 115, 120, 121, 233.
   ascension of, 30, 98, 99, 101–103, 119–121, 155, 233, 234.
   baptism of, 117.
   body and blood of, 115, 155, 156, *see* Symbols (blood, bread, wine).
   born of Virgin Mary, 30, 96, 98, 99, 101, 116, 117, 155, 208, 213, 215, 228–230, 232–235, *see* Jesus.
   conceived of Holy Ghost, 30, 96, 116, 216, 230, 233, 234, 235.
   cross of, 99, 100, 105, 111, *see* Life, tree of.
   crucifixion of, 30, 98, 99–101, 117, 118, 155, 206.
   death and burial of, 30, 98, 100–102, 118.
   descent into hell of, 30, 98, 101, 102, 118, *see* Hades.
   Epiphany, 228, 229, 233.
   events in life of, as eternal processes, 30, 96, 99–102, 115, 121, 155, 230, 235.
   faith in, 115, *see* Faith.
   fast of, forty days, 102, 119.
   flight into Egypt, 117, *see* Egypt.
   glorification of, 119.
   the historic, *see* Jesus.
   incarnation of, 49, 91, 208, 215.
   judged by law of, 30, 98, 103, 120.
   life of, not historical, 153–155, 206.
   our Lord, 30, 96, 98, 230, *see* Adonai.
   man regenerate, 98, 99, 212, 216.
   and Mary, 116, 230, 231, 233, 234.
   merits of, 119, 120, 122.
   resurrection of, 30, 98, 99, 101–103, 118, 119, 155, 223, *see* Resurrection.

INDEX

Christ Jesus, Saviour of man, 98, 103, see Salvation.
    sojourn on earth of forty days, 102, 119.
    only-begotten Son of God, 30, 96, 98, 118, 119, 228, 230, 233.
    the Spiritual Principle, 50, 97.
    sufferings of, 30, 98, 99–101, 233.
    temptation of, 117.
    wounds of, five, 118.
Christianity and Buddhism, 20, 21, 23, 24, 87, 95, 96, 144, 223, 224, 239.
    and Hermetic gnosis, 71, 72, 77, 127.
    and Karma, see Karma.
    mystical, 14, 17, 18, 20, 21, 23, 29, 30, 72, 96, 97, 140, see Catholic Church.
    orthodox, 7, 10, 18–20, 28, 36, 49, 50, 54, 97, 153–155, see Jesus, the historic.
    and re-incarnation, 144, 145, 223, see Bible, Re-incarnation.
    and other religions, 71, 86–89, 94–97, 102, 107, 108, 125, 185.
    salvation of, 219.
Church, Christian, is Catholic, 95, see Catholic Church.
    militant, 109.
    and the Mysteries, 32, 89.
Clothed With the Sun, 6.
Colours, 41, 42, 186.
Common-sense, 28.
Communion of Saints, see Saints, Communion of.
Conception, Immaculate, of B.V.M., see Virgin Mary.
    of Christ, see Christ Jesus.
Consciousness, divisible and diffusible, 72–75, 198–102, see Being, Memory, Spirit.
Controls, see Spirits, extraneous.
Copernicus, 100.
Correspondence, law of, 74, 77, 175, 189.
Counsel, Spirit of, see Spirits of God.
Creation, 146, 147, 197, see Evolution.
    or manifestation, 70, 72, 94.
    object of, 98.
    and redemption, 70, 91, 99, 146.
Creed, Apostles', 29, 32, 41.
    Athanasian, 31, 124, 243.
    of the Elect, 30–32.
    is esoteric, 29–32, 36, 96, see Catholic Church.
    is not historical, 32.
Creeds, interpretation of, 91.

Cripps, George, 65–69.
Cross of Christ, see Christ Jesus.
Crucifixion of Christ Jesus, see Christ Jesus.
    of the two thieves, see Thieves.
Cruelty, 157, see Animals, Food, Justice, Vivisection.
Currie, Col. and Mrs, 61–64.

David, 235.
    House of, 137.
Death, see Life, Man, dissolution of.
    eternal, 30, 31, 241.
    of Jesus, see Christ Jesus.
Demeter, 108, 128, 138.
Destiny, see Karma.
Devolution, see Evolution.
Diana, 130, 136, 137, see Artemis, Isis.
Dionysius, St, 4, 148, 220.
Dionysos, 42, 108, 128, 138, see Bacchus, Iacchos, Spirits of God.
Dionysos-Zagreus, 128.
Divine Knowledge, see Knowledge.
Divine Pymander, 78.
Dogmas, see Catholic Church.
Dominions, 122.
Duality, see God.

Earth (matter), 109, 118.
    fruits of, see Cain.
    and heaven, see Heaven.
Eden, four rivers of, 184.
    lower, 188, 189, see Elysian Fields.
Edom, seven kingdoms of, 109, 110, 237, 241.
Effects, see Causes.
Ego, differentiation of, 192, 197, 198, 199, see Consciousness, Man.
Egypt, as body, 102, 117.
    flight from, 102.
    into, 117.
    religion of, 71, 72, 94, 95, 107, 111, 158, 159, see Hermetic gnosis.
Elect, see Saints.
Elemental forces, see Titans.
Elijah, 209, 212.
Elohim, see Archangels, Gods, Spirits of God.
Elysian Fields, 102, 180, see Eden, lower.
Ends and means, 163.
Enoch, 209, 212.

En-Soph, 105, 107.
Esau, 110.
Esoteric Buddhism, 14–16, 18, 20–22, 27, 40, *see* Sinnett, A. P.
Esoteric Christian Union, 58, 63.
Eternal death, *see* Death.
    life, *see* Life.
Eve, curse of, 56, 57, 113, 230, 231.
    fall of, 113, 131, 132, 231, 232.
    promise to, 231.
    as soul fallen, 97, 129, 130, 231, *see* Adam, Persephone, Virgin Mary.
Evil, animals, *see* Animals.
    cause of, 168.
    is negative, *see* Good.
Evolution, creation by, *see* Creation, Matter, Soul.
    and devolution, 109, 168, 169, 177, 236, 237, 241, *see* Animals.
    object of, 98, *see* Perfection.
    and suffering, 52, 108, 212.
Existence and Being, 176, 189.
    fourfold, 198.
Expediency, *see* Principles, Utility.
Experience, 55, 83, 85, 121, *see* Intuition.
    is suffering, 178, *see* Evolution.

Faith, 76, 117, 121, 150, *see* Belief, Knowledge.
Fall, the, 28, 79, 91, 99, 231, 232.
    effect of the, 79.
    of soul, 129, 130, 131, 231, *see* Eve, Persephone.
    of spirit, 70.
Fate, *see* Karma.
Fear of the Lord, Spirit of, *see* Spirits of God.
Food, flesh-eating and stimulants, 54, 78, 79, 193.
    flesh-eating and veil of blood, 56, 57, 80.
    pure, necessary, 54, 78, 80, *see* Intuition.
Force, centripetal and centrifugal, 177.
Forces, elemental, *see* Titans.
Forgiveness of sin, *see* Sin.
Freemasonry, 106.
Freethought, *see* Thought.
Freewill, *see* Will.

Gabriel, 42, 120, *see* Isis.
Galileo, 100.
Gates, twelve, 106.
Genius, *see* Angel, guardian.
George, St, and the dragon, 26, 27, 100.
Ghost, Holy, *see* Holy Ghost.
Gilgal Neschamoth, *see* Re-incarnation.
Glorification of Jesus, *see* Christ Jesus.
Gnosis, the, 75, *see* Hermetic gnosis.
Gnostic defined, 75.
God, 50, 79, 94, 100, 101, 176, *see* Spirit, Substance.
    altar of, 107.
    Creator of Heaven and Earth, 30, 94.
    duality, Father and Mother, 30.
    three expressions of, 139, *see* Trinity.
    Father Almighty, 94, 119, 230.
    gift of, 76, *see* Life, eternal.
    good, 176.
    ignorance concerning, 74, 78.
    just, 241, *see* Justice.
    knowledge concerning, 74, 75, 76.
    is Love, 180.
    and man, substantial identity of, 74, 75, 83, 114, 121, 124, 146, 220, *see* Soul.
    two modes of, 230.
    Mother of, *see* Virgin Mary.
    polarisation of, *see* Virgin Mary.
    sons of, 30, *see* Christ Jesus.
    Spirits of, seven, *see* Spirits of God.
    spouse of, *see* Virgin Mary.
    union with, 124, 125, 126.
    unity of, 30, 74, 187, 202.
    is within, 74.
    word of, 1, 147, 148, 153.
Gods (or Elohim), 7, 12, 42, 51, 54, 122, *see* Archangels, Spirits of God.
    nine abodes of the, 105, 106, 112, 134.
    A. K. and the, 51.
    Greek, *see* Phoibos, Hermes, Aphrodite, Dionysos, Ares, Zeus and Hera, Kronos.
    images of the, 141.
    mundane, 80, 118.
Good and evil, 163, 176–178, *see* Evil.
    tree of knowledge of, *see* Knowledge.
Gospels, see Bible.
Greece, religion of, 71, 89, 94, 95, 96, 102, 106–108, 111, 125, 127, 128, 133, 135, 143, 158, 159, 184, 185.
Guardian Angel, *see* Angel.

INDEX

HADES, 99, 103, 107, 118, 129, 191, see Christ Jesus.
Harris, T. L., 193.
Healing, science of, 158–160.
Heaven and Earth, 30, 41.
   kingdom of, 30, 41, 106.
Hebrew mysteries, see Judaism.
Hecate, 75, 103, 106, 134, 135, 138, see Isis.
Hell, see Christ Jesus, Hades.
Hera, see Zeus and Hera.
Herakles, 103.
Heredity, 220, 221.
   spiritual, see Karma.
Hermes, 25, 35, 123.
   four implements of, 133.
   as Thought, 73.
   as Understanding, 26, 27, 41, 42, 133, 134.
Hermetic doctrine, nature of, 27, 70, 72–79, 146, 240.
   gnosis, 25, 70–72, 79, 95, 96, 225, 226, see Christianity.
   Society, 2, 3, 24–26, 28, 35–37, 44–47, 58, 208.
   lectures, see Lectures.
Herod, 100, 228.
Hindoo religion, 71, 95, 96.
History and religion, see Religion.
   no such thing as, 151–153, 206, 207, 213, 214.
   times, places, and persons, see Mysticism.
Holy Ghost, 41, 104, 106–109, 230, see Spirit.
   to be born of, 78, see Christ Jesus, Regeneration.
   descent of, 99, 119, 120, 233.
Hoomi, Koot, 216.
Horos, 127.

IACCHOS as power, 41, 111, see Bacchus, Dionysos, Spirits of God.
Ideal, the, 53.
Idolatry, 34, 56, 188.
   veil of, 56, 57.
Ignorance, see God.
Illumination Light of Wisdom, 83, 135, see Revelation.
Images of the Gods, see Gods.
   interpretation of, 91.
   what are, 141, see Symbols.
Immaculate Conception, see Conception.
Immortality, see Life.
   of animals, see Animals.
Impurity, see Purity.

Incarnation of Christ, see Christ Jesus.
Initiation, 7, 30, 32, 71.
Inspiration, 83, see Illumination, Revelation.
Intellect, mode of mind, 76, 92.
Intelligence, 105, see Spirit.
Interpretation, key for, 91, 141, 142, 145, 231.
   mystical, see Mystics, method of.
   of Scripture, see Scripture, Bible.
Intuition, inborn experience, 55, 83, 85.
   and flesh-eating, see Food.
   loss of, 33.
   mode of mind, 28, 76, 92.
   organon of knowledge, 76, 78, 82, see Knowledge.
Involution, see Transmutation.
Io (Soul), 73.
Isis, 127, 135–139, 158, see Artemis.
Isis Unveiled, 5, 10.
Israel, 109–111.
   kingdom of, 109, 110, 237, 241.
   in wilderness, forty years, 102.

JACHIN, 105, 107.
Jacob, 110–112, 235.
   ladder of, 51, 109–111, 113, 237.
Japheth as mind, 187.
Jechidah, 82, 184, 185.
Jerusalem, 106.
   New, 106.
Jesus Christ, see Christ Jesus.
   the historic, 50, 71, 86–89, 95–97, 152–155, 205, 206, 213, 214, 218.
   birth of, 206, 208, 209, 211, 213, 215.
   not denied, 71, 153, 155, 205, 206, 208.
   memories of, 206.
   former lives of, 71, 208.
   and re-incarnation, 77, 212.
John the Baptist as Intellect, 117.
Jordan, river, 102.
Joshua, 102.
Judaism, 71, 86, 87, 89, 94, 102, 108, 111, 143, 159.
Judgment, 30, 98, 103, see Christ Jesus.
Juno, 137, see Zeus and Hera.
Justice, 41, 50, 51, 52, 163, 176, 179, 180, 181.
   and mercy, 238.

KABALAH, 39, 40, 50, 105, 184, 237.

Kardec, Allan, 5.
Karma, 5, 50, 75, 81, 82, 106, 129, 134–136, 138, 143–145, 188, 189, 220, *see* Artemis, Hecate, Isis.
    Christianity and, 135, 143, 144, *see* Sin, original.
    redemption from, 134, 220, 222.
    and re-incarnation, 41, 134, 143, 221, 222, 224, 237.
Kether, 105, 107.
Key, the, 90.
Killing, *see* Food.
Kingdom of Israel, *see* Israel.
Kingdoms of seven spheres, 109, 110.
Kings of the East, 13, 225, 228, 229.
Kingsford, Anna, Apologia of, 49–51.
    and Catholic Church, 17, *see* Catholic Church.
    death of, 52.
    and Edward Maitland, 54, 55.
      mission of, 3, 5, 6, 51, 55.
    health of, 45, 47, 48, 51, 52.
    and Hermetic Society, *see* Hermetic Society.
    Illuminations of, concerning origin of Gospels, 86–88.
    Lectures of, *see* Lectures (A. K.'s).
    post-mortem communications from, 43, 44, 52, 59, 66, 67.
    recognition of, 12, 22, 39, 57–59.
    as reformer, 182, 183.
    source of knowledge of, 3, 7, 15–16, 49, 50, 53–55, 184, 190, 193, 194, 240.
    and Theosophical Society, *see* Theosophical Society.
    Vision of Three Veils, 56.
Knowledge, 91, 92, 117, 121, *see* Belief, Faith, God.
    acquisition of, 178.
    Anna Kingsford's, *see* Anna Kingsford.
    of facts, *see* History, no such thing as.
    interior, 1, 207, *see* Intuition.
    no limit to, 76.
    recovery of, 83–85, *see* Memory, Soul.
    Spirit of, *see* Spirits of God.
    tree of, 99, 104–106, 109, 111, 117, 135.
Koré Kosmou, 127, 139.
Krishna, 86, 87, 193.
Kronos as Fear of the Lord, 42.

LAND, promised, 102.
Law, one, 115, 202.

Lectures (A. K.'s) on Bible Hermeneutics, 45, 146–156.
    to British National Association of Spiritualists, 8, 157–183.
    on the Credo of Christendom, 2, 27–29, 32, 33, 36, 39, 40, 44–46, 94–126.
      abstracts of, 2, 39, 45, 70, 94, 96, 98, 104, 109, 114, 121.
      publication of, 40, 48, 59, 65, 66.
    on Esoteric Christianity, *see Perfect Way, The*.
    to Hermetic Society, 2.
    on *Koré Kosmou*, 44, 127–139.
    on The Method of the Mystics, 44, 140–142.
    MSS. of, 2, 46, 62–65, 67–70, 121.
    on the Nature and Constitution of the Ego, 45.
    on the Systematisation of Psychic Truth, 170–183.
    to Theosophical Society, *see* Theosophical Society.
Lectures (E. M.'s), abstracts of, 39–45.
    on A Forgotten View of Genesis, 45.
    on Esoteric Christianity, *see The Perfect Way*.
    to Hermetic Society, 2, 27, 39, 44–46.
      publication of, 53.
    on History and Character of Hermetic Philosophy, 27.
    MSS. of, 46, 63.
    on Mystics and Materialists, 33.
    on Revelation the Supreme Common Sense, 28, 91–93.
    on The Higher Alchemy, 45.
    on The Intention and Method of the Gospels, 44.
    on The Nature and Constitution of the Ego, 45.
    on The New Illumination, 46.
    on The Revival of Mysticism, 44.
    on The Symbology of the Old Testament, 44.
Levi, Eliphas, 39.
Life eternal, 30, 41, 51, 76, 110, 237, *see* Animals, Death.
    one, 241, 242.
    rule of, 170, 173, 175.
    tree of, 99, 104–106, 109, 111, 118.
Life of Anna Kingsford, 2, 60, 62.
Light, 7.
Limbo, 102.

Logos, 197.
Lord, 180.
  our, see Christ Jesus.
  fear of the, Spirit of, see Spirits of God.
  the, see Adoani.
Love, 41, 124, 125, 157, 162, 179, 180,
  power of, 76, 202.
Lucifer, 112.

MACROCOSM, 220, 221.
Magi, see Kings of the East.
Magic, black, 8, 157, 158, 160–164, 167, 169.
  white, 159, 160, 162, 163, 169.
Mahatmas, see Theosophical Society.
Maitland, Edward, 60–65, 69, 70.
  and A. K., see Anna Kingsford.
  lectures of, see Lectures (E. M.'s).
  source of teaching of, 3, 15–16, 53–55.
Malkuth, 105, 107, 109, 112, 135, 136.
Man, see Animals, Ego, God.
  definition of, 74, 75, 168, 234.
  dissolution of, 192, 199, 200, see Death.
  fourfold, 74, 75, 81, 85, 103, 112, 128, 148, 184–187, 232, 233.
  nature of, 81–83, 97, 113, 114, 170, 174, 177, 184, 192, 202, 234, see Microcosm.
  nothing but, 106, 178, 242.
  place of, 80.
  regenerate, see Christ Jesus, Osiris.
  in seventh sphere, 220.
  and woman, 78, 79, 105, 106, 110, 113, see Rex and Regina.
Manifestation, see Creation.
Marriage of B. V. M., see Virgin Mary.
  the divine, 189.
Mars, 41.
Mary, pure soul as, 97, see Virgin Mary.
  ever virgin, 129.
Mass, see Catholic Church.
Massey, C. C., 4, 11–13, 23, 24, 29, 197.
Materialism and Atheism, 157.
  and Mysticism, see Mystics and Materialists.
Materialists, 171, 173, 174, 179, 180, see Mystics.
Matter is evolved, 146, see Evolution.
  is not illusion, 73.

Matter lowest mode of Spirit, 70, 73, 146, see Spirit.
  redemption of, 70, 73, 146.
  is temporal, 73, 146, 171.
Mead, G. R. S., 71, 95, 139.
Means, see Ends.
Mediumship, see Spirits, extraneous.
Memory, 192, 193, see Consciousness.
  of past lives, 84–86, 192, 212, see Soul.
  and religion, 82, 83.
Mercy, see Animals, Justice.
Merits of Jesus, see Christ Jesus.
  of Saints, see Saints.
Metempsychosis, see Re-incarnation.
Michael, 42, 120, see Zeus and Hera.
Microcosm, 220, 221, see Man.
Mind, modes of, see Intellect, Intuition.
Minerva, 130, 137, see Pallas Athena.
Miracles, 76, 123, 160.
Mithras, 87.
Moses, 4, 102.
  "on Sinai," 3.
Mysteries of B. V. M., see Virgin Mary.
  Church and the, see Church.
Mysticism, 37–39, 226–228.
  Christianity and, see Catholic Church.
  defined, 226.
  and forms, times, places, persons, and events, 18, 96, 140, 141, 148, 149, 226, 227.
  and Materialism, see Mystics and Materialists.
  and Occultism, 40, 104, 115, see Occultism.
  and Orthodoxy, 115, 140, see Christianity, orthodox.
  revival of, 140.
Mystics and Materialists, 33, 36.
  method of, 27, 140–142, see Interpretation.

NATURE, 38, 78–80.
  fourfold, 128.
  seven planes of, 147.
Nemesis, 75.
Nephesh, 81, 184, 185, 199.
Neschamah, 82, 84, 184, 185, see *Anima divina,* Soul.
Nirvâna, 143, 144, 189, 192, 201.
  of the Amen, 30, 31, see Amen.
  the celestial, 30, 31.
  first and second, 114.
Noah (or Nous), 108, 187, 188.
  Ark of, 107, 187.

Noel, Hon. R., 4, 57, 192, 197–199, 200, 205, 212.
"Now and Within," 91, see Interpretation.
Numbers—
  1, see Unity of God.
  2, duality, see God.
  2 thieves, see Thieves.
  3 Magi, see Kings of the East.
  3 measures of meal, 103.
  3, see God, Trinity.
  3 veils, see Veils.
  4 children of river Styx, see Styx.
  4 implements of Hermes, see Hermes.
  4 interpretations, see Bible.
  4 living creatures, 184, 185.
  4, man fourfold, see Man, Pantomime.
  4, Nature fourfold, see Nature, Existence.
  4 planes, see Nature.
  4 rivers of Eden, see Eden.
  4 suits of cards, see Tarot.
  5 senses, 147.
  5 wounds of Christ, see Christ Jesus.
  7 astral powers, see Astral.
  7 kings of Edom, see Edom.
  7 planes, see Nature.
  7 spheres, 30, 40, 41, 42.
  7 Spirits of God, see Spirits of God.
  7 worlds or stations, see Man, Soul, Worlds.
  9 abodes of the Gods, see Gods.
  10 Sephiroth, see Sephiroth.
  12 degrees of regeneration, 187.
  12 fruits of the Spirit, see Spirit.
  12 gates, 106.
  12 labours, 187.
  12, solar number, 186, 187.
  13, Luna number, 186, 187.
  15 Mysteries of the B. V. M., see Virgin Mary.
  30, age of, 117.
  40 days' fast, see Christ Jesus.
  40 days' sojourn on earth, see Christ Jesus.
  40 years' ordeal, see Israel.

OBSESSION, see Spirits, extraneous.
Occult World, The, 5, see Sinnett, A. P.
Occultism, 53, see Mysticism.
Oceanus, 111.
Olcott, H. S., 3, 11, 17, 22, 24, 26, 27, 55.
Orifiel (or Satan) 42, see Kronos.
Original sin, see Sin.
Orpheus, 108.
Orthodoxy, see Christianity, orthodox, Mysticism.
Osiris as Man Regenerate, 87, 128, 132, 138, 139, see Christ Jesus.
Overshadowing, spiritual, 83, 84.

PAGANISM, 95, 96, 102.
Pallas Athene, 112, 118.
Pantheism, 96.
Pantomime, characters of, 185, 186.
Paradise, 102, see Adam.
  first step to, 79, 80.
Paul, St., 4.
Perfect Way, The, 3, 7–10, 12, 15–16, 23, 37, 40, 50, 55, 62, 84, 198.
Perfection, possibility of, 110, see Evolution.
Peri-soul, see Ruach.
Persephone, fall of, 130, 131, see Eve.
  mundane soul, 106, 108, 111, 114, 115, 127–129, 135.
  rape of, 106, 127, 130, 131.
  sought by Demeter, 134, see Demeter.
  Virgin of the World, 127.
Personality, 199, see Consciousness.
Persons and places, see Mysticism.
Peter, St, 41.
Phantom, 83, 84, 191, 199–201.
Phanuel, 111, 114.
Phoibos Apollo, wisdom as, 41, 42.
Physician, see Priest.
Places and persons, see Mysticism.
Planes, four, see Nature.
Planets, 42, 112.
Pluto, 130, 131.
Polarisation of God, see Virgin Mary.
Pontius Pilate, 100.
Postel, Guillaume, 39.
Power, 76.
  Spirit of, see Spirits of God.
Powers, 122.
Prayer, 123.
Predestination, see Karma.
Priest and physician, 158–160.
Priesthood, the corrupt, 100, 188, 218.
Principalities, 122.
Principles, 18, 19, 140, 141, 180, 181, 227.
Promised land, see Land.
Prophet, 82, 83, 135.
Pryse, J. M., 89.
Psyche, see Soul.

INDEX

Purgatory, 102, 107.
Purity, 1, 7, 55, 56, 75, 76, 78, see Food.
Pythagoras, 50, 95, 123, 193, 212, 214.

RAPHAEL, 42, see Hermes.
Re-birth, see Regeneration, Reincarnation.
Redemption, 33, see Creation, Karma, Matter, Salvation.
  of the body, see Resurrection.
  in Hebrew mysteries, 102.
  of soul substance (spirit) from matter, 70, 103.
Regeneration, 70, 77, 78, 114, 155, 211, 212, 220, 232, 235.
  twelve degrees of, 187.
Regina, see Rex.
Re-incarnation, 5, 191, see Bible, Christianity, Karma.
  downwards, 168, see Evolution (and devolution).
  end of, 76, 144.
  necessity for, 77, 85, 143, 189, 195, 196, 220, 223.
  of soul, 30, 41, 50, 51, 76, 77, 82, 84, 85, 111, 188, 189, 192, 207, 212, 220, 236, 240, see Animals.
Religion is esoteric, 18, 91, 96, 97, 126, 140, 216, 226, see Christianity, Interpretation.
  is not exoteric, 140, 150.
  and history, 18, 20, 27, 29, 30, 50, 88, 91, 96, 97, 115, 125, 126, 141, 216, 231, see Bible, Christianity, History.
  memory and, see Memory.
  new, not required, 18, 39.
  and science, 115.
Religions fundamentally one, 15, 20, 71, 94, 126, see Christianity.
Renunciation, 125.
Restored New Testament, The, 89.
Resurrection, 114.
  of the body, 30, 41, 103.
  of Christ, see Christ Jesus.
Revelation, divine, 71, 85, 150, 151.
  divine, from within, 82–85, see Illumination.
  new, not required, 39.
Rex and Regina, 104, 107, 114, 116, 120, see Man and Woman.
Righteousness, spirit of, see Spirits of God.

Rites and ceremonies, 48, 49, 91, see Symbols.
Roman Catholicism, see Catholic Church.
Rosary of B. V. M., see Virgin Mary.
Row, T. Subba, 23, 24.
Ruach (*Anima bruta*), 81, 103, 184, 185, 188, 192, 199–202.

SACERDOTALISM, see Christianity, orthodox.
Sacraments, see Catholic Church.
Saints, 124, 193.
  Communion of, 30, 41, 121–126.
  merits of, 122, 123.
Saintship, 220, 222.
Salamiel, 42, see Dionysos.
Salem, 118.
Salvation, potential, for all, 30, 31, 32, 223, see Animals.
  no vicarious, 97, 100, 123, 141, 150, 151, 155, 156, see Atonement.
Saturn (or Satan), 41, 201.
Science, modern, 179.
  and religion, see Religion.
  and sorcery, see Magic, black.
Scripture, interpretation of, 91, 141, 142, 145, 231, see Bible.
Secret Doctrine, The, 23, see Blavatsky, H. P.
Sem (or Soul), 187.
Sephiroth, ten, 105, 107, 122.
Seraphim, 122.
Shells, 197–200, 241.
Sims, G. R., 59.
Sin, 112, 113, 232.
  forgiveness of, 41, 77, 78, 122, see Karma.
  original, 135, 155, 224, see Karma.
  Mary free of, see Virgin Mary.
Sinai, see Moses.
Sinnett, A. P., 4, 5, 7–9, 14–16, 18–24.
Solidarity, 51, 80, 239.
Solomon, Seal of, 40, 46, 99, 104–109, 114, 117, 121, 122.
  Temple of, 105, 106.
Sons of God, see God.
Sorcery, see Magic, black.
Soul, 192, see *Anima divina*, *Neschamah*, Spirit.
  acts of, 115.
  consciousness of everlasting, 199, 200.
  defined, 200, 236.
  evil, punishment of, 168, see Evolution (and devolution).

Soul, evolution of, 51, 192, 240, *see* Evolution.
   fall of, 129–132, *see* Eve, Fall, Persephone.
   human, seven stations of, 115, 116.
   as Mary, *see* Mary.
   illumination of, 135, *see* Illumination.
   individuation of God, 79, 112, *see* Virgin Mary.
   knowledge of, by intuition, 55, 76, 82–85, *see* Intuition, Knowledge.
   memory of, 135, 192, 201, *see* Memory.
   mundane, seven abodes or conditions of, 46, 104, 106, 109–112, 114, 115.
   one, modes many, 237, *see* Animals.
   two modes of, 129, *see* Eve, Mary.
   permanent self, 82, 188.
   pure, *see* Virgin Mary.
   as Queen, 107, 110.
   redemption of, *see* Redemption.
   transmigrates, 50, 82, 84, 188, 189, 192, *see* Re-incarnation.
   universal, 237.
   as " the Woman " in man, *see* Woman.
Souls, 236, *see* Animals.
   passing through of, *see* Re-incarnation.
   in prison, 122.
Spedalieri, Baron, 39, 40, 66.
Sphinx, 237.
Spirit, is absolute consciousness, 73, 198, 199, *see* Consciousness.
   descent of, 70, 85.
   Dionysos as, *see* Dionysos.
   fruits of, twelve, 231.
   Holy, *see* Holy Ghost.
   is Intelligence, 107.
   as King, 107, 110.
   -man, 173–174.
   and matter, 171, *see* Matter.
   all things modes of, 70, 73, 198, 199, *see* Substance.
   polarisation of, *see* Virgin Mary.
   pure, is God, 76, 83, *see* God.
   and soul, 128.
   is uncreated real and eternal, 70, 82, 171.
Spirits, extraneous, control by, 83–85, 203, 204.
   of Counsel, 41, *see* Anael, Aphrodite.

Spirits of Fear of the Lord, 41, *see* Kronos, Orifiel (or Satan).
   of God, seven, 30, 41, 42, 107, 185, *see* Gods.
   of Knowledge, 41, *see* Ares, Zachariel.
   of Power, 41, *see* Dionysos, Salamiel.
   of Righteousness, 41, *see* Michael, Zeus and Hera.
   of Understanding, 41, *see* Hermes, Raphael.
   of Wisdom, 41, *see* Phoibos Apollo, Uriel.
Spiritual knowledge, *see* Knowledge.
   sphere, 195.
Spiritualism, 8, 53, 85, 170, 188, 203, 204, 219.
Spiritualists and Materialists, 174, 175, 207.
   the true, 170–176, 179, 181.
   and vivisection, 8, 168, 172, 182.
Stars, power of, 80, 134, 144, 220–222.
Stead, W. T., 25, 58, 59.
Steiger, Madame I. de, 4, 13, 19, 58, 217.
Styx, river of existence, 111, 112, 114, 118.
   four children of river, 112, 118.
Substance, unity of, 157, *see* Spirit.
   differentiation of, 197–200.
   of God, 30.
Suffering, *see* Evolution, Experience.
Sufferings of animals, *see* Animals.
   of Jesus, *see* Christ Jesus.
Summer Land, 188, *see* Eden, lower.
Swedenborg, 77, 193.
Symbols, 88, 91–93, 141, *see* Rites and Ceremonies.
   altar of God, *see* God.
   angel (Soul), 185.
   ark (microcosm), *see* Noah.
   blood (Spirit), 108.
   body and blood of the Lord, *see* Christ Jesus.
   bread, 115.
   cap of Hermes, 133.
   cards, *see* Tarot.
   colour, *see* Colours.
   cross of Christ, *see* Christ Jesus.
   diamond (Spirit), 186.
   dove, human soul as, 185.
   dragon (Materialism), *see* St. George.
   eagle (Spirit), 185.
   earth, *see* Earth.

Symbols, east, *see* Kings of the East.
    Egypt (body), *see* Egypt.
    events (processes), *see* Christ Jesus, Mysticism.
    frankincense, *see* Kings of the East.
    gate, 107, *see* Gates.
    gold (Spirit), 142, *see* Kings of the East.
    ground, fruits of, *see* Earth.
    Herod, *see* Herod.
    hexagon, 100, 105, 107.
    hexagram, *see* Solomon, Seal of.
    House of David, *see* David.
    interpretation of, *see* Interpretation.
    king, *see* Spirit, Rex and Regina.
    Kings of the East, *see* Kings of the East.
    ladder, *see* Jacob.
    lamb, 115.
    land, *see* Earth.
    leaven, 233.
    lion (astral spirit), 185.
    mirror, 107.
    moon (Malkuth), 107, 109, 134-137, *see* Malkuth, Artemis, Hecate.
        full, 42.
    mount, 27, 109, 206, *see* Moses.
    myrrh, *see* Kings of the East.
    ox (body), 185.
    Paradise, 3.
    persons (principles), *see* Mysticism.
    places (conditions), *see* Mysticism.
    planets (stations), 101.
    princess (soul), 26.
    prison (Hadean sphere), 107, 121, *see* Hades.
    promised land, *see* Land.
    queen, *see* Soul, Rex and Regina.
    rivers, *see* Eden, Jordan.
    rock (understanding), 41, *see* Understanding.
    rod, 185.
        and staff, 111.
        of Adonai, *see* Adonai.
        of Hermes, 133.
    salt (matter), 113.
    sea, celestial, 109, 179.
        (*Maria*), 129, 235.
    Seal of Solomon, *see* Solomon.
    serpent (astral), 105, 106, 112, 113, 232.
    stone, 111.
    sun, 41, 42, 100, 101, 105, 109, *see* Woman "clothed with the Sun."
Symbols, sword of Hermes, 133.
    times, *see* Mysticism.
    tree of knowledge, *see* Knowledge.
    tree of life, *see* Life.
    triangles, *see* Solomon, Seal of.
    virgin, *see* Virginity.
    Virgin Mary (pure soul), *see* Virgin Mary.
    water (Soul), 129, 211, 235.
    wilderness, 117.
    wine (Spirit), 108, 115.
    wings of Hermes, 133.
    woman (Soul and intuition), 185, *see* Woman.
    worlds (or stations), 101.

TAROT, 186, 187.
Tartarus, 102, 188.
Taylor, Thomas, 130, 137.
Temptation of Jesus, *see* Christ Jesus.
Theosophical Society, 3-5, 7, 11-27, 43, 44, 60.
    and Mahatmas, 3-5, 15-17, 19-22.
    A. K. and E. M. and, 17.
Theosophist, 7, 8, 10.
Theosophy, 4, 14, 18, 226.
Thieves, the two, 144, 223.
Thought, Free-, 53, 54, 79, 134.
    system of, 170, 173, 175.
Thrice Greatest Hermes, 71, 139.
Thrones, 122.
Time, year 1881, 6.
Titans (Elemental Forces), 108, 118.
Torture of animals, *see* Animals, Vivisection.
Transmigration, *see* Re-incarnation.
Transmutation, 102, 103, 141, 186, 209.
Transubstantiation, 50, 155.
Trinity, doctrine of, 197, 243, 244.
    the first, 107.
Trismegistic literature, 71, 95.
Truth is spiritual, 1, 2, 34, 50, 92, 125, 126, *see* Catholic Church.
    is unutterable, 1, 141, 148.

UNDERSTANDING, rock of the, 41, 76, *see* Authority.
    Spirit of, *see* Spirits of God.
    the, 12, 16, 17.
Union, the Divine, 124-126, 223.
Unity of God, 30, 74, 187, 202.
Uriel, 42, *see* Phoibos Apollo.
Utility, 173, 174, 180-182.

VEGETARIANISM, *see* Food.
Veils, three, 55-57.

Venus, 130, see Aphrodite.
Vicarious salvation, see Salvation.
    death, 161, 162, see Magic, black.
Violationism, 157.
Virgin Mary, 230, see Eve.
    acts and graces of, 233.
    annunciation to, 98, 116, 120, 232.
    assumption of, 98, 99, 103, 120, 231, 234.
    to be born of, 78.
    and Christ, see Christ Jesus.
    Christ Jesus born of, see Christ Jesus.
    immaculate conception of, 98.
    coronation of, 99, 103, 231.
    polarises God (Spirit), 98, 234.
    not historical character, 218, 219, 230.
    litany of, 107.
    marriage of, 114.
    Mother of God, 98, 99, 230, 231, 234, 235.
    mysteries of, fifteen, 98, 99.
    rosary of, 98, 103, 231.
    free of original sin, 135, 232.
    pure soul as, 98, 103, 114, 116, 129, 130, 212, 216, 219, 230, 231, see Mary.
Virgin of the World, see Persephone.
Virgin of the World, The, 71, 127, 139, 141, 168, 222, 234.
Virginity, what is, 135, 232.

Vivisection, 157, 158, 162–168.
    Church and, 239, see Catholic Church (and Animals).
    and black magic, 158, 161, see Magic.
    evil means, 163, 168.
    and veil of blood, 56, 57, 80.
Volatilisation of the Fixed, 176, 177.

WILL, free-, 221, 224.
    human, power of, 76, 123, 222.
    perverse, effect of, 31.
Wisdom, Only Begotten, see Adonai.
    Divine, see Woman.
    Light of, see Illumination, Revelation.
    and Love, 180.
    Spirit of, see Spirits of God.
Witchcraft, see Magic, black.
Within, 82, 203, see "Now and Within."
Woman " clothed with the Sun," 42.
    man and, see Man.
    the mystical, 9, 28, 92, 97.
    as Divine Wisdom, 105, 233.
Word, the, see Adonai.
Worlds, seven, 104, see Soul.
Wounds of Christ, see Christ Jesus.
Wyld, Dr. G., 4, 11, 13, 191–195, 205–216.

ZACCHARIEL, 42, see Ares.
Zeus and Hera as Righteousness, 42.

Printed in the USA
CPSIA information can be obtained
at www.ICGtesting.com
LVHW081042140124
768647LV00009B/963